Two Leggings:

THE MAKING OF A CROW WARRIOR

Two Leggings

The Making of a Crow Warrior

Peter Nabokov

Based on a field manuscript
prepared by William Wildschut
for the Museum of the American
Indian, Heye Foundation

Foreword by John C. Ewers

University of Nebraska Press
Lincoln and London

Copyright © 1967 by Peter Nabokov
All Rights Reserved
Manufactured in the United States of America

First Bison Book printing: October 1982
Most recent printing indicated by the first digit below:
1   2   3   4   5   6   7   8   9   10

Library of Congress Cataloging in Publication Data
Two Leggings, ca. 1847–1923.
  Two Leggings.
  Reprint. originally published: New York : Crowell, 1967.
  Bibliography: p.
  Includes index.
  1. Two Leggins, ca. 1847–1923. 2. Crow Indians—Biography. 3.
Crow Indians—Social life and customs. I. Nabokov, Peter.
II. Wildschut, William. III. Museum of the American Indian,
Heye Foundation. IV. Title.
[E99.C92T85   1982]   970.004'97 [B]   82-6979
ISBN 0-8032-8351-2 (pbk.)   AACR2

All maps in this book are by Donald Pitcher.

Published by arrangement with Harper & Row, Publishers, Inc.

In Memory
of William A. Darkey, Sr.
and William Wildschut

Foreword

To the modern traveler by air or auto over or across the grassy plains of Montana east of the Rocky Mountains this sparsely settled ranching and farming country looks like a serene and peaceful land. It may be difficult for him to realize that until less than ninety years ago this was a vast theater of warfare in which more than a dozen Indian tribes of buffalo-hunting nomads—only a few generations removed from the Stone Age—waged relentless intertribal wars. Their many small war parties raided distant enemy camps to steal horses or take scalps. And sometimes rival parties met on the open plains or in river or creek bottoms in bitterly fought, small-scale battles. Even though pitched battles with several hundred Indians on a side were few, war losses were frequent and heavy.

A number of aged veterans of these wars survived until recent years. Around evening camp or cabin fires these elderly men told and retold their war experiences to their children and grandchildren. Yet few —far too few—of their real life stories, rich in vivid detail, have been faithfully translated from the oral literature of the illiterate Indians to the pages of white men's books. These old warriors were of many tribes—Assiniboin, Blackfoot, Blood, Cheyenne, Cree, Flathead, Gros Ventre, Kutenai, Nez Percé, Piegan, Pend d'Oreille, Shoshoni, and Sioux—as well as Crow. But many of the most dramatic episodes were related by old Crow warriors.

The Crow Indians of the middle Yellowstone Valley had a long and proud warrior tradition. They were never a large tribe. But during the late years of the eighteenth century they wrested this fine big-game hunting ground—richest in natural resources of any portion of the entire Upper Missouri region—from the Shoshoni. Throughout the first decades of the nineteenth century they fought to hold their country and to protect themselves from repeated incursions by the many enemy tribes who surrounded them. Caught between the powerful Sioux on the east and the aggressive Blackfoot tribes on the north, the Crow were in the most desperate military position of any Upper Missouri tribe. From the time of George Catlin (in 1832) white traders who knew the Crow solemnly predicted that these Indians would be annihilated by their more numerous enemies. So frequent were Blackfoot and Sioux raids during mid-century that fur traders abandoned their fortified posts in the Crow country. Even the hardiest wilderness traders could not be persuaded to operate a post in the dangerous land of the Crows at that time. During the 1860s the westward-advancing Sioux did dislodge the Crow from the easternmost portion of their Montana homeland. But the United States Army helped the Crow to regain much of their lost territory during the hard-fought Sioux Wars.

So the Crow Indians retreated—for a time—but they survived as a people. They never gave up their struggle. Nor were these stout-hearted warriors content to fight only defensive actions. Nineteenth-century Crow war parties were seen as far south as the Arkansas, on the banks of which they won one of their greatest battles with the Cheyenne, and as far north as the country of the Blood tribe of the Blackfoot in Alberta. They crossed the Rockies to harass the Flat-head and Shoshoni in their homelands, and they struck the camps of the mighty Sioux east of the Black Hills.

This constant struggle for survival against great odds in more than a hundred years of intertribal warfare did not fail to leave its stamp upon the customs and the character of the Crow people. Through-out the first half of the nineteenth century they steadfastly refused white man's liquor and chose to exchange their beaver pelts and finely dressed buffalo robes for firearms, ammunition, and other substantial and useful goods. To increase their numbers they adopted boys and women captured in their wars. Although their young men stole horses from the mountain men, the Crow Indians were known as people who did not kill white traders and trappers as the Blackfoot did. They adopted several traders into their tribe who actively assisted them in their wars against other tribes. Among the Crows alone, the Sun Dance was performed as a sacred ceremony to help warriors gain revenge upon their enemies. Even the laxness of sexual morality among the Crow might be explained as a form of release from the constant ten-sions of a way of life in which life itself might be snuffed out at any moment.

This constant struggle for survival also left its mark upon the individual Crow. Fur traders observed that no other Indians of the Upper Missouri were so well dressed or bragged of their tribal affiliation as frequently or as vociferously as the Crow. And when a tall Crow warrior informed them, "I am a Crow," they knew by his bearing and tone of voice that they were in the presence of a man of courage as well as pride.

Two Leggings, the teller of the story you are about to read, was such a man. He was above all else a Crow warrior. And his story tells us quite as much of tribal values that motivated and guided his actions as it does of his personal escapades. The successful warriors of his tribe were his boyhood heroes. And in his doggedly persistent efforts to win a name for himself by risking his life on repeated war parties over a period of more than two decades, he reflected the strong cultural compulsion upon the males of his tribe to seek to emulate or surpass the brave deeds of older Crow heroes. So strongly did Two Leggings react to these cultural stimuli that repeated failures and limited successes did not discourage him. He was one of the last Crow Indians to abandon the warpath. Significantly also, Two Leggings ended his story with an account of his last war experience. For him it was not the extermination of the buffalo but the end of intertribal warfare that marked the demise of the traditional Crow way of life.

Throughout Two Leggings' story runs the persistent theme of his quest for religious power. It reflects the tribal faith as well as his personal belief in the ability of supernatural helpers, whose aid was obtained through traditionally proper acts, to protect and to assist the individual warrior. It was a strong faith that gave Crow men hope and made the harshness of their life tolerable. Two Leggings' repeated efforts to obtain supernatural power through his own quests for visions, and his settlement for power transferred to him by older and more successful men, reflect both the Crow religious ideal and the culturally acceptable alternative. His war experiences illustrate again and again the reactions of a Crow man of faith to particular critical situations. They reveal the fundamental roles of war medicines and war bundles in the conduct of Crow warfare. And they show us the impossibility of understanding this warfare without a basic knowledge of the tribal religious beliefs and customs.

The reader who has not known aged, illiterate Plains Indians of Two Leggings' generation may marvel at the ability of this elderly man to recall seemingly minute details of his youth and young manhood. But those who have heard other elderly Indians recall their first-hand experiences have learned that illiteracy had its compensations. Forced to rely upon his memory, the intelligent Indian developed this faculty to a remarkable degree. And repeated retelling of experiences over a period of years helped to fix the details in his mind.

Nevertheless, Two Leggings' vivid memories would have been lost to us had not William Wildschut recognized that the personal experiences this aged Crow Indian related to him comprised a primary source for an understanding of Crow Indian life which was worth preserving for future generations. We are indebted to Mr. Wildschut for his foresight in recognizing this fact, as well as for his painstaking care in transferring Two Leggings' verbal reminiscences to paper. Peter Nabokov has not only edited the Wildschut manuscript, but he has provided a series of introductions which relate the adventures of Two Leggings more closely to the experience of the entire Crow tribe. And so these three—Two Leggings, William Wildschut, and Peter Nabokov—have combined their knowledge and talents to present us with a book that the general reader should find both fascinating and understandable. At the same time the book is a contribution to biography, to history, and to ethnology.

John C. Ewers
Senior Anthropologist
Smithsonian Institution

Introduction

A FAMOUS MAN, whose life has figured in events of historical moment, writes his autobiography to clarify those events, give personal interpretations of their significance, and detail his own participation in them. Everything he describes—even the most trivial recollections—will shed light on personal characteristics and public choices which affected history.

The ordinary man, whose existence is far removed from centers of power, is rarely prompted to recall his days. He finds it hard to understand why his life story should have an audience. While men of renown have always documented their experiences, or storytellers have done it for them, only recently have representatives of a culture been asked to relate the rhythms of their lives. The request has come from anthropologists, whose primary concern is with revealing the social behavior of a people, not individual peculiarities. A "great" man, to the extent of his influence, becomes supra-cultural and is only of specialized use to them.

Two Leggings' story is a hybrid of these approaches. Intended by both its subject and William Wildschut, the Museum of the American Indian's field researcher who transcribed the original material, to be the first, more traditional variety, its real value lies in the picture it yields of key motivations in Crow male life.

Two Leggings was only a minor leader. His war record was not spectacular. Despite the frequent "Chief" title applied by Wildschut and others, he does not appear to have risen past the rank of pipeholder, roughly the equivalent of a platoon lieutenant. None of his fasts yielded the life-guiding medicine which he describes as the prerequisite for public success. And his eventual resort to obtaining such important medicine property through the humbling and second-rate procedure of purchase is tantamount to a confession of personal failure.

To compensate for the lack of great battle recountings Wildschut filled his manuscript with Two Leggings' elaborate, hopeful preparations for such feats. His rise to the rank he finally attains earns him many of the attributes of an establishment cog—lack of imagination, destroyed individuality, and increased dependence on ritual. Two Leggings' life story is about a man whose ambition is completely culturally defined and, what is rarely the case with an extraordinary man, culturally predictable. What Wildschut managed to get on paper was the *process* of this ambition being instilled and the *process* of the sanctioning which formed its release.

Two Leggings divulges no surprising ethnological data. All the ceremonies have been documented in detail in Robert H. Lowie's comprehensive monographs for the Museum of Natural History. Nor is any startling historical information revealed. Two Leggings' adventures seem quite insular, in marked contrast with many of his Crow contemporaries who served as scouts for the United States military during important campaigns and who touched pioneer life more intimately.

The book is a series of an old man's backward glances. People alter events in retelling. Often this is not dishonesty but the memory picking out what it enjoys remembering, how it likes to think of what has happened. The choice memory makes, what constitutes the *completeness* of a story, would be different for a Crow than for a member of our culture, and that choice is in evidence throughout Two Leggings' recollections. They are the *Crow* idealization of a coming-of-age struggle—singularly parallel to coming-of-tribal-membership. Two Leggings believes, from his hoary vantage point where he thinks he can survey the totality of his existence, that he is seeing a Crow legend brought to life, Crow truths borne out. His earlier raids were unsatisfactory, he is convinced, because he had not gone through prescribed cultural channels, and whatever problems arose to disturb the success of his later raids could be chalked up to a faulty performance of his mentor's formulas for successful war parties. He sees himself as having paid dearly for once fabricating a buffalo-hunting medicine and remembers the ultimate gratification at discovering that there are no shortcuts to divine approbation and that one must bow to earthly authority in order to succeed.

With Two Leggings remarking so often to Wildschut how the disrespectful young Crows never harken to the old ways, we have watched the entire cycle of a Crow life and have witnessed at close range the mechanics of the control that tribal membership entails.

A Dutch-born businessman, William Wildschut made his home in Billings, Montana, from the fall of 1918 to June 1929. During this time he conducted various ethnological projects among the Crow Indians. The Museum of the American Indian, Heye Foundation, has published two compilations of his collections and notes, *Crow Indian Medicine Bundles* and *Crow Indian Beadwork*, both edited by John C. Ewers.

After meeting the River Crow Two Leggings in the summer of 1919 at a return celebration for three Crow World War I veterans, Wildschut began making periodic visits to the old man's home seven miles south of Hardin along the Bighorn River for the purpose of writing his life story. Their contact and this project were maintained until Two Leggings' death in April 1923.

Usually these talks were held at Two Leggings' homestead, a house made of timbers from old Fort Custer and a tipi along the river where Two Leggings preferred to spend his time. Mrs. L. A. Taylor, Wildschut's sister-in-law, who occasionally aided as a stenographer, remembers three week-long winter sessions during which Wildschut rented a hotel room for Two Leggings.

Sometimes Bull Does Not Fall Down, a childhood companion of Two Leggings, would join these sessions, verifying incidents and enjoying memories. Often Wildschut brought steaks for his hosts and candy for their children. Each talk began with the customary smoke.

As his interpreter, Wildschut employed Jasper Long, a Crow Indian of St. Xavier. Mrs. Ellen D. Wildschut, the author's widow, thinks he might also have used Thomas H. Leforge, the famous "White Crow Indian." An interview lasted the duration of a single episode or until, after some three hours of continuous talking, Two Leggings grew tired. Since Wildschut did not speak Crow, the Indian would talk to Long, complementing his narration with the illustrative sign language which Wildschut apparently could understand. When Mrs. Taylor assisted, she took Long's translation verbatim in shorthand. When Wildschut was alone she believes he wrote as rapidly as possible. To me, Long alleged that he wrote out an English version for Wildschut, and on occasion conducted his own interviews which he then mailed for a fee.

Later—Mrs. Wildschut could not recall how much time usually elapsed between interview and rewriting—Wildschut would work this material into the original story, being careful not to distort or change any meanings. While Wildschut stated that he read back his stories to Two Leggings until there was agreement, Mrs. Taylor could provide no indication as to how this was accomplished. The episodes had been related out of chronological order, which was imposed on the final draft.

A copy of the finished 480-page manuscript accompanied the other Wildschut papers in the archives of the Museum of the American Indian. Although Wildschut had hoped it would be published as a separate book, he privately expressed dismay that the public had lost interest in American Indians.

In the fall of 1962, Dr. Frederick J. Dockstader, the Museum's director, told me of the manuscript. After reading it, I submitted a letter of suggestions concerning its preparation for publication as a Museum monograph. Two years later I handed him a rewritten 280-page version. An appendix on page 213 describes and illustrates my treatment of the original work. Dr. Dockstader believed the book deserved more general circulation than a Museum publication would receive and generously located a publisher.

Dates for Two Leggings' birth, as for all early Indian life on the fringes of pioneer society, are not precise. Wildschut maintained that Two Leggings was seventy-six years old when their talks began in 1919. This would make him eighty years old when he died, according to Wildschut, on April 23, 1923. Two Leggings' obituary in the Billings *Gazette* states that he was seventy-six years old when he died, which would place his birth date in 1847. In Volume IV of Edward S. Curtis' *The North American Indian*, p. 207, Two Leggings is recorded as having been born about 1848. Finally, Two Leggings' individual history card in the Crow Indian Agency files gives his birth year as 1851 and his death date as April 20, 1923. His mother is recorded as Strikes At Different Camps, his father as No Wife. Although Wildschut has Two Leggings remembering his father's name as Four, this discrepancy could be an example of either the common ownership by a man of two or more names or of the wide spectrum of relations classified as "father."

In a hearing held September 9, 1924, to determine the claims to Two Leggings' holdings, Ties Up Her Bundle, Two Leggings' wife, testified that they had married around 1880 when she was fifteen years old. They never had any children but adopted Red Clay Woman because she was the daughter of his wife's sister. When she gave birth soon afterward they adopted her son, Sings To The Sweat Lodge, also named Amos Two Leggings. Ties Up Her Bundle stated that she knew of only one brother of Two Leggings, Chases The Enemy

Wearing A Coyote Hide On His Back, certainly the Wolf Chaser of the manuscript, and said that he had long been dead.

In August 1962, I searched out Amos Two Leggings. A tall man, quiet and dignified in spotless cowboy garb, he had nothing but warm memories of his adopted father and through an interpreter related a few as we drove to the location of Two Leggings' homestead. Nothing remained but some rusty agricultural hardware buried in high grass. When he located the site of Two Leggings' sweat lodge he recalled being sent to fetch the old man and finding him dead inside.

Other Crows wondered why I was bothering with such a minor leader, a man who had never achieved the stature of a Bellrock or a Plenty Coups. The Billings *Gazette* obituary reported: "Although Plenty Coups was the ranking chief since the death of Medicine Crow, Two Leggings had equal influence although both as a rule worked in harmony." However, Crow informants implied that their relationship often went against this rule, understandable when one views Two Leggings' unrelenting concern with status and Plenty Coups' established fame. In addition, they belonged to rival warrior societies.

Most writers on the Crow of Two Leggings' time have given him passing mention. In Curtis there is this abbreviated biography of Two Leggings: "Having no great medicine derived from his own vision, he was adopted into the Tobacco order by Bull Goes Hunting who gave him his medicine of a fossil or a stone, roughly shaped like a horse facing both ways. Two Leggings thus became a war-leader. In pursuing some Piegans who had captured a woman in the Absaroke camp opposite Ft. C. F. Smith on the Bighorn, he counted dashke [coup] and captured a gun by the same act—a high honor. Led two parties against the Hunkpapa Sioux, each time taking scalps. Captured fifty horses from the Yanktonai at Ft. Peck and with Deaf Bull led a party that brought back eighty horses from the Teton Sioux." —*The North American Indian*, Vol. IV, 1909, p. 207.

Like Curtis, Lowie noted Two Leggings' relationship with his medicine father: "Looks-at-a-bull's-penis made medicine for Two-leggings, asking him to choose between killing a person and capturing horses. Two-leggings chose the latter and brought two horses, one of them a buckskin."—*Religion of the Crow Indians*, p. 390.

Thomas H. Leforge, whose memoirs as a Crow squaw man were recorded by Dr. Thomas B. Marquis, first came in contact with his future hosts in the spring of 1865 when "Two Leggings and some other heads of families had their buffalo-skin tepee lodges pitched near the village [Bozeman]."—*Memoirs of a White Crow Indian*, 1928, p. 14. But he does not mention Two Leggings again.

During a visit to the Crow reservation in September 1965, I was told a story about Two Leggings in his later years. It was related a bit defiantly, as if this book would put an unworthy man on a pedestal. In fairness I promised to include it.

When Hardin, the largest town on the reservation, planned its first rodeo, all the Crow chiefs were invited. Accordingly Two Leggings showed up in full dress. But the gatekeeper refused to admit him because he lacked an invitation. Two Leggings argued that he was a chief, but the keeper was adamant. Weeping in the street outside the rodeo grounds, Two Leggings made a curse. According to my friends, the Hardin rodeo has been plagued with rainy days ever since.

The distant ancestors of Two Leggings and his people were a Siouan-speaking group who migrated out of the northern Midwest to meet the Mandan Indians. Soon named the Hidatsa, this tribe evolved an origin myth in which their founders climbed a grapevine out of the bowels of the earth and emerged from the waters of Devil's Lake, in present-day North Dakota, before traveling westward. At the mouth of Knife River the Mandans taught the new arrivals how to build circular, semisubterranean earth lodges and helped them cultivate corn, squash, pumpkins, and black beans, a diet augmented by sporadic hunting. A trivial incident after such a hunt gave the Crows their separate identity. An argument between the wives of two chiefs, quite possibly clan leaders, over the contents of a buffalo's stomach blossomed into a major schism. Following a brief battle, one leader, No Vitals, led his people farther westward to territory north of the Missouri in present-day Montana. Conjectures differ widely as to the possible date of this separation, the fur trader Edwin Thompson Denig placing it as recently as 1776, Lowie as long as five hundred years ago, and Curtis, by a backward count based on the average duration of a head chief's term of office, dating it around 1676. Crow acquisition of horses probably did not antedate the separation but very likely occurred soon afterward, easing their transformation from a horticultural people to buffalo-following nomads. The prominent anthropologist-historian of the Upper Missouri, John C. Ewers, feels these events occurred within the eighteenth century.

The secessionists were to be known by their Missouri-dwelling kinsmen as They Who Refused The Paunch, and came to call themselves the "Absaroke," or Children Of The Large-Beaked Bird, a

xvi

species no longer seen in their country. From this came the French mistranslation, *gens de corbeaux*, hence Crow.

Once they had moved south of the Missouri—it is uncertain whether as Shoshoni conquerors or Blackfeet victims—they established hunting rights to the land they hold today. As one chief is reported to have described this country during an early treaty conference: "I have but one tipi. It has but four poles. It is held to the ground by big rocks. My east lodge pole touches the ground at the Black Hills, my south, the ground at the headwaters of the Wind River, my west, the snow-capped Absaroke and Beartooth Range, the north lodge pole resting on the Bearpaw Mountains."

Possibly a group followed No Vitals' secessionists to become the second Crow band; otherwise the division between River Crow, or Black Lodges, and the more numerous Mountain Crow, or Many Lodges, occurred after the tribe was in its new territory. The former usually hunted north of the Missouri; the latter, together with their offshoot, the Kicked In The Bellies, roamed between the Bighorn Mountains and the Wind River in present-day Wyoming.

Around this country of high mountains, rolling plateaus, fertile valleys, and deep canyons, ranged numerous other tribes with whom the Crows had relationships of varying amity and hostility. The Crow legend of the Crow/Hidatsa severance ends with the resumption of peaceful relations. To the northeast these *Earth Lodges,* in the translation of the Crow name (Hidatsa, also called Gros Ventres), lived with the *Lodges At The Extreme End* (Mandans). From the northwest the Crows were beset by the three Blackfeet bands. Also to the north dwelt *The Hairy Noses* (Atsina, known as Prairie Gros Ventres) and the *Yellow Legs* (Assiniboines). Westward the Crows alternately traded with and stole from the *Poor Lodges* (Flatheads), the *Grass Lodges* (Shoshonis), and the *Pierced Noses* (Nez Percés). Southward they encountered the *Black Lodges* (Utes), the *Striped Feather Arrows* (Cheyennes), and the *Many Tattoos* (Arapahoes). But from the east came their greatest enemies, *They That Cut Off Our Heads,* the fearsome Teton Sioux.

The sons of the French fur trader Pierre G. V. La Verendrye appear to have been the first white men to see the newcomers. On September 18, 1742, Mandan guides led them to a people they named "Beaux Hommes," believed to be the Crows.

A description of the Yellowstone River, written by the fur trader Jean Baptiste Trudeau in 1796, told of a Canadian trader, one Menard, who had visited "the nation of the Crow, a numerous people," also in

Mandan company. A decade later the first account of Crow life was written by the Northwest Company fur trader François Larocque. Having traveled with the tribe for two and a half months during the summer of 1805, he recorded such features of their culture as nomadic patterns and their attachment to medicine bundles. From then on the Crow country saw commercial activity. At the junction of the Yellowstone and Bighorn rivers the enterprising Manuel Lisa built the first Crow trading post in 1807. After passing into the hands of the Missouri Fur Company in 1809, it was abandoned in the summer of 1811. A second Missouri Fur Company post was built on this same site in 1822 but folded a year later.

Once he had purchased the Columbia Fur Company in 1827, Pierre Chouteau greatly expanded the operations of his American Fur Company. In 1832 his field agent, Alexander McKenzie, built their first Crow post, Fort Cass, three miles below the mouth of the Bighorn River. From there the Crows were paid to annoy the competition, the Rocky Mountain Fur Company, which had enjoyed good relations with the Crows. In 1835, the same year that Fort Cass was abandoned, the American Fur Company built its second post, Fort Van Buren, near the mouth of the Tongue River. Eight years later it was abandoned. A third post was erected by this company in 1839, opposite the mouth of the Rosebud River. Before it too was abandoned, the Missouri Fur Company built its final Crow post, Fort Sarpy, which stood five miles below the mouth of the Bighorn River until 1860. But Blackfeet and Sioux harassment kept the Crows dissatisfied with these trading centers. Desirous of the fine Crow robes, the companies found the most fruitful trading method was to send representatives with small amounts of goods to travel with the tribal bands.

In 1864, when the Bozeman trail was blazed to the gold country of western Montana, three military forts were spaced across the Crow country, one the Fort C. F. Smith mentioned by Two Leggings.

After Larocque's entries, Crow life continued to be written about by fur traders and other travelers. Prince Maximilian of Wied-Neuwied's record of his 1832-34 western journey included descriptions of the Crow villages, their chiefs Long Hair and Rotten Belly, and the Crow warrior societies. A mulatto named James Beckwourth, who had lived with the Crows between 1820 and 1830, had his memoirs published in 1856. While flagrantly exaggerating his own exploits, Beckwourth presented an authentic picture of the military aspect of Crow life. During the winter of 1855-56 Edwin Thompson Denig wrote "Of the Crow Nation," based on two decades of familiarity with the tribe during their visits to Fort Union. As a section of his *Five Indian Tribes of the Upper Missouri,* this work devoted itself to those historical and cultural features which were uniquely Crow. And another fur trader, Robert Meldrum, provided valuable data on the tribe in 1862 for the journal of "the father of American ethnology," Lewis Henry Morgan.

During the first half of the nineteenth century the Crows were not entirely ignored by the Federal Government. In midsummer 1825, a year after the establishment of the Bureau of Indian Affairs, a peace commission headed up the Missouri toward the trade center of the Mandan villages. The resident Mandans and Hidatsa played host to two Crow delegations, a Mountain Crow band led by Long Hair and the River Crows under Rotten Belly. But Brigadier-General Atkinson's uneasy escort troops marred the occasion by training cannon on the visitors' encampment. When the Crows spiked the guns a brawl ensued. Rotten Belly was not as easily placated as his fellow chief. Even after singing a medicine song which brought a downpour upon the Mandans' earthen roofs and rotted their crops, he refused to sign the first Crow friendship treaty of August 4, 1825.

In this document the Crows recognized fealty to the United States Government, agreed to remain within its territorial confines, and submitted to its regulation of all their trade—a counter to the strong British commercial inroads. Finally they would undertake no "private revenge" but would refer all injustices to the proper authorities. In return for this surrender of an entire way of life, they were to receive occasional "acts of kindness." Although these clauses were totally unrealistic at the time, they would spell the end to Crow freedom half a century later.

When Secretary of War Lewis Cass attempted in 1834 to define his Indian agencies and substations with greater geographical accuracy, he found little information on the diversity, territoriality, and culture of the northwestern plains tribes. He established a sprawling "Agency of the Upper Missouri, to include all the Indians and Indian country west of the State of Missouri, north of the Western territory."

Until 1851 the Upper Missouri agents limited their annual reports to redundant, ill-informed, and mildly critical comments on the nomadic habits of their charges, their proclivity for alcohol (with the notable exception of the Crows), and their ceaseless intertribal warfare. That spring Congress appropriated one hundred thousand dollars for the holding of a great council of "the wild tribes of the prairie." Assisted by Agent Tom Fitzpatrick and the celebrated missionary-explorer Father Pierre de Smet, Superintendent D. D. Mitchell managed to gather, on September 1, eight to twelve thousand souls. The Cheyennes, Arapahoes, Snakes, and several Sioux branches arrived en masse, while the Crows, Arikaras, Gros Ventres, and Assiniboines were represented by delegations—the Comanches declined for fear of losing horses to the Crow and Sioux. During the eighteen-day encampment, Mitchell wrote: "The different tribes, though hereditary enemies, interchanged daily visits, both in their sectional and individual capacities; smoked and feasted together, exchanged presents; adopted each others' children."

The document signed there established federal right to build roads and military posts in Indian country, fixed tribal boundaries, and provided for the annual payment of fifty thousand dollars in goods for a fifty-year period. When the Senate chopped this to ten years, only the Crows refused to sign; thus, the treaty was never ratified.

In 1867 M. Simonin, a French mining expert, copied the translator's version of Sits In The Middle Of The Land's reply to the Fort Laramie Peace Commission in which he referred to the 1851 document: "Several years ago the whites came to buy from the Crows the route to California, which passed by Ft. Laramie. For this route they were to pay fifty years of indemnities . . . you have not observed the one [treaty] you signed at Horse Creek." Although the gathering yielded no new Crow signatures, Simonin concluded in his journal: "They agreed upon a conference 'in seven moons, when the grass was green,' that is, in the calendar of civilized peoples, toward the fifth of June, 1868."

A treaty drawn up on May 7, 1868, at Fort Laramie was quickly ratified by Congress. It was signed by only the Mountain Crow chiefs, and the Crows therein relinquished all their lands and accepted a permanent reservation extending westward from the one hundred and seventh meridian to about Yellowstone Park, the Yellowstone River being the northern and western limits and the Wyoming line the southern. Besides designating the construction of an agency complex, the treaty's twelve articles dealt with encouraging the Crow to farm and with compulsory schooling for Crow children, and stipulated the distribution of annuity goods.

It took another twenty years for the buffalo to disappear, for inter-tribal warfare to end, and for the Crows to resign themselves to the sedentary life. Their agency was moved twice, in 1875 to Absaroke and in 1884 to its present location a mile from Custer Battlefield on the Little Bighorn River. Continually the Crows were pressed by Sioux hostiles and Blackfeet raiders, and it is the feeling of some that without federal protection they would have been annihilated. Two Leggings' memories terminate in 1888. After that, "There is nothing more to tell." The Crow way of life, which had probably lasted for little more than two hundred years, was over.

In order to place Wildschut's manuscript in the proper historical and cultural context, I have dipped freely into more volumes than are listed in the bibliography. Included there are only those works which focus on the Crow tribe. Without Robert Lowie's extensive work it would be impossible to interpret much of what Two Leggings recalls. The photographs and text in the "Absaroke" half of Volume IV of Edward S. Curtis' *The North American Indian* were likewise invaluable. In person, through his annotated editions of Wildschut and Denig, and in his own writings, John C. Ewers has given this layman much-needed guidance. The books of Frank Bird Linderman, excellent popular accounts of Crow life and legend, also yielded important comparative material.

Dr. Frederick J. Dockstader, Director of the Museum of the American Indian, Heye Foundation, unhesitatingly extended the initial trust, sustained patience, and constant encouragement which brought the project to life. To him and his staff, in particular his chief photographer, Carmelo Guadagno, I am profoundly grateful.

On the Crow reservation I am indebted to Joseph Medicine Crow, Chester Medicine Crow, Carl Crooked Arm, Jasper Long, Edison Real Bird, Eloise Pease, Ray Bear Don't Walk, Otto K. Weaver, Andrew Loveless, and Robert Zang. They either kindly delivered information, patiently translated it, or graciously provided the facilities for obtaining it. Amos Two Leggings was killed in an automobile accident four months after our meeting. I had hoped this book would have thanked him for his help.

Mr. and Mrs. Laidlaw Williams housed me for two summers, during which the bulk of the work was done. For research assistance I am grateful to Nancy Strowbridge, Mrs. Margaret C. Blaker, and Sarah Macmillan. Through the four drafts, Ian Lowson, Peter Perrin, Richard Freis, Hugh Rawson, and William A. Darkey were judicious readers and editors. I also wish to thank Mrs. L. A. Taylor and Mrs. Ellen D. Wildschut for remembering those early years when Crows camped on their living-room floor.

Contents

Foreword   vii

Introduction   xi

Two Leggings: The Making
of a Crow Warrior   1

Selected Bibliography   198

Notes   199

Appendix   213

Index   218

Illustrations

MAPS

Crow hunting and roaming territory during Two Leggings' early years, xxvi
Yellowstone and Bighorn River basins, the Crow heartland, xxvii

PHOTOGRAPHS

(following page 98)
Two Leggings in 1919, wearing pipeholder's war shirt
Sees The Living Bull, Crow medicine man
Crow tipis along the Yellowstone River
Crow representatives at first agency near Livingston, Montana
Two Belly during 1879 visit to Washington
Crooked Arm
Crow treaty delegation, 1872
Bull Does Not Fall Down
Medicine Crow
Spotted Horse
Two Leggings' first war medicine bundle
Crow Tobacco Society procession
Frame of Tobacco Society adoption lodge
Doll that White On The Neck tore down during Sun Dance

xxiv

Doll used by Two Leggings during first Sun Dance

Rattle, scalp ornament, and whistle from Show His Face's Sun Dance bundle

Skunk-skin, apron, and raw-hide container from Show His Face's Sun Dance bundle

Big Shoulder

Hunts The Enemy

Medicine sweat lodge of 104 willows

Common sweat-lodge frame

Braided Tail medicine bundle

Sees The Living Bull's medicine of coyote-head moccasin

Hairy Wolf

Long Otter

Other Bull, Old Horn, Old Coyote, Old Jackrabbit and Two Leggings

Two Leggings shortly before his death

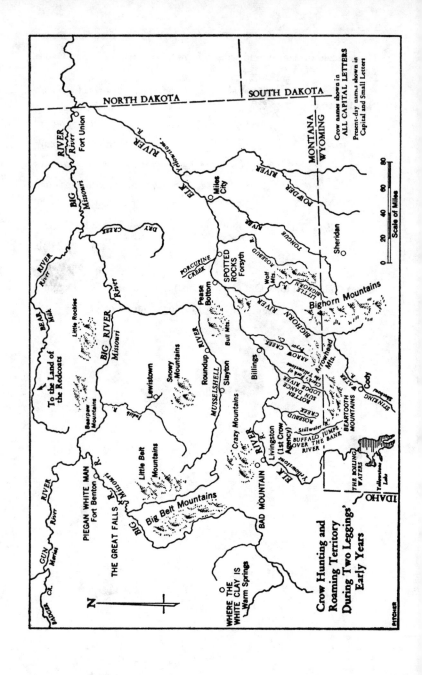

Crow Hunting and Roaming Territory During Two Leggings' Early Years

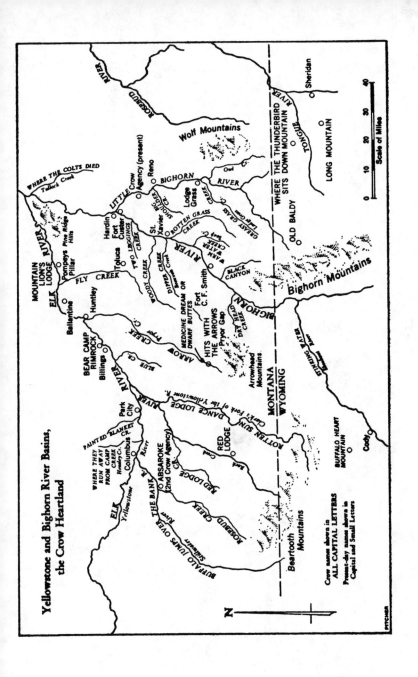

Yellowstone and Bighorn River Basins, the Crow Heartland

Two Leggings:

THE MAKING OF A CROW WARRIOR

Chapter One

In 1844, within a tipi pitched along the banks of the
Bighorn River, a woman named Strikes At Different Camps
got down on her knees, gripped two stakes, and spread her
thighs to give birth.

One of her attendants was known to have received a dream
telling how to mix rubbing herbs and concoct root beverages
which relieved pain and hastened delivery. This woman measured
off three fingers on the wet umbilical cord and sliced it. With
the brown baby at her breast, the mother was handed dried
buffalo meat dipped in fat. At that moment Four, the father, like
all men forbidden to approach the tipi, was selecting the
midwife's payment from his horse herd.

Two days later the mother heated a steel awl and pierced
the baby's earlobes, leaving a greased stick in the openings.

Four days after birth, during a momentary halt on
their journey to Fort Union, Four invited a revered fellow
member of the Whistling Waters clan to become the name
father. After covering the baby's face with sacred red
paint, this man lifted him four times while Four held smoking
bear root to his wincing eyes. Then, referring to some sacred
person in a long-ago dream, this man named the baby Big Crane.

MY MOTHER TOLD ME that when I was a few days old [1] our camp
moved to where the Elk River flows into the Big River. My father
traded for gunpowder from the trader there and when he came home
spread it close to the fire to explain its use to my mother. It exploded,
giving him such bad burns on his head and chest that he soon died.

After my mother died my older brother, Wolf Chaser, cared for me. In those days I was called Big Crane. I was poor, my clothes were always ragged, and I seldom wore moccasins.

My earliest memory is of our tipis pitched along both banks of the Elk River below the present town of Miles City. One day my brother asked me to join him on a visit across the river. After staying a few days we left to visit the trader at the mouth of Elk River.

My brother had given me a bow and some small arrows and on this trip taught me to shoot grouse, rabbits, and prairie dogs. With his full-sized bow he killed a buffalo and showed me how to boil meat without a kettle. Digging a hole he placed a piece of green hide over it and staked it down, allowing enough slack so that the hide would touch the bottom and sides when filled. After pouring water into the hide sack he built a fire in which he heated large stones until they were red hot. Carrying them with a forked stick, he dropped them in. He kept replacing the cooled stones with new hot ones.

When we arrived at the trader's I remember the store seemed strange to me. I could not understand how anyone could live in such a stuffy place with such a low roof.

In those days our tribe had three divisions: Sore Tail led the Black Lodges, Red Bear the Many Lodges, and Grey Dog the Kicked In The Bellies. Long Horse was head chief of all the Crows. At this store we met some men of the Black Lodges and my brother decided to visit their camp.

It must have been close to snow-melting time because I remember Wolf Chaser warning me to keep off the ice in the rivers. We had brought no provisions; game seemed everywhere and the Black Lodges were only a few days away. But we were unlucky and did not kill a deer until two days later when the sun was a tipi height in the west. Immediately we struck sparks on some punk with flint and steel, added small pieces of dry wood, and soon had a cooking fire.

The next morning two more Crows joined us and we reached the Black Lodge village two days later.

One day there the men went hunting buffalo and I followed, carrying my bow and arrows and a knife my brother had made from a piece of iron with a wooden handle bound with buffalo sinew.

I tried to keep the hunters in sight, but all the running and climbing tired me. Finally they disappeared over a distant ridge.

As I sat down to rest I noticed a horse grazing a short distance away. I had no rope, so I drove it toward camp. It was tame and after walk-

2

ing it into the horse herd I watched it for a long time. If it turned out to be a stray I could keep it. Until now I had never owned anything. When I told my brother, he could not find any owner's marks but walked it from tipi to tipi, announcing the way it had been found and asking everyone to look. I followed, afraid that at any moment my new property would be claimed. But when no one had spoken Wolf Chaser told me to care for it and made me a buffalo hide lariat to picket it.

A few days later Wolf Chaser decided to return to our home camp on Elk River. My horse was in poor condition and I led it the entire trip.

I took care of that horse, and my brother trained it to become a good buffalo chaser. As I grew older he showed me how to shoot buffalo on the run, singling out fat calves for me to kill.

When I was about thirteen years old, our camp was on the move to Bear Creek. When we came to a high bluff with sides and coulees thick with berry bushes it was decided to stop, because the women wanted fruit for the winter supply.

As camp was being set up, a man named White ran down the bluff, calling to the women about to pick to stay there. Scouting along the ridge he had seen a bear sitting on its haunches and staring at our traveling camp. Then the bear had sung a medicine song four times, raising one front paw toward the camp each time and patting the ground with the other. After scraping up some mud and rubbing it on its head, it made one streak under each eye. Finally the bear began dancing and moving its paw toward the camp as if to embrace someone. White had run to warn us that this bear would kill anyone who came near.

Although Black Head, one of our Wise Ones, and some other older people tried to hold us back, we slipped away. Halfway up the bluff we saw the bear on top, rising on its haunches as we approached. When we all shot arrows it ran into the bushes. We thought we had wounded it and despite the older people's shouts from down below, we ran into the bushes where it had disappeared. Just as Pretty Hawk and another boy reached a fallen tree the bear charged out. They threw off their blankets and started running but Pretty Hawk caught his foot in the dead branches. The bear hugged him around the shoulders, shook him, and then dragged him off by one arm.

White yelled for us to save our friend; Pretty Hawk was screaming. Black Head carried his gun into the bushes and another man followed behind. The bear was growling, but now Pretty Hawk was silent.

Someone called for me to stay but I crept behind the two men, listening to them encouraging each other. Then I saw Pretty Hawk lying in a clearing with the bear mauling him. When Black Head shot the bear in the back it walked slowly away.

One of Pretty Hawk's eyes was hanging out, his lower jaw was crushed, and on one side his ribs showed through. He moved his hand to touch his face but his shoulder was broken and he clawed the air. It was a long time before he died.

The bushes were fired but the bear was gone. We broke camp immediately, traveling along the Big Horn River until we camped near another canyon where more berries grew.

I spent a good day picking with some other young people, each of us boys helping a girl. Toward evening we swam our horses across the Big Horn River. During our meal on the other side we heard noises and grew afraid enemies might be around, so we rode closer to the mountains, making camp after dark by a little creek. I chose a sleeping place by some thick chokecherry bushes so I would be able to fill my bags quickly the next morning. Medicine Thunder was with me, and we spread our saddle blankets under a large box-elder tree and covered ourselves with robes.

A little before daybreak I felt a weight on my feet and woke up. My robe was over my head and my arm around Medicine Thunder. When something pulled at my robe I held it tightly around my neck. As the tugging continued I let the robe slide off and raised my head. A black bear was sitting partly on my legs, facing in the direction of the other boys and girls just waking up. I dropped my head and tried to squeeze under Medicine Thunder's arm. When he told me to let him sleep I put my fingers to my lips and motioned for him to look. Then he pulled his robe over his face and tried to hide under me. The bear just moved a little more onto my legs, its attention still on the other voices.

When our friends called us, the bear grew restless and moved off my legs, but still did not notice us. It was almost sunup when it finally began walking away. Medicine Thunder suddenly rolled over and we ran, yelling to our friends to get their guns. As we looked back the bear was standing near some underbrush. We caught our horses, raced back to the main camp, and returned with some men. Eats The

Ear rode too close and the bear bit a piece out of his horse's hindquarters. As it turned to escape into some bushes Medicine Arrow shot an arrow into one of its forelegs. It raised itself on its hind legs and pawed the air, crying like a human being. Then we all shot and soon it was dead.

There is not much to any boy's life. Even the gathering of wisdom is play. Many of our games had a purpose in those days.

We especially liked the arrow-throwing game which taught us accuracy and developed our arms and shoulders. An older man would call six or eight of us together at the edge of camp, each with a throwing arrow about his own height. The man threw his arrow, which was our target. Then we threw ours, one after another, and the closest won. People from camp would watch, offering prizes for the winner. Sometimes I was lucky and won a blanket, which I needed because I was poor. The people also placed bets on us and when some well-known warrior picked me I would try hard to win for him.

We also played the hoop-and-arrow game. A small rawhide hoop was rolled along the ground and we tried to shoot through it from far away. The winner was usually given a prize, and the people betting would give something to the boy who won for them.

We boys played war along the river bottoms, separating into two parties and striking each other with willow sticks. I could run through brush without making any noise, ambush someone, and suddenly appear in front of another boy to strike again. Sometimes the older warriors offered prizes for him who struck first or struck most.

In the winter we slid down high slopes on sleds made of buffalo ribs fastened together with rawhide, while one of our girl friends held on behind. In summer we used those same sleds on steep grassy hills. Sometimes we spun tops on the ice. We were also allowed to join in many of the dances, usually held when we had visitors from other clans [2] or when successful war parties returned. I enjoyed this and was considered a good dancer.

Chapter Two

*The legends which helped to form Big Crane's
ambitions followed certain patterns. For Two Leggings, as
Big Crane was later renamed, the Bear White Child tale
must have held particular significance. He saw his own life's trials
and triumphs fitting the general outline of the impoverished
orphan who, after earning supernatural support, wins status
and wealth.*

*A second motif common to Crow oral tradition,
that of the camp bully who lords his power over his fellows,
was also woven into this tale.*

*But the line between myth and reality is hard to
draw in Crow literature. Often a real personage or an historical
incident slips into the realm of legend. Two Leggings asserted that
this was a true story, and there are accounts from the early
nineteenth century of antagonism between the Whistling Waters
clan and the Treacherous clan. The very name of the latter
clan is traced to a certain leader named One Eye, who so mistreated
his own people that his clan was renamed the Piegan, or
Treacherous, clan because its members behaved like enemies, or
Piegans, to their tribesmen.*

As a boy I spent my evenings listening to the stories of our warriors
and medicine men. I wanted to be just as brave and honored, and the
following day would train myself that much harder, running and
riding and playing war games with my friends.

When we were young we did not speak, we listened to our Wise
Ones. Sometimes we were told what to do and sometimes we learned

6

through stories of true things that happened long ago. I will tell you the story of Bear White Child [1] because it contains the most sacred instructions which can be given to a young man who hopes to become a chief. After it was told to me in those early days I swore I would never be revengeful against my own people.

Early one night in leaf-falling season a full moon shone over a Crow village pitched along the ridge of a big coulee. Old Man Wolf, a Whistling Waters clan chief, walked through the camp calling certain men to his tipi for a smoke. When all were gathered, Old Man Wolf said that he wanted to smoke under grandmother moon. Buffalo robes were spread outside and the men sat in a half circle. After the pipe was passed, Old Man Wolf said that since game was scarce they would move next day to where buffalo had been sighted nearby.

It was still dark face—the period just before dawn begins to color the eastern horizon—when the crier woke the camp, telling the women to prepare their men a good breakfast.

A Treacherous clan chief, One Eye, also lived in this village. It was believed he could not be killed because he had been adopted by Bear Up Above, one of the most powerful supernatural persons. His clan members would abuse members of the Whistling Waters, knowing they were too afraid of One Eye to fight back, and One Eye himself often started feuds between the two clans.

A poor boy lived in this village, whose mother was his only living relative. But they belonged to the Whistling Waters clan; its members provided them with food and clothing.

Old Man Wolf had forgotten to invite One Eye to his meeting and the clan leader brooded over this insult. He knew the boy was well liked by all the Whistling Waters, and planned his revenge.

The hunters left at dawn, followed by the skinners and women. As the sun rose it became hotter. Everyone grew thirsty and around the middle of the day they stopped at a small spring where the water flowed cool and clear. After a short rest everyone went for one last drink.

The boy followed the older people, lying flat on his chest and putting his mouth into the water. Then One Eye, standing to one side, pressed his foot onto the boy's neck. All the people saw it but were afraid to do anything. One Eye talked loudly, pretending to give orders for the hunt. When bubbles came to the surface One Eye took his foot away and joined his men.

7

Although the Whistling Waters members were angry, they were afraid of One Eye's power and of causing trouble in the tribe. Pulling the body from the spring, they laid it under a pine tree, covering it with a buffalo robe.

Late in the day they returned to bury him and were surprised to find the body gone. At first they thought some bear or mountain lion had dragged it off, but no tracks could be found. The next morning they carefully searched the surrounding hills, but discovered no signs.

Soon after being placed under the tree the boy had woken as if from a sleep. Instead of returning to his people he walked toward the mountains where he fasted and prayed. One night, at a place known as Bear Camp, he was told in a dream that Bear Up Above would adopt him in the new grass moon. All that winter the boy remained in the mountains, protected by the Without Fires. In the meantime he was almost forgotten in his village, although some felt that One Eye should be punished.

One day, as the boy was resting on a rock, a bird appeared and told him to be ready because Bear Up Above was going to adopt him. The bird said he should not be afraid, Bear Up Above would not hurt him.

As the boy remained on the rock, watching the setting sun, he noticed a black cloud, as if a storm were about to break. The cloud grew larger and more threatening. He felt strong gusts of wind and saw streaks of lightning. It began to rain very hard and he was afraid the large hail stones would kill him. As he ran for a place to hide, a voice told him not to fear, that he was about to be adopted.

The hail fell all around, but the boy was not touched. Again he looked in the direction the storm had come; a black cloud hung in the middle of the hail. The cloud's center began taking shape and he saw the head of Bear Up Above. At the moment the upper half of the bear's body appeared the hail stopped. The bear sang a song as it reached down to embrace the boy. It lifted him into the air and when it finished singing, put him down.

After doing this four times, a fine-looking young man suddenly stood before the boy; he knew it was this same bear. The man said that he had adopted One Eye, but having seen One Eye's acts he had decided to take away his power. He had brought the boy back to life and had tested him. He said he knew how the boy had kept himself from the comforts of camp during the worst part of the year. He would reward him with the power he had once granted to One Eye. He gave the boy the name of Bear White Child.

8

The young man told Bear White Child that upon his return to the village he was to build four sweat lodges and invite everyone to enter them. He told the boy to offer a smoke to him there and said he would like this very much. Then the boy was to make One Eye miserable until the day came to kill him. For this he gave the boy bear sinew, a piece of which he was to throw into a fire. As it shriveled up One Eye's body would also shrink until he died. The boy could kill all his enemies this way.

After telling Bear White Child where the camp had moved, the young man disappeared, leaving behind him a clear blue sky.

During the winter Bear White Child had grown into a young man. As he took the return trail he felt strong and happy. He made himself a bow and arrows and on his way killed a deer, but ate very little. Reaching the outskirts of the village he sat down to rest. Then he rose, walked into the tipi of an old Whistling Waters clan member, and asked him to announce his return throughout the camp and to request his clan members to help him build four sweat lodges. The others in the tipi were surprised to see the boy grown up. After they had smoked, the old man announced the boy's return and repeated his request. The people thought he was crazy, but soon Bear White Child appeared, bringing in willow branches for the sweat lodges. One Eye was among the onlookers and was heard to say that the boy must have had some great dream and that he was glad to see him back. Actually, he was sure he had killed the boy and was afraid. Although One Eye flattered him in every way, Bear White Child ignored him.

After the sweat-lodge ceremony Bear White Child left the fourth lodge, lit his pipe, and offered the smoke to Bear Up Above. When a streak of lightning shot from the bowl to the sky, the people knew he must have some great power and were afraid of him. Then Bear White Child went to his mother's tipi where she was crying with joy at his return.

Nothing more happened until one night, in a dream, Bear White Child was told to fast on Long Mountain.

Early the next morning he told his mother he was leaving and to prepare him a good meal. Understanding that her son had some strong medicine power, she asked no questions. He had told a friend that he was fasting to the spirits, whose chief tipi was on Long Mountain, and his friend had asked to come. They climbed to the top and fixed their sleeping places. That night Bear Up Above appeared in the form of the fine-looking young man. He told Bear White Child that he had made him dream, and was appearing on the first night because he did not want to see Bear White Child suffer. Now was the time for Bear White Child to steal One Eye's youngest wife. Bear Up Above told him not to be afraid, for no one could harm him until he wanted to take Bear White Child back forever.

Bear White Child woke at daybreak and called to his friend that he was returning. When he told about his dream his friend was glad because he hated One Eye.

After their return the crier announced that on the following day camp would move. That night Bear White Child stole One Eye's youngest wife, the prettiest girl in the tribe. Many young men wanted to marry her but had been afraid of One Eye's power. The news spread the next morning as the crier announced that camp would remain there because Bear White Child was to be married. The crier also told the women to make the new wife a deerskin dress covered with elk teeth. When someone asked One Eye what he was going to do he said that both were young, that Bear White Child was a nice man and his wife good looking. He said he could not blame him for stealing her and he thought they would be happy.

But One Eye sent her a message, warning that if she did not come to him something bad would happen. Bear White Child told her that there was no need to be afraid; One Eye could do nothing. When she walked into One Eye's tipi he was feeling good and said that he hoped she would be happy. As a wedding gift he gave her the pony that was her favorite and said he liked her husband. The people were surprised; they were sure One Eye would try to take some revenge.

As the season passed Bear White Child stole One Eye's three remaining wives, and still One Eye did nothing. When autumn came the Whistling Waters members urged Bear White Child to take his final revenge. Soon afterwards he asked his friends to build him a fire. When it was blazing he threw in his piece of bear sinew, saying that it was One Eye's body. As the sinew twisted in the heat One Eye, who was standing a few tipis away, suddenly fell groaning on his back. Everyone saw his body shrivel away and he died.

Then Bear White Child told the whole camp about his dream and said that he had thrown in all the sinew because he never wanted to use that revenge again.

Chapter Three

*The Crow boy quickly learned that the arenas
for achieving success were the fasting place, the raid,
and the council of chiefs. Everything he saw and heard made
him yearn to begin the series of offices: a war party's
helper, scout or "wolf" as the Crows called them, leader of scouts,
pipeholder, chief, and head chief. But rarely was the
progression so regimented; an outstanding exploit or a notably
powerful vision could land a man almost anywhere on the
ladder.*

*To become a pipeholder, or The One Who
Owns The War Party, it was necessary either to experience
a vision which the accredited pipeholders would accept
or to purchase an acknowledged pipeholder's war medicine bundle.
However, only a warrior who had completed four prescribed
battle feats was eligible for this office. During ceremonies on his
raiding trip the pipeholder opened the pipe which was his
badge, and from his personal war bundle he learned where to
lead his men and how to act. When someone disobeyed
this medicine's commands, or when the pipeholder received an
ominous dream, the raid was cut short.*

I WAS GROWING restless shooting rabbits and longed to join the war
parties I watched going out. In the evenings I wandered through the
village until I found a tipi where some old man was telling stories of
famous raids. If I was not invited in I would sit outside, my ear pressed
to the skin wall. Later that night, in my brother's tipi, I would imagine those same things happening to me. When I asked my brother

11

to let me join a raiding party he only laughed, but watched closely to make sure I did not run off.

I was about fourteen years old when we were camped on Bear Creek, a tributary of the Musselshell River, near where it empties into Big River. One day I heard that Shows His Wing, Two Belly, and Bank were leading a war party to recover some horses stolen by the Piegans.[1] My brother would not give me his permission to go, which I knew Shows His Wing would require. Three elder brothers were also helping him watch that I did not run away.

I strolled to the edge of the tipis, carrying my bow and arrows. When my brother turned around, I ran behind a tipi and into the bushes. Arriving at the top of a nearby ridge, I hid behind some rocks while the war party walked by.

I was afraid to join right away but showed myself when they stopped for their noon meal. Shows His Wing asked what I was doing and I answered that I wanted to be their helper. He said I was too young and chose four men to take me home. Although I begged, my words were like the wind to him.

When we could see our village they told me to go on alone. I sat on the ground, watching them disappear over the ridge. Then I looked at our tipis. If I returned I would never have a chance to improve my life. I would rather be killed on a raid than do nothing in camp. I ran until I saw the four men again and started walking slowly behind. When they reached their camp at nightfall, I hid as close as I dared.

It was late in leaf-falling moon and snow covered the ground. As I watched their fires my feet grew numb, but I was only worried whether Shows His Wing would let me stay. The men had built four shelters of tree branches covered with brush and blankets and I could hear them talking inside. When someone walked out of the firelight I did not think he would see me, but the clouds parted and the full moon lit the country like day. I had to answer when he called, and he led me to Shows His Wing. The men were resting after their meal and told me to cut a piece of fresh elk and broil it. As Shows His Wing watched me eat he kept saying that they were walking far and I was so small.

I did not feel that small but he told his men they should have taken me into the village. When I finished eating Bob Tail Wolf and Wolf Cap accompanied me back a second time. But at dawn, when we reached the location of their last noon camp, they said I knew the way.

Again I waited until they had disappeared and again I walked in their tracks. Soon I found the remains of their fire and built it up to warm my feet. It dried my moccasins but made me fall asleep. When I woke it was sundown. After warming up again I followed their tracks in the moonlight, walking across ice, through groves of cottonwoods, and along the river banks.

When we are young we are all cowards. I was alone for the first time that night and the owls scared me. Stopping for a moment, I would hear strange noises and start to run.

Soon I smelled cooked meat and knew I was close. I was afraid to get too near, but once again someone noticed me and took me to the pipeholder.

Shows His Wing said that I was like a coyote trailing behind their party. Boys are always looking for excitement, he said, and his men should have taken me directly to my brother's tipi. But since I had shown my eagerness to go, he allowed me to stay. I was happy and could not speak.

A fat buffalo had been killed and Shows His Wing told me to eat. When he learned I had only a spare pair of my brother's moccasins, he told me to throw away those and my own torn pair. Then he asked some men for extra moccasins but none fit so he cut down my brother's pair and sewed them up again. We had no coats in those days and I wore only a thin shirt, a pair of ragged leggings, and an old buffalo robe with most of the fur gone. I was an orphan and although I had three older brothers I was very poor.

Shows His Wing had a white part of a Hudson's Bay blanket and sent me to Two Belly's shelter for another piece. There I was told that I would be given the cloth for tobacco.[2] Although Shows His Wing had little he sent me back with some and I returned with a narrow strip from a black-and-white blanket. When I wore the jacket the men made I looked like an eagle with white breast and black wings. Breath brought more cloth and after arguing what to make they sewed it into a cap, tying it to the jacket, and then made mittens and attached them to my sleeves. In the morning Shows His Wing led us where he thought the Piegans had gone and we soon found their tracks.

The men were watching to see if I got tired. But I had trained myself and even kept up when we ran one entire night because our scouts had discovered we were catching up. The following sunset we sighted their group of brush shelters.

Our party consisted of only six experienced warriors, two younger men, and myself. We three were told to stay behind and when it grew dark the others crawled out. After they had left I tried to persuade the young men to join me, but they said they were too young for real fighting.

I was excited and also began crawling out. When our men stopped to spread out I lay behind them. It was nearly daybreak when they noticed me, whispering that I must get back. But I was a man now and wanted to see what kind of people these Piegans were.

White Buffalo thought it was too dangerous and someone else warned that if the Piegans chased us I must not cry out.

Then Does Not Turn Back said that I might be braver than any of them and remembered how well I had run. He told me to stay by him.

By the time the sun touched the treetops we had surrounded their camp. I was told again to go back but I stayed, holding tightly to my bow and arrows.

However, the Piegans had discovered us and had slipped away. We quickly picked up the trail and soon saw seven men riding our horses toward the mountains. Then they dropped out of sight.

Shows His Wing led us on a shortcut across the hills, arriving at the mountain pass at sunset. They had not yet crossed and we hid among the trees. Since he was not expecting the Piegans for a while, Shows His Wing told us to rest. But I could not sleep. While I watched the pass, a dog we had brought to carry our few belongings lay next to me.

When it lifted its nose and began growling, I looked closer. Men walked out of the darkness and I put an arrow on my bow. I heard the heavy breathing of my friends sleeping behind me, but never thought to wake them up.

The dog barked, someone shouted, and the Piegans ran down the hillside. Our men were awake and running in the opposite direction, but three stood with me, waiting to see if more Piegans showed. We saw none, and it was too dark to follow into the thick timber. Breath was with me and he yelled for the others to pick up their blankets.

When they crowded around I spoke with a serious face, telling them that one man had walked right up to me and that when he felt my arrow he had screamed. Then I had looked around and only three were with me. Someone said that they had been trying to send me home and now I had proved myself the bravest. Two Belly said they had not acted properly and should return home.

We returned a few days later and my brother scolded me as soon as I walked into his tipi. But he must have heard how I had behaved because after that he did not treat me like the small boy he had always known.

Although on that first war party we did not fight or steal horses, it was the beginning of a new life.[3]

The following summer our camp was farther upstream on Bear Creek. One day I was leaving to hunt birds and had just reached the edge of the tipis when I heard a man shouting. He was too far away to be understood but I could see him wildly waving his arms. Some men galloped past me, heading for him. My brother's horse was tied close by and I jumped on without saddle or blanket. I recognized those riding beside me: Black Earth, Plain Weasel, Stays Among The Birds, and Rolls Himself. Pulling up, we saw a body.

The two men had been surrounded by a small group of Piegans. The hair was gone from one side of the dead man's head, but his friend had fought so hard the Piegans had left after stealing their horses. Stays Among The Birds said that the dead man had been brave and that we would take revenge. His friend pointed the direction the Piegans had fled. That body lying on the ground made me very angry.

The Piegans had ridden so hard that their horses were soon short-winded, and we came upon them whipping their quirts. As they tried to reach some trees we could hear their cries. Now both sides were shooting but no one was hit. Two Piegans could not get to the trees and dismounted, shooting from their knees. As Sharp Lance rode by he yelled for me 'to stay back. Stays Among The Birds caught hold of my reins, saying I was crazy. Sharp Lance rode in close and a bullet hit him in the chest, coming out the back of his neck. When this did not stop us, one Piegan lost his head and began running around in circles. The other pulled out his knife and stabbed his friend until he fell. I wanted to shoot this remaining man but Stays Among The Birds held my horse.

Lets The Women Stand raced past before the Piegan could shoot and grabbed his gun. Then Stays Among The Birds dropped my reins. As I rode up the Piegan pulled his knife out of his companion's body and stood ready. I had an arrow on my bow but decided to ride him down. He got so excited he dropped his knife and just as I was almost on him someone shot him in the head.

Since it was getting dark we did not follow the others into the trees.

We scalped the two Piegans and every man carried a piece. But the death of Sharp Lance stopped our victory songs. We packed his body on a horse and began our return. Soon it started to rain and we rode slowly through a downpour. At dawn we buried our friend on top of a rocky bluff, wrapping his body in a blanket and covering it with poles and rocks.

When we arrived in camp I went to my brother's tipi. He was angry and said that I was too young to go on fighting raids. But my friends said that I was a brave young man and that if I was not killed I would become a great warrior. My brother's words meant nothing when so many spoke like this. I would not disappoint them and would leave the next time I had the chance.

Soon after I returned from the fight in which Sharp Lance was killed I was walking around camp and noticed a group of men and boys talking excitedly. Sends Him Home was holding an unbroken bronco, blindfolded, without a saddle, its hind legs tied. I overheard him offer four arrows to the boy who could break it. Someone said that here was a boy who was not afraid of anything. I told Sends Him Home that the horse held no gun or knife and that I would ride it for those arrows.

Some men holding the horse pulled off the blindfold as soon as I was on its back. When they handed me the reins the horse stood still, its muscles trembling. Then it snorted, bit at my legs, and reared. But the hind legs were tied; it spun around and I landed on my back. After they had roped it I told Sends Him Home to untie its legs.

As soon as I was on its back again it ran and bucked. I tried to head it toward the flat area above camp but I lost control. When the people cooking their evening meal saw us coming, they scattered. The horse seemed to enjoy kicking apart their fires.

I felt myself slipping and a hard buck threw me at the entrance to my cousin's tipi. My back hurt and Sends Him Home, who had followed on his horse, told me to lie still. Then my cousin came out and covered me with a blanket. We have a custom that if someone falls in front of a relative on his father's side that relative must give him a present. In the excitement I had forgotten.[4]

Sends Him Home gave me the four arrows anyway because I had not been afraid. But my back was stiff for a few days.

Chapter Four

Two Leggings has mentioned three "elder brothers," besides Wolf Chaser, who tried to keep him from stealing away on dangerous war parties. English designations of kinship do not exactly mirror Crow relationships. A man's clansmen, according to their age, would also be called elder or younger brothers. The same term would be used in speaking to any of his mother's brothers.

Not only would a Crow boy have addressed his real mother as "mother," but also both his mother's and father's sisters. He would use "father" interchangeably for his real father, a stepfather, his paternal uncles, his father's maternal uncle, and the son of his father's sister. Then, too, he would call his aunts' husbands "father," and finally he would use the word when talking to any ceremonial or adoptive fathers.

Later on, Two Leggings remembers a "brother-in-law" who lent him a horse during a foray against Piegans. If he had been married when this fight took place the term could have included his wife's mother's brother, his wife's brother, as well as a blood sister's husband. However, he was barely nineteen, unmarried, and with Wolf Chaser as his only surviving blood kin. The term is either a mistranslation, or the chapter a slip in Two Leggings' mental chronology.

ONE DAY in grass-growing moon, when I was about sixteen, Big Boat announced a raid. My brother wanted me to wait for a few summers, but it was time I made a name for myself. I found Big Boat preparing to leave with nine men and asked to go. He wanted to know what my brother thought. After telling him I added that I could ride and shoot and run as well as anyone in our village.

Some of his men told him to let me come because I could carry the food, go for water, and collect firewood. I said I would be glad to be their helper.

Big Boat said I could come if my brother approved, and I ran back and begged until he finally agreed. At home I gathered a few pairs of moccasins, a buffalo robe, a new bow and twenty new arrows which my brother gave me, and an old knife traded from the Gros Ventres.[1] Long before dawn I was waiting in the dark outside Big Boat's tipi.

The sun was just rising as we left. We kept our faces north, crossing the Musselshell River and then the Big River. The first night out Big Boat chose a camping spot and, after ordering me to bring in some firewood, sat down to watch me. Then he told me to carry some water from a creek. When I had the fire going he seemed satisfied.

Rolling up in my robe that night I thought that now I was poor and unknown, but soon people would be talking about me. And if I was not killed some day I would become a chief with many honors and horses and property.

We traveled north for many days, even into the country of the Red Coats, but saw no enemies. We wore out our spare moccasins and cut up our robes to make new ones. Finally we were killing prairie dogs to stay alive, and Big Boat decided to turn back.

After many days we reached the Gun River. It was too high to ford so we tied driftwood poles together with rawhide, laid cross poles, and tied on our clothes. We fastened buckskin strings to each raft and held the ends in our teeth as we swam across with other poles under our arms.[2] The current was so strong it carried us far down river, and when we reached the other bank I was exhausted. But we had no time to rest and continued home.

As I was walking in the rear someone called out that he saw a person and started running. As soon as the Blackfeet knew they had been discovered they began yelling. All carried guns while we had only three. One of our men was shot in the arm. Another, hit in the hand, shouted for us to stand or be killed. Throwing off my pack, I knelt and shot at the nearest Blackfeet, my arrow going through his neck

18

and spinning him around. When I shot a second arrow into his arm he tried to pull it out. I shot a third into his shoulder and it bounced up and down as he ran back to his friends.

We entered a small coulee. Soon a man looked over the ridge nearest us and asked in our language who we were. I shouted back that I was a Crow. He told us to go home because they had finished with us. One of their dogs walked close and I shot an arrow through its chest, yelling that if he came near I would kill him like that.

A little later we watched them disappear into the hills. If they had been riding we would probably have all been killed.

We had lost our robes and were nearly naked. We walked the rest of that day and long into the night before sleeping.

The next day we ran into a buffalo herd and then had enough meat for our trip back and hide to patch our moccasins. We were happy men a few days later when we walked into our village at the foot of Snowy Mountain.

There was much singing on our return and I was mentioned as the only one who had wounded a Piegan. I had to tell my story to the friends and relatives who visited my brother's tipi. The two wounded men recovered but the one man's hand was stiff for the rest of his life.

Soon after our return, Long Horse, Chief of all the Crows, fell off his horse and died from the injuries. Crooked Arm was chosen in his place.[3]

Our camp packed up after his death and moved in easy stages to Big River. During this entire trip our men hunted buffalo.

Wolf Chaser had gone to visit the Many Lodges camped near the Arrowhead Mountains, and I stayed with our village as far as Big River. During this time I would often sit on a hilltop outside camp, imagining the things I would do someday. I wanted excitement but no one seemed to want to go raiding. When I heard that three men were leaving to visit the Many Lodges at Arrowhead Mountains I asked to go. Perhaps there I would find a pipeholder to join.

When we arrived we learned that their chief, Grey Dog, had just been killed. The new chief was Sits In The Middle Of The Land and next to him in rank was White On The Side Of His Head.[4]

The Many Lodges traveled to the Bighorn River, following it downstream until they camped near the present town of Hardin. Buffalo were plentiful in the valley and every day we hunted, keeping the women busy cutting meat into thin strips, laying them on racks to dry, and cleaning skins.

When the buffalo moved off we traveled over the Pine Ridge Hills to Elk River Valley and down Arrow Creek to the Arrowhead Mountains again. I had been staying with Wolf Chaser and while I was here he gave me a flintlock he had bought from an old man.

I made a powder horn by boiling out the core of a fresh buffalo horn, carving a driftwood plug to fit the large end which I fastened with hardwood pegs. I also made a buckskin bullet bag and hung both on a strap over my shoulder.

So when Half Yellow Face announced a raid against the Shoshonis I was ready. I quickly got his and my brother's permission to go, this time as a warrior.

It was a beautiful morning in grass-growing moon as Half Yellow Face led eleven of us west, on foot because we hoped to steal horses for the trip back.

We followed Arrow Creek, crossing the flats and walking along the river for many days, but we met no people. Our moccasins wore out and we had to kill elk and use the skin to cover our feet. We ate grouse and bear because we could not find any buffalo, and walked so far the weather grew hot. We had long since passed the place where the town of Cody now stands and were following the mountain ranges farther west. In this country we found no white people. We even crossed the big mountain range, and then, one day towards nightfall, we found ourselves at the edge of a lake so large we could not see the other shore.

I woke first the next morning to a sound like a faraway drum. After the others were up we tried to see the camp we were sure was close by. Half Yellow Face pointed to a wooded mountaintop and told us to hide there until dark.

All day we kept watch, but though we still heard the sound, no people appeared. Toward evening someone saw smoke rising from the lake shore, and Spotted Horse, one of our bravest men, crawled down.

He returned very excited and told Half Yellow Face that it was not fire smoke but steam from boiling water that bubbled out of the ground; the drumming was its noise. When we followed and saw the boiling water we did not like the place. Half Yellow Face led us homeward but game was scarce and we traveled for days with nothing to eat. Finally we walked out of the mountains near the present site of Cody and saw four enemy tipis on a hilltop. People stood around them. Then we noticed a number of horses, separated from the tipis by a steep ridge.

We all agreed that it would be better to be killed than to starve to death. Although we almost never cut horses in daylight, we could not wait. When the enemy corralled them for the night they would be even harder to steal. Then we saw the people go inside to sleep during the hot part of the day.

Half Yellow Face had us move up and chose Short Horn and Wolf Goes To Drink, both good runners. We watched them crawl up to the grazing horses, taking advantage of every cover and holding sage bushes before them.

After disappearing into the herd, they shortly returned leading two horses. Four more men then crawled up and brought back eight more horses. While our men kept returning for horses I stayed behind with two men to guard the growing herd.

By the time we had twenty-four head the sun was far past the middle, and we began to worry they would wake up. Half Yellow Face said we had enough, and once we had quietly walked the horses a safe distance we allowed ourselves no rest until we reached our village on the banks of the Bighorn River.

We returned in leaf-falling moon, almost naked, without any ammunition, and starving. But we had twenty-four horses and all of us were alive. Our people had been afraid we were dead and there was much feasting and dancing. Our story was told among the campfires, the victory songs mentioned our names, and again I was noticed.

Chapter Five

*When the Crow Wise Ones told Two
Leggings these creation myths, each was laced with lengthy
dialogues, tangential episodes, and personal
variations on well-known themes. Every tale, whether of
the remembered warpath, mythological heroes, or
supernatural figures, required an entire evening to unfold and
was adorned with a great variety of stylistic
devices in word usage and dramatic emphasis. Even then,
when the fire was down to glowing embers and the
raconteur received no audience "aho" to a particularly masterful
expression, his story was dropped until the following
night.*

*Throughout his talks with Two Leggings,
Wildschut interrupted the narrative to ask for a rationale
behind the bare description of events, customs, and
ceremonies. Initially the old man feared that such intimate
disclosures would cause his death. But Wildschut was
patient, and later he sprinkled these abbreviated pieces of sacred
lore into his manuscript. They have been combined
here to give the Crow world view, without which, Two
Leggings told Wildschut, "much would remain like a
starless sky."*

Now I MUST TELL you some sacred stories which were told to me by
our chiefs and medicine men and came from their many winters. So
I will begin at the time when there was no earth, when there was
nothing but water.

We have always believed in one creator of everything and call him

First Worker.[1] One day First Worker was looking over the world and did not like all this water. He made a duck dive down and bring him some mud. After rubbing this between his palms he blew it everywhere, creating the land and mountains and rivers. First Worker wanted to make human beings and formed the mud into many groups of clay people. To test them he made arrows and stuck them into the ground pointing east. When he ordered the first group of clay people to charge the arrows, they fell back. The next group also stopped when they met the arrows. Although the last group were pierced by the arrows, they ran on through. These different clay peoples became the different Indian tribes, and the bravest, who had charged through, became the Crows.

First Worker was proud of them because they were not afraid to die. He told the other groups to spread out and live in different places but he placed the Crows in the center so that whatever direction they traveled they would always meet other tribes.

First Worker also created two boys and ordered them to teach the Crows how to live and to give them their religion. These boys were First Worker's servants and that is why when we dream and have visions we receive both a medicine and a sacred helper to guide us through life. Except for important ceremonial occasions and when we fast for visions, we address our prayers to our sacred helper, who will pray for us to First Worker. These helpers are different for each of us as we all have different dreams.

Our medicine men, the chiefs, and our parents wanted us to fast for a medicine when we felt the need. Sometimes powerful dreams were seen by a child who did not understand them until years later. But the stories we heard in the winter tipis and around the summer campfires were usually enough to make us want power and protection in our future lives and war trails.

Once I remember a leading medicine man asking through the camp for our young men to fast in the mountains. Our enemies had been repeatedly successful. He hoped one of us would receive a medicine and take revenge.

Many of our women fasted and some obtained powerful medicines. But usually they did not fast until they had married or were old enough to be married, and then it was because they were mourning someone's death or because of an unhappy love affair.

The sweat bath was the first medicine First Worker and his two boy servants gave us.[2] In the old days it was our most sacred medicine and came before all fasts and important ceremonies. It cleansed our bodies, and when we burned incense inside the sweat lodge while praying to First Worker, it cleansed our souls.

The two boys told us that the sweat lodge represented First Worker's body. The steam from the heated stones, or the smoke from the incense, was his image. It used to be taken as a cure for an illness, but now it is used at any time, like a bath. They still pour the four, seven, ten, and countless number of cupfuls on the red-hot stones, but many do not know what this means. The first four cupfuls are First Worker's arms and legs. They are also the four main supporting willows of the sweat lodge. The next seven are the pipe-pointer star [the Big Dipper]. The ten cupfuls represent the cluster stars, and the countless number means the Other Side Camp, where we live after we die.

If we were preparing for a fast we followed the sweat bath by carefully washing our bodies in a stream and scrubbing our nails. Then we purified ourselves in a sacred smudge of burning pine needles. After that we took no food or water. This also cleansed our minds and took away as much as possible our human smell. The Without Fires do not like the smell of men, and we fasted for them to favor us.

The two boy servants taught us to weep and pray as we fasted for our own medicine. If there was no reason to weep we were to torture ourselves and sprinkle the earth with our tears and blood. We were told that First Worker's birds like to eat, and when we cut a piece of our flesh it softens their hearts so they will help us and perhaps become our medicine.

If we fasted on a mountaintop we built a small bed of rocks running east and west, spread it with pine branches, and faced east as we lay down. Then we covered ourselves with a freshly tanned buffalo robe rubbed with white clay to show cleanliness. For four days we lay there, sleeping and watching the sun until we saw our vision.

The two boys sent by First Worker taught us how to make medicine bundles after we had received our vision. The bundles contained the skins of animals we had seen in our dreams. If the sun, the moon, clouds, or other things appeared in those dreams, the boys showed us how to represent them in different ways.

The two boy servants taught us that there is another world like our earth, the Other Side Camp. The same animals, birds, fishes, and plants live there. The same rivers flow and the same mountains rise to the sky.

The Other Side Camp is divided into two clans and together they are called the Without Fires. One contains the animals, the sun and the moon and the stars, except for the star with a tail which sometimes appears during the summer months, and the souls of the dead —the little whirlwinds which dance over the plains. All the water animals of both our world and this Other Side Camp world belong to this clan, and so do the birds, the thunder, and the dwarfs. Old Man Coyote is its chief.

The other Without Fires clan is made up of everything that comes from the earth: the plants, flowers, trees, and rocks. This earth clan has four chief spirits: the wind, the fire, the water, and the earth itself.

The earth is our mother; our body is born from it and returns to it after we die. Our breath is wind and it is also our soul. Our words are our breath and they are sacred.

Each of the two clans is divided into many clans represented by different Without Fires. When we receive a medicine we join the Other Side Camp clan of our helper. Sometimes we fasted many times, dreaming of different helpers. Then all these and the dreamer made one personal medicine clan.

The Without Fires chiefs also have their servants. The sun is the chief of all the sky beings and its most important servant is the eagle. The moon is a lesser chief and has the owl for its servant. The lightning, wind, and rain also have birds as their helpers.

The chief helpers of the most powerful Without Fires can choose who among the lesser Without Fires will belong to the dreamer's medicine bundle. He will be told this in his vision. The objects within a medicine bundle are the actual dwelling places of the members of the dreamer's medicine clan. Many different things are found in each bundle because every item represents one of the Without Fires or something the dreamer was promised; only he can explain them.

I have seen a shield on which there were pictures of the sun, rain, clouds, and an eagle with lightning striking from its claws. The dreamer who was told in his vision to make that medicine may have only had a vision of an eagle. But the sun, lightning, wind, and rain belonged to the eagle's Other Side Camp clan and he pictured them also.

Certain things in a medicine bundle always mean the same: Horse-hair represents the hope for horses, elk teeth or beads mean wealth, and a strip of otter skin means water because the otter is the chief of all water animals.

All Crows have a sacred helper from the time of their birth, but some do not know him because they never receive their own medicine or because their dreams are not powerful. In that case they can buy a duplicate medicine bundle from a well-known medicine man or warrior. Some of us bought powerful medicine bundles from well-known medicine men even if we had a vision of our own because we wanted their power and their sacred helpers. But the owner would rarely duplicate all of his bundle. He would hold a little power over his copies, as was right.

We are fond of gambling and the two boys taught us this. The two Without Fires clans like to gamble against each other and their stakes are the lives of the Indians they have adopted through the medicine dreams. When a clan member loses, his adopted child is "eaten" [3] by the winning clan.

The man who dies fighting is lucky. He was looked after with special care by some Without Fire father who had won his life in the gambling. After he dies his soul is dressed with all the honors of a warrior. He becomes one with the helper who won him and will live an honored life in the Other Side Camp.

We did not want to receive a vision of the sun because he is a bad gambler. Although the dreamer usually became a powerful medicine man, he almost always died young. We preferred the moon which gambles often but rarely loses; its adopted children lead long lives.

The clans of the Without Fires also have a servant. He looks like an Indian but has pine trees growing out of his lower eyelids. He arranges war parties, brings enemies together, and leads the souls of the dead to be adopted by the winning members. If no one is killed in these battles he is disappointed and tired as he returns home.[4]

Old age is not as honorable as death, but most people want it. It proves that a sacred helper was powerful and fond of his child. It also shows that he was a good gambler and never lost a game during his child's earlier life. When the time comes and we old men go to the Other Side Camp to live in peace and happiness, we are one with our sacred helper.

Many men die young on the battlefield. This shows that their sacred helper was not very powerful and lost his game early in the life of his adopted child. Or perhaps the adopted man did not obey his sacred father. When we receive a medicine our sacred helper gives us certain instructions. Sometimes we must not do certain things, like eating certain foods. If we disobey we may have bad luck or sickness or suffer a wound in battle. If we keep disobeying our sacred helper he will grow angry and place the life of his child as a stake against some powerful opponent who always wins. The souls of people who die this way are of a lower kind, but they are allowed to enter the Other Side Camp. However, the souls of suicides and murderers must roam the earth as ghosts.

When the Black Robes came to us they talked about the devil but we could not find him in the things we knew. We think that everything is good and bad and that no person or thing is all good or all bad. I have known many men who had the ghosts as their medicine.

But we are afraid of ghosts because they may have a grudge against someone and plant a cactus needle in his body, making him sick. This can only be pulled out by a medicine man and that costs many presents.

Rock medicines were also given to us by First Worker's two boy helpers. Before First Worker created people there were only himself, Old Man Coyote, and a man who was the spirit of all rocks.[5] This man wandered over the earth looking for a mate, but without any luck. Then he met Old Man Coyote and told him about his search. Old Man Coyote advised him to go to the tobacco plant. Inside its husk were seeds, and Old Man Coyote said that these were the female people. The spirit of all rocks went to the tobacco plant and entered the husk. There he found a mate and took her to his home. They were the origin of life.

When the two boy helpers gave the Crows the sweat lodge and the Sun Dance they also gave us the tobacco-planting ceremony and the rock medicines. Four is our sacred number and that is why they gave us four medicines.

Rock medicines are both male and female because they began with the marriage of the male rock and the female tobacco plant. Sometimes we place a male rock medicine with a female one and do not disturb them for a year. By that time a little rock will have come into the medicine bundle.

If we pass a strangely shaped rock we will often stop and pray to it, asking it for good luck and health and happiness. Sometimes we will carry that rock home, hoping it may appear in a dream. If we do

not dream about it, we forget it. But if we do, we believe it is a medicine rock. We make it into a bundle and pray to it.[6]

Our bundles, the songs belonging to them, and the ceremony for
using them were all taught to us in our dreams. Together they made
our medicine. A man who ordered his life with this help was a good
and happy man and lived for a long time.

Chapter Six

Fleeting moments of peace, such as the one brought about in this chapter through the intervention of a Piegan child-captive who had escaped to his own people, occurred between the Crows and their most hostile enemies.

But with the Shoshonis, Nez Percés, and Flatheads the Crows enjoyed long intervals of amity. The permanent alliance between the Crows and Shoshonis began in 1876 when two hundred Crow lodges arrived to sound Chief Washkie on his attitude toward the Sioux invaders.

Although Looking Glass' Nez Percés joined the Crows in a battle against the Sioux in 1869, eight years later Crows were scouting for General Howard in his pursuit of Chief Joseph's and Looking Glass' bands.

Before 1867 the Crows had made a lasting treaty with the Blackfeet allies, the Atsina. With the Mandans and their own cousins, the Hidatsa, they were always friends.

One famous truce with the Kiowas, established just after the Crow separation from the Hidatsa, produced intermarriages and the transfer to the Kiowas of such cultural traits as the Sun Dance doll, individual medicine bundles, and warrior societies. The two tribes exchanged visits; Kiowa parents sometimes left their children with Crow families for years.

DURING THE WINTER after my return from the Boiling Waters we camped for a while on the flat between the junction of the Little

29

Bighorn and Bighorn rivers. On the first clear morning after many days of snow Pretty Face asked me to join him hunting. Everyone was short of food, and also I was tired of sitting in camp.

Pretty Face was married to a much older woman and brought her, his saddle horse, and his pack horse. I took two horses and carried my flintlock.

I walked first, Pretty Face came behind with his bow and arrows, and his wife drove our horses in the rear. The snow slowed us as we climbed a bluff—where Fort Custer was later built[1]—to look down into the Bighorn Valley. Small buffalo herds were pawing through the snow for grass. The wind was right and we managed to get close to one bunch.

I singled out a fat-looking two-year-old bull and wounded it. At the shot the buffalo stampeded, my bull straggling after them. But it soon fell and I ran up. Then it got to its feet, trying to catch up with the herd, but soon slumped again. This went on until finally it fell still beside a tree. By now Pretty Face and his wife were out of sight.

Walking up I saw its tail move, and before I could raise my gun it charged. I shot wild, threw the gun down, and ran. When I thought I heard it stop, I turned. Something slammed into my chest, throwing me on my back in a little hollow. The bull swerved to avoid me, then tore past. It also ran into the little cutbank and stood there for a moment, staring at me and shaking its head. Red froth dropped from its mouth and its eyes turned red. But it would not fall. Whenever I tried to roll over, it pawed the ground and switched its tail.

My blanket had fallen when I hit that bank and I was feeling cold. Each time I reached for it the buffalo stepped closer. The day was ending, and while I prayed to the Great Above Person the cold grew worse.

Then I heard Pretty Face telling his wife that he could see my tracks from the top of the cutbank and then saying that he saw my body. When he called out I was afraid to answer. Pretty Face said I must be dead and they began to cry.

He tied his blanket to his rope. As he dropped it down, the bull charged. Then I called out, and while he dragged the blanket along the cliff I scrambled up the bank.

Pretty Face told the bull that it had almost killed his friend, then put an arrow through its heart. We built a fire and soon were eating and laughing about my running into the bank.

That night I dreamt buffalo were standing all around me, pawing the ground and making the snow fly. I was on my back growing very cold. When I woke up my robe had fallen off and I was shivering. The next morning I found my gun. We loaded our horses with meat and returned to camp.

Not long after that hunt our village was at the mouth of the Musselshell along the banks of Big River. Some of us had gone hunting and chased one bull into the river. I rode a little distance downstream, dismounted, and began swimming with my knife in my teeth. When the bull saw me it tried to hook me but moved clumsily in the water. I grabbed the long rump hair and climbed onto its back, stabbing it in the side with all my strength. When I could not kill it I tried to push its large head under water, but it was too bulky.

My friends had followed along the shore and I called for a rope, which I tied to the horns. While they pulled I ripped its sides open, but it did not die until we were close to shore. I was glad to slide off its back and never did that again.

That season many things happened. A few weeks after the killing of the buffalo in the river a party of Piegans stole some horses. The weather had grown colder and ice sealed the creeks and rivers. A revenge party was organized and my brother let me join. I put on my warm clothes and took my flintlock. Leaving before sunrise, we quickly found their tracks. We rode all day and all night, allowing our horses only enough rest to keep moving. Soon after daybreak we discovered a burned brush shelter. The Piegans must have thought the cold weather would keep us at home.

Later that same day we came around a bend in a creek and they were whipping their horses. Seeing us, they dropped the stolen herd, but we kept up the chase. I was in the lead as they turned for the river. Someone shouted for me not to follow them onto the ice.

But I kicked my horse off the bank and immediately we began sliding. Four Piegans escaped up the opposite bank and I was about to ride down the remaining two when they dismounted. Even though their rifles turned out not to work, I jerked on the reins. My horse slipped and I was thrown, giving the Piegans time to remount and reach the other side. They rode halfway up a hill with a steep cliff on one side, meeting their friends on a ledge so narrow only one man could ride at a time. My friends had caught my horse and we rode to the top of the hill and built a fire. I was excited and joined Hard To Camp With at the cliff edge. The Piegans were directly below,

31

but we did not want to show ourselves. We were arguing over how to kill them when the cliff collapsed beneath me. Suddenly I was on a Piegan's back, grabbing his powder-horn strap and pulling him to me. Just as the strap snapped, Hard To Camp With slid down, snatching the man's gun. The Piegan joined his friends at the far end of the ledge. I grew afraid and tried to scramble back up.

But the Piegans were even more surprised than we. One ran off the cliff and was battered to death on the rocks; the others tried to hide in a shallow cave.

When the rest of our men slid down my courage returned. Before the Piegans could protect themselves we killed them all.

On our return a great dance with victory songs was held and the Wise Ones and warriors praised us. My brother changed his opinion of me. From then on I took the danger trails whenever I wished.

Not long after the killing at the cliff, Piegans killed one of our men who was out hunting. When I joined the revenge party my brother gave me a shield with a two-headed bear painted on it. He also gave me a fast roan mare, and I carried my bow and arrows. We galloped hard for several days and long into each night. Then the Piegan tracks were less than half a day old; finally our scouts reported riders just ahead. My horse was a good runner and I was up front when we saw them. As we raced over a ridge they were forcing their tired horses up a high hill. When they reached the top I and three others were a few horse lengths away. I put an arrow on my bow and yelled as I chased them down the other side.

Suddenly we were almost in the middle of a Piegan camp, and a large group were riding to help their friends. As we hurried back up I kept turning to watch one Piegan with a white-painted face, whose hair was tied in a knot on top of his head.[2] I got ready to shoot but an elder brother, riding beside me, caught hold of my bridle rope so I could not turn. The Piegan dismounted and his arrow struck the edge of the shield hanging on my back.

Another Piegan stood beside this man as I was aiming and shouted in our language for me not to shoot. When he asked about his brother, Poor Wolf, I recognized him.

Several years earlier our warriors had captured some Piegan children, and I had known four well: Poor Wolf, Strap, Rise Up, and Lie In A Line. They and a few others had escaped just before this raid and must have alerted their people that we were coming.

The Piegan who had shot an arrow now aimed a gun but Strap

knocked it away, breaking it against a rock. As we drew near, a Piegan asked if I was wounded and I said no. If they had not gathered around so quickly I would have killed the man who had shot at me.

We told Strap that his brother had also left camp and must be lost. Later I learned that he finally reached his people after living for days on roots and berries because the gun he had taken did not work.

After my return Wolf Chaser said that everyone thought well of me and that I seemed to have no fear. When people spoke like this it made me even more anxious to become a chief and a pipeholder.

My left shoulder was raw from riding with that heavy shield swinging about. From then on I only carried the shield cover, or a miniature shield, because their medicine power was just as much protection. But I still displayed the shield in parades.

We had made friends with those Piegans, but it did not last long. Many times they promised they would not shoot our buffalo or steal our horses. But they always lied and soon afterwards we found them again in our country.

Chapter Seven

On a raid the Crow novice-warrior
risked his life to perform defined deeds. Two Leggings
listed the four important "coups" in this order: Most
praiseworthy was the striking of an enemy with a gun, bow,
or riding quirt; then came the cutting of an enemy's horse
from a tipi door; next, the recovery of an enemy's weapon in battle;
and finally, the riding-down of an enemy.

Specific insignia advertised these
honors. The winner of all four could decorate his deerskin war
shirt with four beaded or porcupine-quill strips,
one running from shoulder to wrist on each sleeve and
one over each shoulder from front to back. Merely earning
the first coup enabled a man to trail a coyote tail
from one moccasin; from both if he performed the feat twice.
Eagle feathers tied to a man's gun or coup display stick
revealed the number of scalps he had taken. A knotted rope hanging
from his horse's neck told of the cutting of an enemy's
picketed mount. And the number of horses captured could be
read from the stripes of white clay painted under his
horse's eyes or on its flanks. From a white clay hand on those
flanks one learned that the owner had ridden down an enemy.

THE WINTER after we had made friends with the Piegans was very severe and I do not remember any war parties going out. The snow was deep and the cold so bad that several horses froze to death. We stayed close to the mountains on Red Cherry Creek, not far from the present town of Red Lodge.

34

At snow-melting time we moved to Arrow Creek and then our scouts reported many buffalo with thick fur in the Bighorn Valley. Sits In The Middle Of The Land gave orders to break camp and we moved through the Pine Ridge Hills. Finding great herds roaming in the valley, we easily killed enough for meat and robes.

When I had my share I could hardly wait to hear of a raid being organized. During the long cold season I had not visited the white trader for ammunition. But I had traded with the Gros Ventres for some hickory sticks and had made myself a strong bow, covering it with rattlesnake skin which I attached with glue boiled from buffalo bones. I also made arrows from chokecherry wood and straightened them with a stone arrow straightener.

After everyone had enough meat and skins, Sits In The Middle Of The Land led us back to Arrow Creek country. On our way we camped at Woody Creek and I heard of a raid to be led by Sews His Guts—once a bullet had opened his stomach until his intestines were falling out and his friends had sewn the hole with sinew and awl.

Sews His Guts let me join and early one morning twenty of us walked out of camp. I took my gun, as we hoped to stop at the trading post on the upper reaches of Big River [Fort Benton].[1] Sews His Guts carried his rock medicine as well as his pipe. Inside was a rock the size of a man's fist with a human face carved on it. It was a powerful medicine and had brought him through many battles.

We crossed Elk River just east of the present town of Billings. As we came up the bench north of the river we were held back by large buffalo herds. After killing some buffalo for meat we walked on to the Musselshell River, forded it, and continued north to the foothills of the Snowy Mountains. Then we began moving carefully because we were nearing Piegan country.

One day when the sun was in the middle of the sky we noticed a man on a nearby hill making smoke signals for us to come over. We could not see whether he was Piegan or a Crow from another clan. Eight men started towards him but we called them back, laid down our packs and heavy robes, and began walking in a body. Immediately men dashed out from behind rocks and bushes around the signaller, carrying muzzle-loading rifles and firing as soon as they were within range. We found cover but kept advancing. As they fell back to reload, I ran out screaming a war cry.

One hung behind and I shot him in the shoulder. Reaching back, he jerked out the arrow, broke it, and threw it on the ground. He pulled out his knife and ran at me. Jumping aside, I shot him in the breast. He also pulled out that arrow, broke it, and threw it down. I tried to keep out of his reach, yelling to get him excited. Then I shot a third arrow into his stomach. He made a growling sound, but after he broke that arrow he made signs for me to go back. I made signs that I was going to kill him. Then he made signs for me to come closer so he could fight with his knife, and I made signs that I would not.

He was almost dead and there was no reason to be afraid, so I suppose I played with him. He was my enemy and had probably killed some of my relatives. He tried to dodge my next arrow but it went into his chest and came out of his lower back. Blood ran from his mouth and nose as he walked slowly towards his friends. I shot once more. He stumbled and fell and died a moment later. Then I scalped him and tied the hair to my bow. After yelling to our men far ahead, I sang my first victory song.

Taking his warbonnet out of its rawhide case I put it on my head and danced around his body. I never thought that a Piegan might surprise me. I was only a boy and now I had my first coup. I sang and thanked the Great Above Person. I danced until the sweat ran down my body.

Eight men came back, and when they saw the Piegan they divided the rest of the scalp and joined in my singing, shooting arrows into the body. Then we ran to meet the others returning over the hill. I told of my fight but would not go back with them. After they all had shot arrows into the body they wrapped it in a robe and laid it on a rock.

The Piegans had been chased away and nobody was killed. Sews His Guts decided to return to camp, which had moved to the Bighorn Valley near the present Mission of St. Xavier.

We were singing as we walked into the village, and I held a long willow stick with my scalp tied to the end. For two days and nights the women danced the scalp dance and my name was spoken as the one who had taken revenge on the Piegans. After our celebrations we settled down to our usual life of hunting and playing games.

The Piegans must have grown very angry that season. Two other parties returned shortly after with more scalps. During the night we posted scouts to prevent their crawling into camp, but those Piegans were very clever.

Following the herds over the Little Bighorn River to the present site of Reno, we continued down river to its meeting with the Bighorn and the present site of Fort C. F. Smith.[2] There the men hunted again to supply their families with meat and winter robes.

One night my brother and I woke to a woman's screams. Running outside, I heard her just beyond camp, yelling over and over that her mother had been killed.

Torches were lit and men were running around and jumping on horses. When I arrived at the place the woman was wailing and tearing her clothes, her mother's body beside her. Piegans had surrounded them as they left the circle of the tipis.[3]

The daughter began pushing a knife into her forehead, and blood ran down her face. Then she sliced her arms and legs. We took the knife away so she would not kill herself. Our people behaved like this when a close friend or relative died, but she did not know what she was doing.

I wanted to join the riders chasing the Piegans, but the ground was covered with snow and I wore only leggings and no moccasins. I ran back, dressed quickly, loaded my gun, and while I was looking for my horse someone excited me by yelling that we must kill Piegans. Jumping on the first horse I found, I whipped it hard to catch up. The dark-face period had passed and with dawn we could make out the Piegan tracks. My brother-in-law rode a beautiful long-winded horse, and when he noticed mine faltering he gave it to me.

They turned out to be seven men on foot. Their bullets whistled by and they fell back, trying to reload. As I was almost on top of one man he yelled and lifted his gun barrel. It caught between my left arm and body. A bullet burned a hole through my deerskin shirt. Riding over him, I grabbed the gun but could not dismount to scalp him because Piegans surrounded my horse. One swung at my head with his rifle. When I dodged, the butt struck my shoulder, almost knocking me off.

The man I had ridden down was only stunned. But as he got to his feet Bull Does Not Fall Down rode up and killed him.

I noticed the feathers attached to his hair. The other Piegans were far enough away so I dismounted and scalped him. Singing a victory song, I mounted again and waved the scalp. The six remaining Piegans were soon chased into a buffalo wallow, lying flat while we rode around them. One by one we killed them all.

Later on we built a large rock pile where this fight occurred, and it is there today. When we rode into our village we were singing and holding willow poles with Piegan scalps hanging from the ends. There was a big celebration and a dance, but I was too tired and went to bed. Then the drums woke me and I dressed to watch a woman's dance, all the girls wearing their best clothes. I thought that perhaps I should stop killing and find myself a wife and make my own home. I could still go out on raids, I told myself, but only for horses.

Then I started thinking that the time had come for me to fast for a medicine. I walked back to my tipi and lay down, trying to make up my mind. If I were to become a chief and a famous warrior, I realized that I could not think of marrying and staying at home. But it was still some time before I fasted.

Chapter Eight

On these early raids Two Leggings has been tempting fate; he has been warring without a "medicine." Throughout literature on American Indians this word is the translation for a variety of terms meaning "imbued with sacred power," perhaps because the curative aspect makes most sense to us.

As Wildschut interpreted the word: "The Indian who is visited in his vision by a personified animal, plant, rock, or spirit, accepts this visitant as his sacred protector through life, but he never forgets that it was First Worker who first gave his sacred helper the strength to do this. This power, known among the Crows as 'maxpe' [maash-pay], and commonly translated, 'medicine,' was given in greater or lesser degree to all things."

The Crows walked in a world where anything could be brushed with this mysterious potency. Ordinary objects, if they figured in a dream, would suddenly become sacred and valuable. Anything which demonstrated the potential for determining the course of life was considered medicine. The trick came in harnessing these latent powers to one's aid, in the container of a medicine bundle, and carefully keeping at bay their harmful aspect through strict adherence to that bundle's taboos.

AFTER THE PIEGANS killed the woman outside camp, we moved to the part of Wyoming near the present town of Cody. It was still early in grass-growing season and on our way we stopped at the junction of the Stinking Water and the Bighorn River.

While we were there a war party returned from the Sioux country with horses. I watched the dancing in their honor and could wait no longer. I told some friends that I was going after horses, not scalps,

39

and seven were willing to join. We needed a pipeholder so I asked Three Wolf, one of the youngest pipeholders and always ready for a raid. In a dream some nights before he had been promised horses; he said we would not have to travel far.

He chose Wolf Head, Bushy Head, and myself for scouts and led us toward the southern slopes of the Bighorn Mountains. We rode up Old Baldy and before reaching the top killed a buffalo, skinned it, and built a cooking fire. This was our last meal for two days.

We had only been out for two days and did not expect enemies so close, but a scout Three Wolf had sent to an open area up the mountain returned to report people hunting in the valley on the other side.

We rode back with him and saw a large party of Utes and Cheyennes chasing a herd toward our fire. Riding deeper into the mountains, we watched from some thick pines. When the Utes and Cheyennes discovered the smoking wood they began talking and moving their arms, and soon were spreading out to find us. But a trail on rocky slopes, especially in winter, is hard to follow. They returned to the valley, where we watched their women setting up tipis in a large circle. We stayed hidden until dark and then went for our horses picketed deeper in the trees. As we mounted I told my friends that all earth creatures, the birds, and we ourselves must die sometime. Tonight we would crawl into this camp for horses and if we were all killed it was not important. But I said that if we lived our names would be praised and the women would dance.

We dismounted at the base of the mountain and crawled to a dark grove near their camp. They expected a raid and had picketed their horses within the tipi circle. Fires ringed the camp and we saw men wrapped in blankets, carrying guns, waiting for someone crazy enough to try to reach their horses.

Sometimes a guard yelled out, asking us to come and smoke. But they were afraid to leave the fires. Wolf Head whispered that we would get nothing if we just sat there, and started to crawl towards the tipis, taking only a knife and a buffalo-hair rope coiled around his waist. He dropped to his stomach and wriggled straight for a campfire where three men with guns were kneeling. Then he was gone, but we saw his plan. Between him and the fire was a bunch of sagebrush; he had crawled into their shadows. As long as none of the men in the firelight moved, he was safe.

It seemed a long time before we heard a noise behind us, thinking

40

first that some Cheyenne had found our location. But then Wolf Head whispered, and walked in leading a fine black horse. After crawling between two tipis to cut a picket rope attached to a tipi door, he had escaped through the shadows on the other side of camp, making a wide circle back. We admired him and I told myself I would be just as brave.

When Wolf Head announced that he was going home, some younger men grew afraid the Cheyennes would discover the cut rope and left with him. Piegan [personal name], Pozash,[1] and I changed our hiding place. But the fires threw such a bright glare we were afraid to sneak between them.

Then dawn began to show and the firelight paled. Walking along the river bank, I saw three tipis faintly outlined on the other side. I hid behind a big cottonwood and made out the forms of three horses picketed beside them. Sounds came from inside one tipi and I ran back to picket my horse near the river, took off my clothes, and laid down my gun. Then I began to wade, holding my knife, bow, and arrows over my head. But swimming made too much noise so I dressed again.

Beavers had built a dam there, forming a deep pond. I wrapped a blanket around myself and my bow and arrows so only my eyes showed. I crossed and passed between the two nearest tipis. People were talking inside and I smelled smoke.

Walking slowly up to a fine bald-faced horse I tossed my rope. The animal was nervous and snorted. I looked at the tipi door, but it was still. As I tried to rope the horse's neck better a gun went off next to my ear.

At the same moment I felt the air of the bullet the horse reared, knocking me to the ground. The man who had quietly slipped out of the tipi must have thought he had killed me. I woke to his shouts and saw men with guns running towards us. Racing to the river, I leaped from the bank to the beaver dam. When the Cheyennes started shooting from the bank I threw myself flat. Then, when they had emptied their guns, I ran the rest of the way, untied my horse and picked up my gun, and joined my friends in the trees.

They noticed the bullet holes in my leggings and blanket and were surprised I was alive. We pushed our horses higher, looking for a place to hide for a few days before trying again. But when we reached an open area we saw below a large party of Cheyennes leaving their tipis and soon heard the men in front yelling as they found our tracks. Their horses were fresh, and they quickly chased us out of the trees and up the steeper slopes.

My horse could hardly walk and by the time I reached the top it would not move. The Cheyennes were close, singing and yelling, and one called us women in our language.

I had my gun in my belt, my quiver under my left arm, and my bow ready. Piegan, Pozash, and I scattered. The man speaking Crow was Wears A Mustache, well known among us. When he called us women again, challenging us to fight, I became angry. My horse had started to walk and I just hoped it could reach some nearby woods. I turned to shoot at Wears A Mustache, but was out of breath and the arrow fell short.

I called out to Piegan, a little ahead of me, that we should die fighting rather than be killed like this. He looked back but kept riding as Pozash and I dismounted. Then Piegan dismounted and ran towards us. First I took my muzzle loader, but after one shot it would be useless so I also grabbed my bow and arrows. As I ran towards a thick pine grove I saw Pozash hit with a bullet.

One Cheyenne, holding a large feather-fringed shield, was running after me and another kneeling man shot at me, his bullet kicking up dirt between my legs. I took my gun but changed my mind. When I hit him with an arrow he limped back to his horse.

I had been running and dodging bullets but calmed down when I wounded this man. As I headed again for that pine grove another bullet just missed me. Cheyennes were running to head me off, but then I entered the trees and they seemed afraid to follow. I shot at them once with my muzzle loader, and while they ducked I ran like a deer and was soon out of sight.

By the time I made my way to the next slope I could see Cheyennes in the lower meadow. I dared them to follow me. They must have been very angry.

I had lost my horse and blanket, my moccasins were torn apart, and my leggings and shirt were in rags. But I still held my gun, bow, and arrows. Piegan appeared ahead of me and together we headed home.

That night we were caught in a rainstorm and were miserable without any blankets. There was little shelter in those mountains, and anyhow we could not stop because Cheyennes might be behind us.

After killing a buffalo the following day we ate a little meat and packed some and patched our moccasins. When we reached the Bighorn River where it enters the canyon we built a raft, tied on our clothes, and pulled it across with thongs held in our teeth. Once on the other side we felt safer and a few days later arrived in our village, still near the present town of Red Lodge. Everyone thought we had been killed since Wolf Head and his men had already come back.

After my return I began thinking over all that had happened and felt afraid. All those Cheyennes had been shooting at me and I had lived. Pozash, who had been in much less danger, was dead. I decided to fast for a vision in which I could see the Without Fire who had been my protector.

When I told Wolf Chaser and Crooked Arm about my escape they said I should stop going out. They were right and I told them I wanted to go on my first fast soon. But I would not promise to wait until I had obtained a medicine before leaving on another raid.

Wolf Chaser was afraid for me and one day gave me a medicine bundle, teaching me the songs and ceremony for opening it and handling it. I was thankful but did not feel it was very powerful. He had never been a real warrior and preferred to live in camp.

Chapter Nine

Prompted by the murder of a close relative or friend, the Crow mourner who pledged to hold the Sun Dance sought through its ordeal the spiritual assistance to wreak successful revenge. Thus the Crow dance was not an annual rite, as among their neighbors, nor was it a demonstration of piety. Describing it here, Two Leggings omits the three days of preliminary rituals, recalling only his painful participation in the ceremony's consummation, the self-torture.

While mourning the killing of his wife and son, the first owner of Shows His Face's Sun Dance bundle received a vision of both his next wife and a Sun Dance doll. A year later, at a ceremony attended by men only, this doll which he had seen was fashioned from the center piece of a white-tailed deer's skin stuffed with a mixture of sacred sweet grass, white pine needles, and hair from the temples and chin of a mountain sheep. The doll, a kilt from a male black-tailed deer's skin, a skunkskin necklace, a buffalo-hide rattle, a hair-lock attachment, and a whistle carved from an eagle's wing-bone—all were enclosed within a boat-shaped container painted to represent the mountains, the earth, the sky, and the rainbow (see photos of this bundle). Before the dance of Shows His Face, the bundle was used in the Sun Dances of Holds The Young Buffalo Tail and Puts Earth On Top Of His Head.

SOON AFTER I returned from that raid when the Cheyennes had nearly killed me, our camp moved to the Bighorn River near the present town of Hardin. During our stay I heard that some young men were leaving to fast in the Wolf Mountains and joined them. After completing our preparations we climbed one of the highest peaks and I built my bed of rocks and pine branches. But my courage failed that first night. I did not receive a vision and walked back to camp.

I was ashamed that I had not stayed the four days and nights and vowed that next time I would not give in so easily.

Then an uncle of mine, Shows His Face, and two of his young sons joined a war party against the Cheyennes. They were unlucky. One of his sons, Crane Goes To The Wind, was killed; the other was so badly wounded he died shortly afterward.

Their father was crazy with grief and for more than a moon sat alone in the hills near camp. We could hear his wailing. I had been fond of my cousins and also left camp to cry over them.

When my uncle finally returned to us he announced that during his time in the hills he had received a dream promising him revenge if he would be chief dancer in a Sun Dance.

He asked his friend, Puts Earth On Top Of His Head, the owner of a Sun Dance medicine bundle containing a very powerful doll, to act as ceremonial chief for the dance. My uncle was glad when his friend agreed.[1]

I took no part in the preparations but watched from a distant hill. Everyone seemed to be enjoying himself except for us who were still mourning.

I told Wolf Chaser that as soon as the Sun Dance lodge was erected I would join the dancers. He thought that if I hoped to receive a vision it would be better to fast on a mountaintop. But the dancing, the fasting, and the torture of the Sun Dance were always considered the strongest way to obtain a medicine. We were poor and I was glad of this chance to know my sacred helper and improve my position. Although my brother tried to keep me from entering the Sun Dance lodge, I would not listen.

When the day came for the lodge to be erected and my brother saw he could not talk me out of it he told me to cut a strong branch of box elder and to borrow a buffalo hide rope. After cutting the branch and borrowing the rope, I stripped to my breechcloth and moccasins and went to the site of the Sun Dance lodge. There I met Crooked Arm, one of the dance leaders, and asked him to prepare me.

First he told me to set my pole firmly in the ground inside the lodge. Then he took a dish made of mountain sheep horn in which he had mixed white clay, sweet grass, and water. Stirring this several times, he ordered me to kneel and sang this song: "They want to have a lot of things."

45

When he finished singing he painted one stripe of the mixture up and down on my chest, one on my back, and one stripe down each arm. After singing another medicine song he rubbed the mixture all over my body and scratched five crosses into the clay with his finger tips, one on my chest, and one at each elbow and each shoulder. Finally he scratched a half circle from one side of my forehead to the other.

After making me lie on my back he pinched up the skin on the right side of my chest, stuck his knife through, and inserted a wooden skewer. When he put another skewer on the left I did not show the pain I felt. He hung a loop of buffalo rope, also painted with white clay, over each skewer and tied the other ends to my pole. He placed a skunkskin necklace around my neck, an eagle feather in my hair, and a whistle in my mouth.

Crooked Arm then told me that if I felt like crying I should, but no longer than necessary. If I felt sick I was to look at the doll, which would give me strength.

Six or seven men singers and three women singers entered the lodge, the drums began, and I started to dance. The singers hardly stopped between their songs and when they became tired new singers took their place. I danced until the ropes were completely wound around my body and then danced to unwind them, all the time leaning my full weight on the thongs. I prayed to the Great Above Person and the Without Fires to pity me, to give me bravery and success in battle and a long life and wealth. Especially I asked for a vision strong enough to help me make a name for myself.

I did not cry. I danced and prayed and sometimes blew my whistle, keeping all my weight on the thongs. The people watching around the dance lodge talked to us to keep us dancing. I forgot time and everything else. Toward morning someone called to me that my partners were resting and told me to lie down.

Then I felt my tiredness and could hardly move. But when I lay down I could not sleep. It seemed only a short time later that Crooked Arm jerked me up by my thumbs, telling me to be ready to dance. The singers filed into the lodge and when the drummers began they started: "Something you dance for is coming now."

We danced again around the pole and my skin seemed to stretch forever. It was not so sore when I kept the thongs taut, but when I let them go slack it hurt very much.

I suffered terribly that day. Many times I thought I was going to faint, but I kept dancing. The sun rose higher, my pain increased with the heat, and my thirst became unbearable. I envied the other dancers when I heard them calling out a horse, a scalp, or some other vision they had seen. I prayed for something soon so my suffering would be over.

As I jerked on the thongs and tried to dance faster the left skewer tore loose and blood ran down my body. Now the right side became very painful. As I danced close to the pole where the rope had wound itself I thought something appeared beside the doll. A vision seemed about to come. I prayed harder and jerked with all my strength. I must have been reeling when I realized that someone beside me was crying. It was a young woman, a cousin, who had been watching my suffering. She stabbed herself in the forehead until her face was covered with blood. When I noticed her what I thought was going to be my vision went away. I tried to dance, but I could hardly move and felt about to faint.

Crooked Arm had been watching and now walked over to tell me to stop. Holding me over a smudge of evergreen needles, he sang this song: "Now I am just coming."

He cut two poles to support me under the arms, telling me to watch the sun until it fell below the earth.

This was about noon. For the rest of that day I stood and watched the sun, praying to the Great Above Person for his help in the things I would try to do. That night little brush shelters were put up for the dancers and I lay down to sleep.

Crooked Arm woke me the next morning to say that during the night Shows His Face had received a vision of three enemy bodies lying on the ground across the river. He asked if I had received any vision. When I said no he spoke kindly, saying that I had gone through the Sun Dance and now everyone would recognize me as a man. In the future, he said, I would be sure to have better luck. Whenever the leader received a vision the ceremony was over so Crooked Arm helped me back to my brother's tipi. He told me to stop mourning and said that now I should marry.

Soon after this dance Shows His Face led a raid and found four Sioux hunting buffalo at the place in his vision. The Crows attacked and one Sioux escaped on a fast horse. But the other three were surrounded and killed and no Crows were injured. His dream vision was fulfilled through the powerful medicine of that Sun Dance doll and bundle which I later bought.

My wounds healed after a while, but I was disappointed not to have been rewarded with a medicine dream. I decided to fast as soon as possible and hoped the Without Fires would look on me with more favor then.

Chapter Ten

*Although the Sun Dance ordeal made Two Leggings eligible for
marriage, the dual need for a fulfilling vision and a warrior's
reputation became his exclusive drive.*

*The ideal Crow marriage was between a man of about twenty-
five years with honors to his name and a girl just past puberty
who was no clan or kin relation. After offering horses to the girl's
brothers and meat to her mother, the young man received presents in
return. When the couple went to live with his parents before setting
up their own tipi the girl would be presented with an elk-tooth dress.*

*But reality was something else. While fidelity was extolled in
women, a constant man was held up to ridicule. Lovers might meet
during the pairing-off at the cutting of tipi poles, when berry-picking,
or at nightfall at the edge of camp. A woman changed hands through
the wife-stealing rivalry of the Lumpwood and Fox warrior societies
or by the death of her husband, whereupon she might live with her
brother-in-law. She could succumb to the advances of a seducer, or a
Crazy Dog—a warrior sworn to die on the battlefield—could earn
her favors for his daring. However, her reputation declined with each
new partner.*

*Such customs shocked early chroniclers and gave the Crows
a reputation as the most dissolute of all plains tribes.*

TOWARD LEAF-FALLING season we moved from the Musselshell River
to Elk River and then to the Bighorn River, camping near the present
town of Hardin. The valley seemed covered with buffalo and we
hunted for our winter supply. Then we broke camp again, forded the
river, and traveled down the valley, stopping in the cottonwood grove

where our dance hall now stands—a few miles above the present Mission of St. Xavier.

The leaves were turning yellow and we expected the first snow any day, but when we reached this place it was still hot. As we passed the flat before the grove, I noticed thousands of prairie dogs sitting on their haunches and barking at us.

The next morning the men were parading around on their finest horses, singing love songs and joyful songs. The girls, whom I was just beginning to notice, were dressed in their best clothes. Someone told me that a big dance would be held that night.

It was a day to make anyone happy, but I was still disappointed over my failure to receive a vision during the Sun Dance. Without it I could never hope for success on the warpath. So I decided to go on a fast. This time I would stay and torture myself, trusting that the Great Above Person would help me.

In my tipi I wrapped an elkskin shield cover around my shoulders because it was strong medicine. Picking up a newly tanned elk robe, I went to the river, took a sweat bath, bathed, and went to the prairie-dog town.

As I walked among the barking and staring prairie dogs I thought that maybe these earth creatures who live underground as the birds live in the sky could help me receive a powerful medicine.

I found the biggest hill in the dog town and dug away some earth with my knife to make a more comfortable resting place. Then I lay down, facing the east. The next morning I awoke to prairie dogs barking all around me. As I walked around I found a root-digger's stick. I turned toward the sun and drew out my long knife. On the ground I crossed the knife and the stick and then raised my left index finger.

I called the sun my grandfather and said that I was about to sacrifice my finger end to him. I prayed that some bird of the sky or animal of the earth would eat it and give me good medicine because I wanted to be a great chief some day and have many horses. I said that I did not want to stay poor.

Kneeling, I placed my finger on the stick and hacked off the end. Then I held the finger end up to the sun with my right hand and said my prayer again. Finally I left the finger end on a buffalo chip where it would be eaten by some bird or animal.

For three days and nights I lay in that dog town, without eating or drinking. In the dark-face time of the fourth night I heard a voice calling from somewhere. Lying very still, I heard it again, but could not locate it. The next time I heard the words of my first medicine song and I never forgot them: "Anywhere you go, anywhere you go, you will be pleased."

I saw the face of a man who was singing and shaking a buffalo-hide rattle. I also heard a woman's voice but could see only her eyes and the beautiful hair on top of her head. They filled me with joy and I thought that if I ever saw a woman with those eyes I would marry her. Then the voices sang: "You. I am coming. There is another one coming."

Many people seemed to be talking and I became confused. My vision people seemed to be coming from behind a hill. First I saw the man's head and then I saw him from the waist up. After his song he faced east and shouted. Then he shouted to the north and finally to the west. The singing grew faster and I fell back as if drunk. When he shook his rattle I saw a face painted on it. The man was painted with red stripes across his chest and face and other stripes running up and down under his eyes and nose. A mouth opened in a face painted on the rattle, and I began to faint. The woman did not show any more of her face or body but kept singing, and I learned the words to her other song: "I am doing it now. I am doing it now. Discovered Plant.[1] I am making his lodge. I am doing it now."

A voice told me that if Comes Out Of The Water [2] came to me I would have much property. The woman kept telling me that what I was wishing for had come true. I noticed the parting in her hair was painted yellow. Then someone seemed to be driving horses toward me. As they drew closer I recognized Shot In The Face walking behind them. The horses were real and I had woken. Shot In The Face said that he had watched me staggering around but did not realize that I had been fasting. He was sorry to have disturbed me and asked where my blanket was. I saw it was some distance away and then noticed my swollen finger. Although it hurt badly I was more unhappy not to have dreamt all my dream. I had intended to stay another night but felt too weak and returned to camp. My finger was bandaged in my tipi. After eating a little food I slept.

I did not think my dream was powerful, but at least I had some medicine songs I had dreamt myself. These were much more powerful and valuable than the ones I had sung before in battle, which had been bought or given to me. I did not tell my friends or the medicine men about my dream. As soon as possible I would fast again for a stronger vision.

In the meantime I did not want to remain in camp. When I heard that Crazy Sister In Law was going out I found him. He said that he had noticed me in the Sun Dance and wanted such brave men.

Now it was late in leaf-falling moon and the nights were cold. One morning at dawn we gathered on the outskirts of our village. I carried my flintlock, the powder horn and bullet bag were on a strap at my side, and my bow case and quiver hung on my back. But I was not warmly dressed and the men called me Belly Robe because of the old wrinkled buffalo robe wrapped around my waist.

The pipeholder often selected younger men for his scouts so I was not surprised when Crazy Sister In Law chose me. It was a good sign when he gave me the coyote skin to carry. In my last dream my spirit man had carried a coyote skin over his arm. Now I was a scout, soon I would be a pipeholder, and then I would be a chief. But I still said nothing to my friends.

The other scouts, Woman Does Not Know Anything, Spotted Horse, and Medicine Father, picked me as leader because I was the only sun dancer. As soon as we left, Woman Does Not Know Anything and I rode ahead to cover the country for game or enemy signs, arranging with Crazy Sister In Law to meet at a place on the Musselshell River.

The two of us rode all that day without seeing any signs, while the other two scouts kept us in contact with our men. At dusk we headed for the meeting place. Crazy Sister In Law was inside the brush shelter which his helpers had built and he invited me to sit next to him across from the entrance. It was the first time in my life that I sat there and for a while I could not speak. Crazy Sister In Law filled his pipe and after we had smoked I gave my report. No one else had any luck locating meat and we went to sleep hungry.

At daybreak the four of us set out again. I carried my coyote skin and we all painted our faces red. The older men taught us to carry red paint ground from rocks, explaining that it is part of the everlasting earth and would protect us.

For a long time we rode without seeing any animals. Finally we came to a bluff giving us a wide view. Since I had not slept well the night before I told my companions to wake me if they saw anything. The wind was blowing hard and I lay down in the shelter of a little knoll, folding my coyote skin next to me.

I dreamt the coyote skin stood up and began howling. It faced east and then north and finally sang this song: "I am going far. I shall bring some bones."

It howled again, still facing east while it sang another song: "I shall have a good time."

Then it threw a bone into the air which came down covered with meat. I noticed that the coyote's paws and face were painted red. It howled and sang a third song: "My partner. I am going. He is lying still."

This meant that the coyote saw an enemy's body lying on the ground. Then it howled a fourth time, faced south, and sang a fourth song: "This is the land where I used to live. Look that way. I want that over there."

I looked in that direction and a black horse was galloping away. My foot was kicked and Woman Does Not Know Anything was standing over me, saying that the other scouts had already left. That coyote had shown me where to find meat, where I would kill an enemy, and where I would capture a beautiful black horse. But I was sorry I had been woken. I might have learned more. I carefully picked up the coyote skin and followed my friends. On the way I told them to say thank you. After saying it they asked what it meant and I told them of my dream and pointed out a high ridge to the west. On the other side, I said, would be buffalo.

Spotted Horse was on the fastest horse and reached the ridge top before we were at the foot. We saw him looking, and then he took the blanket from his shoulders and waved it at us. We thought he meant enemies and made signs back. But he held up the robe's points, which meant buffalo. Joining him we saw three animals grazing down the slope. Someone said we should pray and sacrifice to the Great Above Person, so we all prayed that we would like to eat some of this meat. If we killed a buffalo we vowed to sacrifice skin from our hands.

The dream had been mine so I did the shooting. Hanging the coyote skin over my shoulders with the head piece over my forehead, I began to crawl on my hands and knees while two scouts circled to drive the buffalo toward me.

At last a buffalo walked close, thinking I was a coyote. As it pawed the ground I killed it with one shot in the left side.

Each of us pinched the skin on the left hand between two fingers, stuck in an awl to hold the skin up, and cut off a small piece with a knife. We made a prayer of thanks as we sacrificed this skin to the Great Above Person. Then we roasted some of the meat for ourselves. The other three butchered the rest and carried the pieces to our starving companions not far behind. I did not carry any because I was the leader. We met no enemies on that trip and soon returned to our village.

Chapter Eleven

*Songs were an integral part of the medicine
power which Two Leggings was attempting to accumulate through
these early fasts. While personal songs received under
these arduous circumstances were considered the most important
kind and were often passed from father to son, songs played an
essential role in every major and minor Crow ceremony
and every Crow social dance. They were also a formalized
means for communicating emotions upon occasions running
from the seduction of one's wife to the preparation for death when
the end appeared imminent.*

*Some songs, such as children's lullabies,
were public property. Others were spur-of-the-moment
creations, quickly forgotten. If a particular medicine song proved
to benefit its owner, less successful warriors paid much for its
rights.*

*Before he ever received his own songs,
Two Leggings gave a buffalo's hindquarter to Bear and his
wife. In gratitude the renowned old warrior permitted the youth
to sing his personal war song: "Friend, we will go there. I would
like to have plenty. I have plenty."*

*"Friend," Two Leggings explained, was
the Without Fire visitor of Bear's medicine dream. "We will go
there" expressed the singer's request that this sacred helper
accompany his coming raid. "I would like to have plenty" spoke
his hopes for that raid, and "I have plenty," his assurance that
those hopes would be realized.*

55

I HAD HOPED for better luck on that war party when I was leader of the scouts, and still felt I did not have a strong medicine. After our return I went deer-hunting for skins for moccasins, and then camp moved from the Musselshell River to the Elk River where I killed several buffalo for robes. Traveling slowly up Elk River, we finally camped close to the present town of Livingston, at the foot of a place we called Bad Mountain.

After those hunts I was more unhappy and took only a small part in the dances and celebrations. My brother noticed this and one night in his tipi asked what was wrong. When I explained he said that no one should go out as often as I did without some protection. I told him that I had fasted and received a vision, but he said I had never told him about it and would be killed if I kept on.

The next morning Medicine Crow, Young Mountain, Blue Handle, Walking Mouse, Bull Does Not Fall Down, and others whose names I have forgotten joined me in a ceremonial sweat bath. That afternoon we started to climb Bad Mountain, each of us carrying a newly tanned buffalo hide painted all over with white clay.

On our climb we passed a spring and stopped to take off our clothing, wash, and clean our fingernails and toenails. Then we built a fire, dropping in some pine needles to purify our bodies with their smoke.

It was a long climb and although leaf-falling moon had just arrived the weather was hot. We were tired as each man selected his spot, built a rock bed, and covered it with fresh pine branches. Then we prayed and slept under our buffalo robes.

That night none of us received a vision, but we continued our fast, praying and weeping through the following day. The second night I dreamt of a man telling me that a bird sitting on top of Bad Mountain would see me the next night. The dream ended as the man disappeared. The following morning I woke to find the others preparing a meal down the mountainside. When I joined them, Medicine Crow said that they had not dreamt and he thought we should break our fast.

I told them that they could return home but I was wanted on the mountaintop that night. Then Medicine Crow decided to stay on, but Little Fire, Young Mountain, Blue Handle, and the others said that they would wait at the foot of the mountain. They lacked the courage to fast one more day.

I chose a new resting place and fasted for three more days and nights, growing very hungry and thirsty. All the time I prayed and my heart pounded like a drum.

After dark-face time of the third night, rain fell, and I crawled from my place underneath an overhanging rock to lie on my back and catch drops. I must have fallen asleep because a voice on my right told me to look at a man over there who was well known all over the world. The voice said that he was Sits Down and that he was sitting on the mountaintop.

Looking up I saw a person with clouds floating in front of his mouth. A ring of clouds hung above his head, but then I saw that it was really a hoop with many kinds of birds flying around it. An old eagle flew and perched on this hoop.

When a voice asked if I knew that I was known all over the earth I did not answer.

The person's face was painted with pink stripes down his cheeks which meant the clouds. Then clouds rolled in front of him, and when they separated, his face was painted with a wide red stripe across his forehead. This meant I would get what I wanted. His eyebrows were painted yellow and this meant sight. He sang this song: "I am going to make the wind come. I am going to make the rain come."

A different voice said that all the birds of the air were going to show their feeling toward me and that it would come true. After some silence this second voice said that it had been told to sing. Now I understood that the second voice was the cloud person's servant who had been instructed to give me a medicine song: "Come. Long ago. Thanks. You will be a chief."

I followed the man-in-the-cloud's pointing arm and saw a large number of horses appear above the horizon.

The words "come" and "long ago" referred to a time years before when I had joined some boys on a fast on this mountain. Although we had tortured ourselves we had been too young and had given up when we became hungry.

The dream was over and I woke to the rising sun. Soon Medicine Crow walked over and pointed down the mountainside to our people breaking camp.

After joining our friends down the mountainside we all walked to the valley. Medicine Crow told me that he was afraid he would never live to be an old man. (But his life disproved this. When he died in the summer of 1920, he was over seventy years old.) He did not tell what he had seen but he felt miserable and was so weak he could hardly walk.

Three other young men who had come signalled with a blanket for us to join them on a ridge top. Before reaching them we came upon some antelope, killed one, and built a cooking fire. We finally walked into camp just as it was pulling out for the Musselshell River.

During the time we camped along that river an old man named Four Dance visited our tipi and told us the story of his medicine dream. It made a great impression on me. This was his story.

I had three older brothers, Passes All The Women, Does Not Care For Women, and Women Leggings. Now they are all in the Other Side Camp.

When I was about seventeen I wanted to make a name for myself. But my older brothers would never let me join a raid. We were living with our grandmother, Holds By The Gun, because our parents had died long before.

Once my brothers were gathering their weapons for a raid. When my grandmother asked them to pity me they said I was too fat to run. She told Does Not Care For Women that they were wrong not to take me and that she would help me.

The next day, after they had left, she called for me. Holding a big bundle, she explained that this powerful medicine had belonged to her grandfather and contained a Sun Dance doll and a skunkskin. If I took it to a high ridge and fasted and prayed she was sure the Great Above Person would pity me because the bundle had brought powerful dreams the few times it had been used.

We were camped along Elk River near the present town of Billings. Some young men and I climbed the rimrocks along the southern shore. My grandmother had loaned me a white-painted buffalo robe and had given me a stick hung with two eagle feathers and painted with white clay. After building my rock pile on the highest place I planted this stick at the head and fasted for four days.

On the morning of the fifth day I woke and thought about going home. Everyone else had left. But I fell asleep again and saw seven men and one woman far off to the west. At first they seemed to be standing on Bad Mountain in the Crazy Mountains north of the present town of Livingston—which we also call the Bird Home Mountains. As I watched they sang a song. The second time they appeared on Snow Mountain in the Crazy Mountains. One man was dancing and wore feathers tied like a fan behind his head. His face was painted with lines across his cheeks and forehead. Then they disappeared, and the third time I saw them standing on Bear Head, one of the bluffs between the present towns of Park City and Columbus. The men held up drums but I could see their painted faces through the drumheads. A skunk inside one drum had fire burning in both ears. The seven men and the woman were singing and dancing but I could not hear the words. They disappeared again, returning a fourth time on the rimrocks north of the present town of Billings, singing: "Buffalo are coming toward me."

Then they stood in front of my rock pile. When they threw off my blanket I lay still. They hid their eyes with eagle feathers and sang again: "Your poles are bulrushes."

Beating their drums, they tried to prevent me from seeing what they held. I thought it was my grandmother's doll but then I saw it was a screech owl. When the owl sat on my chest they sang again: "Beat the drums."

A man stood on my right, his face covered with a large elk robe. Suddenly he threw it off, pulled out his flintlock, and shot the owl. It hooted and I think went inside my body. The man picked up some dirt and put it in his gun, saying that rocks all over the earth are hard but that even if all the guns were aimed at me I would not be hurt.

Then he shot at me, and the owl, which had returned to my chest, jumped aside. I felt myself bouncing up and down. A big black owl flew up from the valley and sat beside me. The man holding the gun told the other people that I was poor and that they might help me.

The black owl sang this song: "I shall run all over the earth."

When he had finished I noticed the trees had turned into people who were all shooting at the owl. A few feathers dropped as it flew away and returned again. Some tree people gave me small pieces of meat. Some of my own horses appeared and I noticed one dead on the ground. I thought it meant bad luck.

When I first woke I thought I had been shot and that my dream had been given by some bad spirit.

After returning to camp I gave my medicine back to my grandmother, but it was not time to tell her about my dream. She seemed worried since the bundle had always brought powerful visions before.

Some of our best-known medicine men thought my dream was very strong and that I would never be killed in battle. Then I told my grandmother.

One day after I had married I was camped close to the Arrowhead Mountains near a good spring. A man rode up to my tipi and, pointing to some willows near the spring, said that enemies had built trenches there. They could not be chased away since the best warriors were hunting. He had heard of my dream and asked me to do something.

I told him to wait and went inside. After painting yellow stripes across my eyes and zigzag lines from my forehead down across my cheeks, I put on a fringed buckskin shirt decorated with large quillwork circles on front and back. I also hung two red sashes under each arm and wore a scalp-lock necklace. When I walked toward the enemies my wife came behind holding one sash. After stopping four times I told her to go back.

They had covered their trench with buckskins and dirt and now raised the cover to fire, but I continued walking. A few feet away one man shot at me but missed. Another jumped out and held his gun muzzle against my chest. But when the gun went off I was not shot. As I walked I made a noise like a hooting owl and sang my medicine song. Behind me our men began firing. The enemies tried to escape from their trenches but then they were in the open and all were killed.

I was never wounded and only once had a horse killed under me. My dream was powerful and though I had been a poor boy I grew to be a chief and a medicine man.

I was excited by this story and hoped to make a name for myself the same way. But I needed a strong medicine to protect me and decided to fast again soon.

Chapter Twelve

*In their youth Two Leggings and his
companions had to elicit visions through rigorous, ritualized
suffering. Later on they received prophetic dreams
without preliminary ordeal and even experienced unexpected
visions.*

*The Crows distinguished four grades
of dreams. In "no-account dreams" one saw when asleep some
incident which merely left a vague sensation.*

*"Wish" dreams contained some
medicine power. However, being little more than hopeful references
to property and different seasons, they did not always
come true. The dreams which Two Leggings' aged guests
give him when they attend his sweat-lodge ceremony are of
this type.*

*Third were the definite "property" dreams.
In them a man saw blankets, shawls, warbonnets, horses, and
the like, which he later acquired through actual events.*

*Finally there were the "medicine dreams"
or "visions." Although Wildschut uses the words almost
interchangeably, their slight difference is demonstrated when Sees
The Living Bull mentions his fourth fast's medicine dream
turning into "a real vision" once he had been woken by rain. In
these the faster received, through his sacred helper, his medicine
and its accompanying instructions.*

DURING THE SNOW SEASON we camped on Arrow Creek, but when the
snow melted and the ice left the rivers we moved to Dry Head Creek

between Arrow Creek and the Bighorn River. Soon after our tipis were pitched, eight of us left camp to fast in the Bighorn Mountains, planning to climb a mountain on the east side of Black Canyon called Where The Thunderbird Sits Down Mountain.

Most of our people were afraid of this place because it was the Thunderbird's home. Long ago a man named Covers Himself With The Grass was traveling through this country. He heard a strange noise and looked up to see the Thunderbird flying down. His horse bucked and when he dismounted, it ran off. With his rawhide rope he tied himself to a tree at the canyon bottom. The rush of air from the Thunderbird's wings was so strong the trees on both sides were uprooted. Covers Himself With The Grass was saved, but his tree was thrown about until he was sure it would pull up.

We decided to fast there because we wanted a stronger medicine. Medicine Crow, Young Mountain, Mouse Walks, Shows His Tail, and I were all close friends, but Young Rabbit, Plenty Screeching Owl, and Yellow Weasel were nearly strangers to us.

Each man carried his own robe painted with white clay. When we reached the foot of the mountain we took a sweat bath and cleaned ourselves. Building a fire we purified our bodies in sweet-sage smoke, and then painted ourselves with white clay. We arrived at the top before dark and built our little rock piles two feet above the ground. Covering them with fresh pine branches, we then laid down flat rocks.

I asked Young Mountain to help me sacrifice my flesh and he lifted the skin on my left arm, cutting out a piece that looked like a horse track. I hoped to steal horses and had asked for that cut. Then I faced east, held the piece up to the sky, and told the Great Above Person that I wished for some animal to eat this and help me receive a powerful medicine. I also asked for a long life.

Plenty Screech Owl had Young Mountain cut a horse track on his arm. His was larger but when I asked Young Mountain to cut me again he said mine was big enough.

Medicine Crow said he was going to cut off the tip of his right index finger but instead had Young Mountain cut horse tracks on his arm. Again I asked to have my cut enlarged and Young Mountain punished me by cutting many small tracks. Then he sliced off the end of his own index finger. We all stood in a row, raised our sacrifices to the sky, and prayed out loud for a long time.

I was surprised that Medicine Crow had joined us again. His father was Sees The Living Bull, one of our most powerful medicine men, who could have made his son a good medicine. But Medicine Crow told me later that his father encouraged him to obtain his own medicine, saying that then he could care for his own children when Sees The Living Bull died.

Stretching out on my back I watched the moon and stars by night, and followed the sun through the next day. As I prayed I grew very thirsty.

After the second night five men wanted to return home. I did not think about giving in and let them leave. Medicine Crow and Young Mountain also stayed on.

We told the returning men to kill an elk at the foot of the mountain, to cache the meat, and then to tell our families we were staying all four nights.

A strange noise rushing up the mountainside woke me early the third day. Immediately I thought of the Thunderbird and grew afraid. As it drew near I pulled my robe around me. I felt better when it proved to be a hailstorm, and cut leafy branches to protect myself. Then all became quiet again. I lay and thought of all the animals of this earth, praying that the Great Above Person would lead one to me in my sleep, that it would eat my flesh and become my sacred helper for the rest of my life.

All the next day I watched the sky and slept. At dark-face time that night the vision of my last fast came again. When I woke it was nearly dawn but one bright star shone above the eastern horizon. After I saw it I covered my head with my robe and fell asleep again. A man appeared above the horizon and a voice which I could not locate spoke to me. The man was waist-high above the horizon where the sun would soon rise. A hawk perched on a hoop on his head. Something red in the right side of the man's hair grew larger and finally colored the entire sky. A streak of the brightest red went up the middle. The man asked if I knew the name of the bird on his head. I lay still without speaking. He said the name of the bird was The Bird Above All The Mountains. In the future, he said, people would hear about me all over the earth.[1] Then I learned my vision man's song: "Thank you. A long time going to be a chief. Thank you again."

Behind me I heard a voice but saw no one else. It told me to look at that man on the horizon whose name was Looks All Over The Earth.

When I saw my vision man again a large black eagle was flying over his head. The hoop where the hawk was sitting was painted partly

63

blue, which meant the earth, partly yellow, which meant the day, and partly black, which meant the night. The man took off the hoop, looked at it, and told me to look around.

After singing another song, he held the hoop before his eyes. Although he was seeing several visions, I saw nothing. The other voice behind me said to look west and asked if I saw the trail.

Through the hoop held before my eyes I had a vision of a trail running from the west, where the wind comes from, and heading east. At its end I saw a tipi and grazing horses. Between us snow covered the ground. Then a big eagle flew over my head and I noticed its claws. The voice behind me said to look toward the Musselshell River. Turning in that direction and looking through the hoop I saw bodies on the ground. The eagle hung over them and pretended to grab one. My dream man sang: "Thank you. A long time going to be a chief. Thank you again."

My vision man said that Wolf Runner was coming to see me. He said that the big eagle was the same one which had visited me on Bad Mountain.

Then the voice behind me said to look east, where I saw a big sweat lodge built of forty-four willows and four small sweat lodges of four branches each, all close to the Bighorn River where my future house would stand. Whenever I wanted to go on the warpath, the voice said, I must build those sweat lodges and sacrifice to him and his kind.

The sun was just rising as I woke, covered with perspiration. My blanket lay apart from me. Standing up, I thanked the Great Above Person for my vision and medicine. Young Mountain came over and asked if I wanted to stay. Since I had received my medicine we left. I had felt weak and exhausted but now my energy seemed to return. My arm had hurt and I had lost much blood but now I hardly noticed it.

Medicine Crow, Young Mountain, and I walked to the foot of the mountain where our five friends were waiting. After enjoying a meal of elk meat we lit a pipe. Someone said that since this was the only time we could speak about our visions we should smoke this pipe and tell what had come to us.

When my turn came I smoked and said that I had seen the same person who had appeared to me on Bad Mountain. I told about the horses but said I did not understand the snow's meaning.

Young Mountain said we Crows knew less than half the earth people; to have them all know me meant something great.

Medicine Crow held the pipe and said he had seen a man and had dreamt a good dream. But then another spirit he could not see told him that the first man was a bad spirit who spoke lies. The second spirit then appeared as a man wearing a buffalo robe with the hair side out. But Medicine Crow could not see his face. Telling Medicine Crow to look toward the joining of the Little Bighorn and Bighorn rivers, he said that something was shining over there. He was to remember this because when that thing would really be there he would become a chief.

(Many years later, when Fort Custer was built near these rivers, we noticed how some windows shone in the light of the setting sun. Medicine Crow became a chief about the time the fort was completed.)

Young Mountain told Medicine Crow he did not think the vision very powerful. Mine had been best, he said, for the world was large and if I became known all over that meant something powerful. He could hardly believe it. I assured him it was true and added that as soon as I was a pipeholder we would not have to follow other men.

When the pipe was handed to Young Mountain he said that although he had cut off his fingertip he had not received a dream.

Shows His Tail was passed the pipe and said he was a man like us. He had seen an enemy's body lying along the creek which runs between the Little Bighorn River and Rotten Grass Creek. He said that when we killed an enemy there he would strike the first coup.

The rest had not dreamt anything so we started back to camp, arriving at sunset. When my brother asked if I had received a vision I said that I had, and he was pleased that now I would have better luck.

Shortly afterward Shows His Tail went on a raid and took an enemy scalp at the place in his dream.

Chapter Thirteen

When Two Leggings bemoans his orphaned state it is more rhetoric than fact. He completely neglects another social group in Crow society, from which no one was excluded.

At birth every Crow baby belonged to the one of thirteen clans to which his mother belonged. Among members of these "lodges where there is driftwood," as the Crows called clans, existed the solidarity of wood entwined. Fellow members feasted together, assisted their clan brothers about to be initiated into the Tobacco society, and aided widowed and orphaned members. However it was forbidden to marry within one's own clan.

Sometimes clans temporarily separated from a larger band for hunting purposes. But unity among all clans was the communal hope. When a conflict arose between two clans, the camp police and neutral clans would try to bring about peace, pleading, "we are one people."

Two Leggings himself belonged to the Not Mixed Clan, so called because when the Big Belly clan was renamed most of its members were war leaders who did not associate with ordinary folk.

Obligations were also due toward members of one's father's clan. A man could not cross a paternal clansman's path without giving him a present, and he would often feast these clansmen and present them with gifts. Sometimes they became a child's name father and, as in Two Leggings' case, a medicine father.

AFTER THAT FAST our camp moved to Hits With The Arrows. On the way I told Young Mountain and Piegan—who was also called Walks Toward The Two Mountains—that I was ready for a raid.

They were my partners [1] and when they asked to join I told them to gather sixteen willow branches and some charcoal and to meet me the next morning.

At dawn we rode to a hill top. With the willows I built four small sweat lodges, crossing the branches two by two and setting them in a row with their openings toward the rising sun This was also toward the Sioux country, which my medicine person had pointed out for my next raid. I powdered the charcoal, mixed it with buffalo grease, and rubbed this all over the branches to show revenge. In tiny holes in the center of these lodges I made little fires and burnt bear root [2] shavings. Then I cut a long slender pole and tied a red blanket with a black circle and four black crosses to the top. The circle meant the hoop I had seen and the four crosses the four directions my vision man had shown me. After planting the pole before one lodge I faced the sun, said "aho" three times, and sang my vision song: "Thank you. A long time. You are going to be a chief. Thank you again."

I prayed to the One In The Sky and to all up there that I wanted a long life, that tonight when the stars were out I wished them to visit my sweat lodges. If I was lucky on my raid I promised to make these lodges again for them, and to make them every time I went out.

When I sat down Young Mountain said that he had never seen sweat lodges made of only four willows. I explained how the voice had shown them to me, instructing me to build them before every raid.

My prayers and sacrifice over, we set out on foot toward the Sioux country. Later that day, as we came upon a small buffalo herd, I crawled within range of a fat cow, rested my flintlock on a forked stick I usually carried, and killed it with one shot. We ate and then cut some meat into strips which we strung on sticks for each man to hang on his back. That night we built a little brush shelter. Before going to sleep Young Mountain said that he and Piegan were worried that I carried no medicine for our protection.

I said that those four sweat lodges had been given to me for a medicine. But I promised that when I was a pipeholder I would carry a medicine whenever I left camp. Reminding him that he had a father and a mother to help him, I said that I was an orphan and had to depend on myself to discover right and wrong. He knew my brother was not a warrior and could not help me. Although many of the Wise Ones in camp would not like what I was doing, I said that if I sat in camp wishing for someone to give me a medicine nothing would ever happen. I must find out for myself and be very careful to avoid bad luck.

67

Only that way would the Wise Ones begin to trust me and look on me as a man. Their hearts would soften and they would help me. I assured Young Mountain that these sweat lodges were my medicine now and would protect us for this trip.

He said that then he wished I had brought them, but since they had come this far they would follow me. I admitted pretending to be a pipeholder without a pipe, but I urged him not to be afraid and promised again to make a medicine on our return.

We traveled east along the Elk River, sleeping several times before finally reaching the country around the present town of Forsyth. There we spotted seven horses grazing on a high hill south of the river. Although we saw no enemies we knew they must be near and hid in the brush of a nearby coulee. After a while Young Mountain went for a closer look while Piegan and I ate dried meat. The sun was in the middle when Young Mountain returned to report that they were strays. Now they were grazing downhill beside some buffalo. He described a fine brown mare with a colt, but said the others looked poor.

Leaving our hiding place we lit some dry buffalo manure and held it in our hands as we walked around the horses. When they tried to smell us and stood still, we slowly approached, walked them to water, and drove them back to a high bank where we roped the brown mare. The rest did not run and we roped one after another, finishing about dark and eating again. Piegan had been looking them over and thought they belonged to a bunch stolen from Cutting Turnip the leaf-falling season before.

Since my vision's first part had come true I wanted to be careful. The enemies who had lost their stolen horses might still be around. At first we were afraid they were unbroken. But after Young Mountain jumped on the brown mare, Piegan and I chose mounts. Riding as far as Porcupine Creek that first night, we made camp close to the river. Two days later we arrived near our village at Rock Pile, close to the Buffalo Heart Mountain and northwest of the present town of Cody.

As we rode into the village in the morning, driving four horses and a colt before us, we sang victory songs and shot our guns into the air. A dance was set up in our honor and the older men praised my name. I was proud, but I did not forget to thank the Great Above Person for the great medicine dream.

I had been careful because my future depended on not hurting myself or those with me. Although few honors were won this trip I had brought horses, which are always valuable, and I had tested my medicine vision. My medicine person had asked me to look east and had shown me horses close to where I found them. My dream was real, and I wanted to go in the other directions to make it all come true.

Some pipeholders did not like my leading a war party without having been accepted as one of them. They said bad things would come of it, but the younger men admired and encouraged me. About this time I was initiated into the Lumpwood warrior society and felt this another step toward improving my standing.

A few days later my brother said that if I had decided to become a pipeholder I should ask a leading medicine man to make me a duplicate medicine. But I still thought I could do all these things alone and would not listen.

When I asked Young Mountain to join another horse-stealing raid he asked where and I said north to the mouth of Wolf Creek as my vision had directed. He asked me to carry a real pipe this time, even if we did not smoke it, and also suggested we take some boys as helpers and scouts. Then it would appear that I was a real pipeholder.

He was right but we would have to find boys I could trust since the chief would never allow me to pretend I was a pipeholder. If he heard about this or the camp police caught me my weapons would be broken and I would be beaten. But if a person who disobeyed was successful all could be forgotten. I was headstrong and would not wait for anything or ask anyone for help. And I was sure I would return successfully.

But I promised to follow Young Mountain's suggestions. That night I stood in front of Rattle's tipi and told him to come outside. When I asked if he wanted to join us he said that he would have to wait until his people were asleep. Then he would take his father's bow and arrows, spare moccasins, and horse.

I offered him some moccasins. Young Mountain walked up and the three of us sat in the bushes, watching his tipi. His father came home, the fire burned lower, and we knew they were asleep.

Rattle crawled into the tipi and a little later came out with the bow and quiver over his shoulder. When his father said something Rattle straightened and ran for his father's horse. Then we heard his father wake his wife.

Rattle reached his horse, quickly tied its mouth with a rope he had borrowed from me, and jumped on. But he had forgotten that the horse was picketed to a stake. The rope drew tight and the horse fell. His father grabbed him on the ground.

Rattle began crying, saying that he was only taking things because he was afraid his father would not let him leave.

His father was not angry but said he should have asked first. Then he called us over and asked us to wait until the next day when he could give his son a good horse and spare moccasins. He said he would not stop Rattle, because it showed he was going to be a man, but that it was not good to steal.

After they had gone inside Young Mountain wanted to leave because if we had bad luck the boy's parents would blame us. He was right and also in daylight the camp police could easily spot us. That night we slipped out.

At sunup I built the four medicine sweat lodges and prayed for success. Then we rode north to the Piegans. After several days we approached their country and began riding carefully from hilltop to hilltop.

Finally, we spotted a Piegan camp in the distance, moving in our direction. Afraid scouts might be in front, we hid all that day in a thick grove of cottonwoods and chokecherry bushes. As the sun was setting we saw them pitch their camp close to a creek and turn their horses out to graze.

Young Mountain asked me to sing a medicine song and to promise that if we had good luck I would make a medicine when we returned. I had the pipe tied to my belt, but did not want to risk the anger of some Without Fire by using it. Besides, I did not even know the ceremony.

It had been dark for some time when we finally left the grove. Soon we heard dogs barking and Piegans talking. When Young Mountain asked me to sing again I told him not to worry and reminded him of my dream of the buckskin horse I was to steal on this northern trip. After promising again to make a medicine when we got back I sang a medicine song in a low voice.

No one seemed to be guarding the horses that were grazing a little apart from camp. Crawling on our hands and knees until we saw them clearly, I pointed to the buckskin I would go after while Young Mountain tried for the pintos. However, I told him to leave with whatever horses he could quickly round up. I could remember when he had crawled right among the tipis, and I wanted no bad luck when I was responsible.

I roped my horse and drove off several others, while Young Mountain caught a good-looking sorrel and also drove away some more.

Together we had twelve and for the rest of that night we rode as fast as we could, continuing through the next day. Then we stopped briefly to give our horses a little grass and water.

Young Mountain picked up a spotted eagle's tail feather on our way, thinking it was better if I carried something that looked like a medicine. For a long time afterward I wore it in my hair.

The morning after the fifth night we came in sight of our camp. I sang another medicine song as we drove our horses through the tipis and the people came out to watch: "I went by here. The last one was the best."

Everybody greeted us and my name was spoken. Young men came to my tipi at night to ask to join my next raid. But I was afraid to let them without the consent of their parents or the medicine men. I had no relatives and as long as I took only one or two friends nothing was said. The old medicine men would shake their heads and say something bad would happen, but that was my worry.

As usual camp life grew tiresome. Piegan had been staying at another camp and when I met him again I asked him to join me on a raid for horses. We made preparations and some days later headed north with two other friends. Since we were on foot and had to keep hunting for food it took us about seventeen days to reach the Great Falls of Big River.

The sun was almost down when we arrived at the foot of what we call Rattle Mountain. Since we were close to enemy country we climbed a hill to look out. The Deer River ran in front of us, and some distance north, at the foot of the Belt Mountains, was a large Blackfeet camp.[3]

After dark we forded the river, found a trail leading up the cliff bank, and carefully approached their camp. There was a bright moon and we found their horses. I told Piegan and another man to try to capture some but warned them first to be sure no guards were near.

They disappeared into the shadows and we waited. Soon we heard barking dogs and shouts. People were lighting torches and running for their horses. As Piegan and the other man ran into sight they yelled for us to get away. Running for the river we could not find the trail down and jumped off the cliff. We dropped our robes and extra moccasins and waded until we could swim. When we were nearly across they appeared on the cliff and began shooting. Little spurts of water popped up but we reached the other side and ran for the cottonwoods. By the time they had crossed we were hidden.

We doubled back and waded for a long time in the shallows. We were lucky that clouds had covered the moon. The first part of the night we could hear men looking for us but by dawn they had gone. All the next day we hid on an island. They must have thought we had headed home and were searching in that direction. At nightfall we left, careful to make it a long journey away from usual trails. When we walked into our camp on the Musselshell many days later, there were no victory songs.

Chapter Fourteen

Sees The Living Bull was also called Goes Around All The Time and Bull That Goes Hunting. As a boy helping his mother butcher a buffalo he had pointed to the animal's penis, which she had just tossed into the river. An alert older man, either out of the characteristically Crow ribald sense of humor or because he saw some spiritual significance in the act, had named the boy Looks At A Bull's Penis, which Wildschut tastefully rendered as Sees The Living Bull.

Born sometime between 1815 and 1820, he led eleven successful war parties, was five times wounded, and once rescued six injured tribesmen. His clan affiliation, Whistling Waters, was the same as Two Leggings' father, placing him already in a close relationship with the boy.

However, he was only Medicine Crow's stepfather, having married his own dead brother's widow when she was pregnant with Medicine Crow, a common practice. Like Two Leggings, Sees The Living Bull had seen this wife in an early vision.

In the fall of 1875, when General Gibbon was recruiting Crow scouts, Sees The Living Bull brought in the largest Crow contingent, but deferred to Chief Sits In The Middle Of The Land for leadership.

Sees The Living Bull's treasury of Crow legends was preserved in 1902, when he was his tribe's second oldest member. Transcribed by S. C. Simms of Chicago's Field Museum, they constitute the first publication of Crow mythology.

IN THOSE DAYS I had many unsuccessful raids because I thought I could do everything just like the older and wiser men. I even failed in my first attempt to marry.

After my return from that trip to Deer River it was chokecherry-picking time and we moved to the Bighorn Mountains, camping briefly at the mouth of Black Canyon. Then we crossed the mountains into what is now Wyoming. The buffalo fur was long and thick and every day we went hunting for new robes, trailing after the herds and finally camping near the present town of Cody.

One fine day in leaf-falling moon while we were still at this place, the young men took out their drums and invited all the girls to a dance. I wanted to ride before the girls in fine clothes and tell the brave things I had done, so I cut a pair of leggings from a red blanket and added long fringes. Then I made a coup stick, tied many eagle feathers to it, and fixed my long human hair attachment to my head.[1]

I rode my large gray horse to the dance ground, intending to choose a woman and have my own tipi. As I rode along the row of girls dancing to the men singing behind them I tried to pick one. When Chief White On The Side Of His Head came out of his tipi he sang a praise song and told everyone to look at me because I had proved myself brave even though I was young. Some day, he said, if the Great Above Person let me live, and when he and the other old men were in the Other Side Camp, I would be their chief.

I rode by one girl and laid my coup stick on her left shoulder. If she kept it there it meant she was willing to be my woman. But she knocked it off, although the other girls told her not to. Everyone saw her refuse me and I was unhappy as I rode back to my brother's tipi.

For a while I stayed at home. Camp moved to the banks of the Musselshell River and then it was decided to visit the Black Lodges, camped along Big River. On the way I joined the hunting for robes and meat in order to forget about war parties. Sometimes I visited girls and thought of marrying, but I did not ask anyone seriously.

I was staying with friends because my brother had already gone ahead to the Black Lodges. But camp moved too slowly and three friends and I left also. I led a big bay horse captured from the Sioux as a gift for my brother.

On our way we had to swim the Big River. To keep our clothing, guns, and ammunition dry we built a small boat of four strong willow branches and rawhide, keeping the center of the hide stiff with the willows and fastening the four corners together in the shape of a bottle neck. We placed two stones in a fold at the bottom to hold it upright. Then we attached two buckskin thongs, held their ends tightly in our teeth, and pulled it across with a pole under one arm for support.[2]

At the Black Lodge camp I rode straight to my brother's tipi. I was sad that evening and we talked late into the night. He wanted to know what had happened and I described that last unlucky war party. Also I told him about my dream but said that I had not been able to capture as many horses as I had seen. However, I added that my vision had been unclear about the proper time for these raids.

When he asked if I had talked with any medicine men I said they wanted me to wait until the next spring and even the spring after the next winter. I said that he knew I could not hope to be a pipeholder if I spent all my days in camp.

He advised me to follow their advice because they had lived longer and understood dreams and visions. He told me not to be so ambitious and to wait for the proper time. Our talk did not satisfy me.

Medicine Crow and I had become close friends and spent many evenings in his father's tipi. One night while camped along the Musselshell he and I returned late from a buffalo hunt and I was invited to his tipi. After our meal we smoked, and Sees The Living Bull listened to our description of the day's kill. Talking about a wounded bull which had almost gored me, I mentioned that my medicine had been with me when Medicine Crow shot it. Then Sees The Living Bull told his son that he remembered we had fasted together on Where The Thunderbird Sits Down Mountain, but that he had never heard about his son's vision.

When Medicine Crow said he had not received anything but that I had dreamt a great vision, Sees The Living Bull was interested.

He was a kind and well-known man and I trusted him. I told him all I had seen and also what had appeared during my earlier fasts.

When I finished he said he believed me but that I had not seen anything great. He said that our guard in the sky, called The White Man Of The Sky or Great Above Person, did everything for us. If I had received my dreams from him my medicine would be powerful and I would always have good luck. But he said mine had come from one of his many helpers without his knowledge and was not powerful. He advised me to stay at home because I would have bad luck if I left again.

Medicine Crow mentioned that the ground in front of the horses had been covered with snow and that I thought this meant I should go out this season.

75

The tipi door was raised and White Around The Edges entered, a medicine man even older than Sees The Living Bull. They both began questioning us and asking for more details of my dream. Finally White Around The Edges said that those horses were on the other side of the snow which meant that I must wait until after this winter when the snow had melted. When he asked which side of the mountains the horses had been on I remembered lying with my back to the east and them to my left. Then he asked whether there had been anything on top of the snow. When I said no, he advised me to stay in camp this winter, to hunt if I had to go out, and not only to wait after this winter but until the following one. Before then, he said, I was sure to have bad luck. As I thought of the boredom ahead I became very unhappy and left the tipi.

Shortly after our talk I bought a new gun which worked with a lever. Twins had carried it on a raid but was unable to make it shoot and had traded it to me for very little. Eight cartridges could be loaded at one time and then it shot eight times in a row. Taking it to the trader at the head of Plum Creek,[3] I traded a buffalo robe for twenty shells and made a buckskin bag to hold them.

Now I could shoot so fast there was no reason to be afraid. I wanted to try the gun out on enemies and kept thinking those horses ought to be mine no matter what the two medicine men had said.

Leaf-falling moon had passed and ice lined the river banks. I had to go out, and asked Young Mountain to join me on a trip to the Piegan country. First I visited the trader for more shells and when he showed me a cartridge belt I traded a buffalo robe for it.

My gun and belt were admired in camp. The guns cost fifty buffalo robes each but that did not stop many from buying them. I had not yet made a real medicine but carried a hawk like the one in my dream. Two boys joined us, and one cold dawn we headed north and west for the Piegan country. After sleeping four times we reached the Crooked River where it makes a big bend. We had to cross twice and the water was very cold. But we built a fire to warm ourselves and felt better as we rode on.

I sent one man to scout ahead, but we saw no enemies or even their tracks and arrived at Loud Sounding River, close to the present Piegan agency. After crossing it we were about to ride on when we saw a howling wolf. Young Mountain said that maybe it was telling us

76

of enemies close by. Although we could not understand the wolf we led our horses into some brush in a coulee.

We saw nothing strange but the wolf walked closer, still howling. As it called to us we grew frightened and whipped our horses toward the head of the coulee. Finally we dismounted near a hill and crawled to the edge. Still we saw no enemies and the game seemed undisturbed. But we stayed on the hilltop until sundown when I decided to move to a higher hill. I was not afraid but felt responsible for the men we had brought.

In the lead with my gun and telescope, I was near the top when a boy yelled out that people were coming. I saw Piegans running around the hill and knew why that wolf had called. Shouting for the boys to run I dismounted and started shooting. Bullets hit all around but I dodged them. When a Piegan shot an arrow at me I shot him off his horse.

Young Mountain had left with the boys but when he saw me surrounded he came back. Lying flat on the ground I shot a Piegan's horse in the hindquarters. When it fell the rider ran off. Young Mountain had returned with my speckled white horse. As the Piegans emptied their guns and retreated we chased them. I shot one off his horse and then shot him again on the ground. When they had reloaded they came back singing medicine songs. Feeling a sting in my arm I saw blood on my shirt. We fell back but as soon as they had emptied their guns we chased them again.

Then a man rode to a hilltop and signalled with his blanket. I called to Young Mountain that their camp must be close and that my arm was no good. He yelled back that he was shot in the hip. It did not matter if we died but we had to help those two boys. As I turned my horse was shot. It stumbled and after I dismounted, it fell over.

When the Piegans rushed me I jumped on a Piegan horse I had picked up earlier in the fight and had tied to my other horse. My left arm was useless and my shells were almost gone.

Occasionally we stopped to shoot, making sign language for them to go back before we killed them. They were afraid of our repeating rifles and hung back. When we picked up the two boys who were waiting for us I told them to run for their horses while we protected them. I told them not to stop even if we were caught by the Piegans.

Another Piegan was signalling with a blanket for help. Young Mountain and I led our horses up a steep hill and then rode down a creek running through a coulee with thick brush on either side. By the time the Piegans had gathered on the hilltop we were on our way home.

Again we caught up with the two boys and began a ride which continued through the night and into the next day. When we arrived at Crooked River that sunset, Young Mountain wanted to rest because he was worried the water would get into our wounds. But I said they would not cross at night and we would be safe on the other side.

Making a skin float we put our clothes and ammunition inside and pulled it across with thongs held in our teeth. The two boys swam ahead with our horses. When we touched bottom and crawled up the bank we were exhausted and freezing. After warming ourselves over a fire, I had the boys find an old buffalo skull, knock off its horn, and bring us some water. We drank but went to sleep with nothing to eat. Before dawn we were riding again, crossing Muddy Creek and riding down Plum Creek to our village.

When I walked into my brother's tipi he said if I kept this up I would surely be killed. Although I was now a man, he said, I was still alone and should marry and have my own tipi. He did not know my first vision had shown me my wife. Whenever I saw a woman who looked like her I asked her name, but it was never the same and I remained unmarried.

Although I still would not listen I also felt I should stay home. If I had more bad luck no one would ever join me.

During that winter I joined eight men from the Black Lodges on a visit to the Many Lodges on the Musselshell River near the present town of Slayton. We hunted with that camp and then visited another camp on Fly Creek near Elk River. Although war parties were occasionally organized I remained in camp.

One day hunting along the Musselshell we saw some Crows riding toward us. They were the people from Fly Creek coming to visit the Many Lodges.

Sees The Living Bull was among them. When he called me over I could see he was displeased. He said he had wanted me to wait at least until the snow was off the ground. If I continued this way my vision man would grow angry and take away his protection. I listened to his warnings but hearing the returning warriors announce their coups made me very restless.

Then a raiding party returned with stolen horses, but one of its members, Beaver, had been killed near Warm Water by enemies who had pursued them. When Sees The Living Bull saw me next he said he knew how it felt to listen to the stories and see the captured horses, but reminded me that I did not want to be killed like Beaver.

He said this for my own good. I was his son's partner and he liked me. Still I hated this quiet life. After hunting buffalo until I grew bored, I would often sit alone on some high ridge and think about the honors a man could win.

Chapter Fifteen

*It was natural that Two Leggings would relate the one Sun Dance
in which he participated; it is not surprising that from a spectator's
vantage point he would here recall White On The Neck's fiasco.
The event burned itself into most Crow memories, for it actually
left eleven men and one woman scalped in its wake.*

*In another version White On The Neck only tore off his Sun
Dance paraphernalia and rushed for water before receiving his
vision. Since he was the pledger this was sacrilege and caused the
disastrous subsequent events. Plenty Coups, who gave Wildschut a
third version of the aftermath, said the bundle was thereafter
discarded. But in 1915 the doll was collected by Robert Lowie
for the American Museum of Natural History.*

*Although the Department of the Interior did
not officially ban the Sun Dance until 1904, its vengeance
motivation among the Crow caused its extinction as soon as the
intertribal raiding was curtailed; the last dance was held
about 1875 in the vicinity of their Rosebud Creek agency.*

*However, in 1941, a variety which omitted
the self-torture was brought to the Crow reservation from the
Wind River Shoshonis and is still performed each
summer.*

NOT LONG after my return from the Piegan country we moved to
Big River. One day a miserable-looking man rode toward our camp
and we recognized White On The Neck. Two moons earlier the
Sioux had raided his village and killed his younger brother. Since

80

then he had been mourning and sleeping in the hills. He told us that just before he had wandered into our village a vision had instructed him to give a Sun Dance. After our chief brought the people together White On The Neck stood before us, faced the sun, and said that the Sioux had killed his brother and now he wanted to sacrifice to the sun which was his grandfather through the ceremony of the Sun Dance.

Then scouts reported buffalo moving toward Elk River. We broke camp and moved as far as the mouth of the Bighorn. But hunting was poor and when we heard of herds roaming in the valley we traveled up river, striking camp near the present town of Hardin.

Grass-growing season had nearly come. When our chief had the camp crier tell the hunters to bring in the tongues of all buffalo killed, we knew that preparations for the Sun Dance had begun. As the tongues came in, White On The Neck gave ten to each of his helpers. The Sun Dance lodge was to be erected farther up river where Medicine Bear now lives because the cottonwood trees there made good Sun Dance poles. Our entire village moved to this place.

It was difficult to find the virtuous woman to serve as tree notcher because many eligible women would not accept the honor. A cooked buffalo tongue with a stick run through it was carried from tipi to tipi until Getting A Sword accepted. The whole camp was present as she walked out of her tipi, carrying the tongue to the center of the village and facing the sun. Raising her right hand over her head she said that the sun up there knew that her husband Onion had bought her in the honorable way and that no man had ever dishonored her. After her prayer she walked back to her tipi and was allowed to eat the buffalo tongue.

That evening the camp crier announced the name of the virtuous woman who had accepted the tongue and said that the other preparations would continue the following morning.

A fresh buffalo hide was next needed. This was always difficult because the appointed hunter had to kill the animal with a single arrow which could not make a second hole in the skin. If that happened the carcass would be abandoned and he would chase another.

Bull Shield was hunter, Bull Water and someone else the butchers, and Shows His Face was the fourth man.

That evening they entered a special tipi and Shows His Face scratched a buffalo track on the earth floor and faced the direction where they expected to find buffalo. All held buffalo-hide rattles in their right hands as they sang this buffalo song: "Buffalo is coming."

Then they sat behind the buffalo track, faced where it led, and sang the buffalo-calling songs until dawn, with some intervals when they went outside to smoke. No one else was allowed in. Long before dawn some of our oldest scouts left camp, each painted with white clay and wearing a wolfskin cap. It was not yet sunrise when we heard their wolf howls telling us they had sighted buffalo. The whole camp cheered this good news.

Bull Shield carried only two arrows as he and his butchers rode out, leading their best buffalo horses. They had not gone far when they saw three buffalo walking towards them. Switching to their buffalo horses, Bull Shield rode up with his butchers close behind. His medicine was powerful that day; his arrow went into the back as far as the feather. Blood ran from the buffalo's nose and mouth and it began staggering. Now each butcher had to tie one eagle feather to the buffalo's head-hair before it fell. This was the most difficult part, but it was done.

Instead of skinning from the belly up they worked from the back down, carefully taking out all the bones and packing them on the horses together with the heart, the liver, the kidneys, part of the intestines, and a little meat.

Our scouts had been on the lookout and raced back as soon as they saw the hunter and butchers returning. Bull Shield and the other two men were not supposed to ride slowly; they galloped hard through the village to the tipi where White On The Neck was waiting. The entire camp was there and received them with shouting and songs. Their horses were held by the underlip but they could not dismount until the meat, bones, and hide had been unpacked.

White On The Neck had covered his hands with white clay. His cheeks were painted black for revenge and he held a knife painted with a mixture of charcoal and buffalo grease. He cut the meat into very small pieces, giving one to everyone. After singing four songs he cut the buffalo hide in half and the ceremony was over for that day.

The next morning Getting A Sword [1] was placed on a horse and given the stone maul and the longest prong from an elk antler. We were all dressed in our finest clothes and followed on foot as her horse walked to a selected tree with four black rings painted around it. We all sang four songs and after each one she pretended to hit the prong with her stone maul. When she really hit it the last time we yelled and fired off our guns. This tree and ten others were cut down by some of the tribe's hermaphrodites.[2] Then all the young men tied ropes to the heavy poles, mounted their horses, and dragged them to the lodge site, each riding double with a girl. Before they started some of the bravest men were put on the poles. Presents were given to their relatives because it was considered something of a disgrace to ride these poles. As soon as they could the men jumped off.[3]

A large woodpile had been gathered at the lodge's center. Three of the heavy poles were laid over it and tied near their tops with thongs cut from the hide Bull Shield had skinned. One was placed toward the north, another south, and a third west. The east was always left open, like the wide opening in the camp circle, and no one could pass through there.

A medicine man had to climb the center pole but only one who had dreamt of eagles could do this. They were hard to find. A pipe was carried around camp and offered to the eligible men, but none accepted. At last Hair Wolf made it known that if the pipe were brought to him he would take it. We did not know he had dreamt of eagles but he was given the pipe and led to a special tipi some distance from the western pole and in direct line with it. He was given four presents and while inside he painted his entire body red. We could hear him singing his medicine songs. When he came out he was wrapped in a big buffalo robe fastened with an eagle-feather quill. He was also carrying an eagle-feather fan in each hand, and an eagle-bone whistle hung from his neck. As he drew near the western pole he sang and moved the fans like the wings on a flying eagle: "I am a bird, coming from the clouds."

After the first song he stopped and blew his whistle, imitating the flying eagle again. Four times he did this until he stood before the pole, whistling and waving the fans. We watched intently as he began walking up the pole. If he fell, bad luck would come into our camp. I do not know how he kept his balance but he arrived safely where they were all tied together and sat down. Now when he whistled and moved his arms, we all shouted at the top of our voices.

Holes had been dug for the butt ends of the three poles and we all rushed up to raise them in place with the help of several long tipi poles tied two and two with rawhide. Hair Wolf sat where they all crossed, like a bird in a nest. We laid the resting poles in place and interlaced them with willow branches.

All the pipeholders had painted themselves according to their vi-

83

sions and were in full dress, wearing their medicines and each carrying a rope and whistle. All together they ran toward the Sun Dance lodge, stopping four times until they arrived at the eastern entrance.

Some of the spectators were singing and others dancing. We watched the pipeholders run around the lodge and then stare at the top. Someone called for silence. A pipeholder yelled that he saw a scalp hanging up there. Another yelled that he saw a horse. Other things were seen by the pipeholders. This way they gave their dreams to the men who were to dance in the days ahead. They knew that those dreams would be seen again by one of the dancers and would aid the revenge.

The Sun Dance started the next day. All the dancers assembled near the lodge and the women brought buckskin thongs painted with white clay. A small pine tree the height of a man had been set inside the lodge. A Sun Dance doll fastened to a willow hoop was tied to the tree's top facing east. Seven eagle feathers in a fan shape hung from the hoop.

Then the dancers entered the lodge, each carrying a whistle, a skunkskin around his neck, and an eagle plume fastened to the back of his head. The medicine men tied white thongs to the skewers piercing the dancers' breasts and attached the other ends to posts planted inside the lodge. White On The Neck stood in front of the lodge, but did not enter until after the first song. Then he stood between the two piles of white clay, a Sun Dance hair lock tied to the back of his head. He wore a buckskin dress around his waist, carried an eagle-bone whistle, and had one eagle plume attached to each of his little fingers. He also wore a skunkskin around his neck, painted with white clay.

When the drummers—one a woman—took their places inside and began the second song, White On The Neck looked at the doll for the first time: "The one you want to dance with is here now."

White On The Neck sang with them and began dancing up to the doll and then back away, blowing his whistle and staring at the doll. When the song was over we all yelled and clapped our hands to our mouths, and then it was sung again. The singing and dancing lasted late into the night until the leader halted it and helped White On The Neck lie down between his two white clay piles. He covered him with a blanket and we all went home for a short rest.

The crier woke everyone early and after eating we returned to the Sun Dance lodge. It was very hot and I heard that White On The

Neck was not dancing well and that his whistling was weak. Later I noticed that he had to be forced to dance. Perspiration was pouring down his body and many times he almost fell. Suddenly he ran toward the tree, tore off the doll with both hands, and fainted.

Everyone was alarmed. Water was brought to wake him and the leader told him that we were holding this Sun Dance because his brother had been killed. Everyone had been willing to help him, but he said that White On The Neck had done a great wrong and now some of us would be killed.

That same day we broke camp and moved to what is now called Two Leggings Creek, camping near the spring a few miles from its mouth. Moving every day for the next three days, we went to Woody Creek, then to Dipper Creek, and on the third day crossed the Bighorn River and camped on Rotten Grass Creek. During the night Sioux stole some of our horses and I joined a party following their trail over the high hills east of Rotten Grass. Some of our men caught up with part of the Sioux at Big Shoulder Creek, killing one there and another on the ridge top.

Before they reached the Little Bighorn River we killed another Sioux, and a fourth was killed as he swam across. On the other side they separated, some riding east and the rest following the river downstream. We went downstream but did not catch up until they reached the location of the present Crow agency. Then we could see their warbonnets and medicines. One Sioux fired his six-shooter and the bullet passed over my head. I heard yells that more were coming and saw a large band across the river. Turning our horses we raced for the foothills where our main party was signalling.

As we joined them we saw two other Sioux driving some of our horses stolen the night before. When they tried to escape we noticed that one was a woman. One Fingered Bear was just ahead of me and we both chased them. The woman's horse was tired out and she cried to the man, but he did not seem to hear. Then One Fingered Bear shot her. The main group of Sioux rode to help the man with the horses. Most of our horses were exhausted and several men were on foot, but mine was long-winded. Waving my gun at the remaining Sioux, I made signs telling them to come closer. Then the stolen herd ran by me and I saw a beautiful gray with split ears and a Sioux shield hanging from the saddle. Driving my horse into the bunch, I changed mounts and led my own.

A little later we all came together and found the stolen horses on

85

a hill where the Sioux had abandoned them. Those of us still mounted rounded them up.

Riding back we kept in a tight group because the Sioux seemed everywhere. We traveled slowly to the Bighorn River, making camp for the night across from the mouth of Two Leggings Creek. Through the next day we rested our horses often because they were still tired from the day before. Late that night, as we approached our village, we heard people crying and singing the death song.

We were told that the morning before some Sioux had stayed behind; once we had left they had shot eleven men leaving camp to join us. White On The Neck's breaking of the rules had caused this.

But he was not driven from the tribe. After a year of not participating in any ceremonies or dances or joining any raiding parties he began to live a normal life. Several years later he led a raid against the Sioux, returning with a large number of horses and several scalps. After that no one mentioned the other thing again.

Chapter Sixteen

*When the Crow chiefs, or
"good men," thought a man's dream outstanding they might
permit him to lead the camp through four trial moves. If
he found enough food and pastureland, if war parties returned
with horses and no casualties, and if the camp were not raided,
he joined the council of chiefs. Then the regular
head chief resumed control.*

*The duties of The One Who Owns
The Camp, or village head chief, were to help the chiefs decide
when and where his followers should move and pitch their tipis, and
each spring to appoint the warrior society to police
the camp.*

*In the more common procedure by which
a man became a chief, a warrior who had struck the four
important coups gave presents to an acknowledged chief on four
different occasions, without divulging his motive. Then, after
making his request to buy the chief's medicine bundle or its
duplicate, he was either accepted or
rejected.*

*Sometimes when the camp was preparing to move
and the chiefs had met to discuss their dreams, an agreement
could not be reached over whose to follow. The camp would
split, and those believing in one chief would leave with
him.*

WE NEVER STAYED where something bad had happened. As soon as
the eleven men were buried our chiefs led us across the Bighorn

River at the mouth of Black Canyon, along the foot of the mountains to Arrow Creek, and then through Hits With The Arrows. Finally we camped at the foot of the Buffalo Heart Mountain, close to the present town of Cody, a well-known fasting place where many important medicine men had received visions.

When Bull Well Known asked me to fast with him I decided to try again. After our preparations we climbed to the top, meeting several others also fasting. This time I did not torture my flesh and just prayed to the Great Above Person. For three days and nights I received no vision, but near daybreak after the fourth night seven people walked toward me from the east. First they were on top of a peak in the Wolf Mountains. Then I seemed to fall asleep and when I woke again they were standing on top of Where The Thunderbird Sits Down Mountain where I had fasted before. As they approached they began to sing, and a voice said that I was seeing birds. Then I understood their song: "The birds are coming to me."

After another victory song they turned north toward the Piegan country. They sang again, and turned toward the Sioux country. When they faced those directions it meant I should go to those tribes. Their songs assured me I would be successful. After this second song I woke. Although my dream had been short I had been given two war trails.

Soon after returning to camp I talked again with Crooked Arm. He said my earlier dream was more powerful and wanted me to wait until the next snow had fallen and melted before going out. Otherwise, he said, I would have bad luck.

Sees The Living Bull agreed with him. But I still could not refuse Bull Does Not Fall Down when he asked me to join him to the Sioux country. Seventeen of us followed the foot of the Bighorn Mountains and by the time we arrived at Tongue River our scouts had located the Sioux camp.

For the rest of that day we hid, and after dark began riding toward their village. While seven of us guarded our horses the rest crawled into the camp and returned with horses that had been picketed in front of the tipis. Although they picked up their own horses and left for home, we did not want to return empty-handed and stayed until the following night. When it was too dark to see, we moved quietly into the tipis. Bumping into a horse, I cut it loose and walked it to our meeting place. The others were already back and we rode into the mountains. As daylight came I saw I had stolen a big bay.

When we got back to camp we found we had thirty head in all. But my bay was in poor condition and never became a good runner.

We also discovered that Wrinkled Face was missing and his relatives soon began to mourn.

Camp moved to the mouth of Red Lodge Creek and ten days after that horse-stealing raid Wrinkled Face appeared on a nearby hill. After becoming separated from the first returning group he had run out of ammunition and had not eaten for several days. His moccasins were worn out and he had cut up his leggings to wrap his feet. Until this time Wrinkled Face had been poor. But now he became successful, bringing back several horses on every war party. He had also been unfriendly. But after this he grew kind and was liked by everyone. Later he told us that during his wandering he had dreamt something powerful.

I planned to stay in camp for the rest of that summer and not take any more chances. Our village moved from place to place until it was decided to visit the Black Lodges at the foot of Three Mountain in the Little Rockies along Big River.

We had a happy time there. Game was plentiful and enemies seemed to be staying away. War parties would occasionally return and this gave us more reason for dancing and feasting. Our two camps together held several hundred tipis and we had to hunt continually for food. We were here for nearly a moon when scouts reported a large herd nearby to the north. I needed fresh meat and the following afternoon rode my buffalo horse slowly out of camp, leading a pack horse. Usually I rode the pack horse to rest my buffalo runner, but I did not think I would be going far.

No enemies had recently been sighted, but I was accustomed to being careful. Before each ridge I dismounted and crawled to the edge to cover the country with my telescope.

Riding into the valley where the herd had been reported, I found nothing. I decided that if I did not see any game from a high hill a little to the north I would return to camp. It was hot and all the dancing and eating of the last days had made me sleepy. Tying my horse to a tree, I lay in the shade and watched the sun set. For a time I forgot what I was doing.

Before me the country was very broken; beyond lay a large meadow and then came more broken country. As I looked over those ridges and coulees I saw something which made my laziness go away.

89

A buffalo herd was running out of the broadest coulee. Looking through my telescope, I knew no wolf pack could chase that many. Soon about six men appeared behind, and from their riding style and headgear I could tell they were Flatheads who had crossed the mountains.

I rode into camp as night fell. I should have informed the chief right away, but we had nothing to fear from a few Flatheads who would have left immediately if they discovered our tipis. I wanted to be the first to surprise them, and told only Young Mountain.

When we set out at sunrise I was on a roan, a good long-distance runner, and Young Mountain was riding a buckskin, also long-winded and fast. Young Beaver stopped us at the edge of camp, calling me brother and saying that I had a better horse. He asked me to kill him a nice cow and promised me the fat.

Young Beaver tried hard to provide for his father and mother but his buffalo horse had just been stolen by enemies. I liked him and his people, and they were my relatives. I told Young Mountain we would hunt before looking for the Flatheads.

We three started north, where Young Beaver had been told to find buffalo. I was sure these were the animals the Flatheads had been chasing. On the way we passed a few Crow hunters already butchering their kills. When we reached a ridge I dismounted to look over the edge. Two Flatheads were chasing buffalo. I ran back to the horses and told Young Beaver to warn our hunters and also to alert the camp. I said I was going to try to kill one and might be out all night.

Young Mountain and I tied our horses and hid behind sage and rocks along the ridge. While I looked through my telescope he watched the two men below. I could not find the other Flatheads but was sure their camp was nearby. Young Mountain pulled my arm; the two Flatheads were chasing a few stray buffalo in our direction.

I looked back but Young Beaver with help was not to be seen. Then I noticed someone skinning buffalo south of us. We galloped over, recognizing Hunts The Enemy and his long-legged sorrel horse stolen from Flatheads. I said that if we killed those two the women could dance the scalp dance for us and we could tell our children about this coup. But I said that if we were killed it would be a good death, for the Great Above Person was looking down to watch our bravery.

Meanwhile Medicine Bear had ridden up on a pinto mare and told me that two more men were just over the ridge. When we called to them Small Heart appeared on a buckskin and White From The Waist Up on a big bay. Returning to the hill we now saw four Flatheads on the other side. I was glad to have collected more men. Then several more Flatheads appeared around a pine grove on a faraway hilltop. We also noticed that the four below were not the men Young Mountain and I had first seen. Those two had wounded a bull, now charging them as they rode in circles. They could have easily seen us but were too busy. We drew back and Hunts The Enemy and I dismounted, handing our horses to our friends. Crawling to the edge again, we saw the two hunters about a rifle-shot away. Hunts The Enemy said that everything dies sometime and that we should think about what we could tell our children and grandchildren if we scalped these men.

We all rode around the hill and into a deep ravine between the hunters and their pack horses. As Hunts The Enemy and I watched from the rim the others waited below. Finally killing the bull, the Flatheads came for their pack horses, one on a white horse and the other on a bay, both men about my age but larger than most Flatheads. They wore breechcloths and held guns. Bows and arrows hung on their backs, but they carried no medicines.

As soon as we crawled back all of us galloped out of the ravine. The Flatheads reined in so hard one horse almost fell backward. Its rider slid off and called for the other man, who was racing down the meadow to his friends.

When the man on the ground fired I tried to pull up, but my horse kept running. I felt a pain in my left shoulder and thought I was dying. As soon as possible I dismounted and he ran up, in signs calling us women.

He was brave but I did not notice that. Blood soaked through the light-colored shirt I had bought from the trader at the mouth of Plum Creek. At first I thought it came from my mouth. When I moved, my left arm hurt badly. I made signs to the Flathead that he was a woman and that I would kill him before I died.

When he saw me back on my horse he caught his again and I grew afraid. I do not know why I felt that way, but I rode back to the ravine. Just as I discovered my friends were gone after the other Flathead, a bullet missed my head. I turned and we began riding around in circles, hanging to the outside and shooting over or just below our horses' necks. Then I heard yelling and was glad to see Bear

Looks and Hunts The Enemy. But it also made me want to earn this coup alone. I reined in and shot from behind my horse. The Flathead also dismounted, keeping up his fire as he walked with his horse in front of him. When I killed it he laid down, shooting from behind the carcass. As I started to ride around him I did not notice that Bear Looks was beside me until he fell from his horse, shot through the spine. Then I raced straight at the Flathead, but I was out of breath and my horse threw its head into my gun as I fired. Before the animal dropped I jumped off. The Flathead tried to grab my gun but I shot his left hand. He tried again and I shot him in the right side. Dropping his gun he rushed at me with a knife. I jumped away and he fell on the ground.

I shot my last bullet, but was so excited I hit his left hand again. I picked up his knife and gun, grabbed his long hair, and was about to scalp him when Hunts The Enemy asked me to help lift Bear Looks onto his horse. Then he stopped wailing over the body and pointed north. More Flatheads were heading toward us. I let the head fall back but told myself I would return. By the time we had Bear Looks' body tied to the horse we had to leave.

My horse was dead and Hunts The Enemy's had run to camp. As we reached a rise we saw Flatheads grouped around the man on the ground. I felt faint from loss of blood, but would kill some of them before I died. I told Hunts The Enemy to give me his gun and cartridges and go on with the body.

The Flatheads were pointing at me and I could find no hiding place so I tried to walk up the hill. Before reaching the top I saw someone on a horse. I held my gun but it was White From The Waist Up. As we rode double over the top I turned to see the Flatheads catching up.

I told White From The Waist Up that if they got too close we should dismount and fight. Then he pointed out Young Beaver riding with men from camp. We all started shooting as the Flatheads rode over the hill. When they spun around to escape, our men raced close behind and White From The Waist Up left me. Feeling weak and in pain, I started walking back to camp.

Men riding home stopped to tell me that the news had passed I was dead. They were glad to see me alive and wanted to see my wound. I rode double into camp. As I passed Bear Looks' tipi I heard his relatives crying. They buried his body in the brakes along Big River.

The chiefs decided to move camp early the next morning. All

night we heard men riding in and singing victory songs. I felt glad because it meant they had been successful without losing any more men. Hunts The Enemy visited me and said they had revenged Bear Looks, returning with three scalps. When I fell asleep I dreamt of a scalp dance in which I was the chief.

(Many years later when we were friends I visited the Flatheads. That man told me that when he was on the ground he felt me lift his head by the hair, unable to move. He had waited for my knife and could not understand what had happened. But he was never able to use his left hand.)

When we arrived at Big River the next day we made rafts for the old men, women, and children and for our clothes and provisions, each pulled by four men with thongs in their teeth and poles under their arms. I could not use my left arm and crossed with the very old men. When the swimmers made fun of me, I yanked on their thongs and ducked them.

We reached the southern shore and pitched our tipis on a sloping ground covered with big cottonwood trees. By the time the sun was in the middle everyone was settled.

Preparations began for a big dance and the old people called the names of different men through the camp. My brother told me to mount up because I had been wounded and had acted bravely and the people wanted to see me.

Painting myself and wearing my best clothes and human-hair attachment I mounted my favorite horse and waited until Old Dog,[1] an old medicine man, came for me. He sang as he led me into the circle of the dancers: "I am going to give you a scalp. I am going to give you a scalp."

Then he asked everyone to stop talking. Speaking my name, he said I was one of their bravest young men. He told them all to look at me and said I would be a chief. From this day on, he said, I would not scold any children and would treat all my people well.

It was a very happy day for me. I was beginning the ceremonies which would finally make me a chief.

At sunset the dancing stopped and a sweat lodge was built of a hundred and four willows, the largest number ever used. I was in my tipi when a boy told me that I was invited to this ceremony. Following him I found Sees The Living Bull, Shell On The Neck, and Old Dog, our leading chiefs and medicine men. The previous day's warriors were also there and in front with me those who had counted coups. Sees The Living Bull tied a red blanket to a pole and set it up for a sacrifice. Then he prayed to the Great Above Ones, which were the sun and moon and stars and all above people in the sky. He said that we were offering this blanket, and asked for good luck, long life, and successful raids for the warriors gathered here.

When we all entered a sweat bath the chiefs prayed for us again. Afterwards we bathed in the river and then smoked and talked over the day before, adding details and remembering the brave things that were done. It was early morning when I returned to my tipi. All was still and the air was warm. Before going in I looked up at the sky, raised my arms, and prayed for all the powerful beings above to look at me. I told them I wanted to be a chief. I asked them to give me a long life and courage when I was in danger. I asked the moon and stars for their help.

Two days later camp moved to Elk River and although I had begun to listen to the older men's advice I was still too young. Parades through our village would be accompanied by older men singing about our brave warriors, and now I was mentioned in those songs. I began thinking about another raid to add more coups to my name.

Chapter Seventeen

The Bear Song Dance was one of a handful of minor Crow ceremonies. It and the Singing of the Cooked Meat—a semiannual occasion for rock-medicine owners to open their sacred bundles—were indigenous. Others, like the Medicine Pipe ritual and the Horse Dance, were the products of visits with other tribes, usually their Hidatsa kinsmen.

The Bear Song Dance performers were knit together by their ability to produce from their mouths parts of a creature or object which had miraculously entered their stomachs during a fast. Revealed were elk chips, white clay, black dirt, owl feathers, ground moss, snails, eggs, feathers from an eagle's tail, a little human being, and, commonly, parts of the bodies of bears and jackrabbits. People owning horses would exhibit horse tails; those who could doctor wounds, buffalo tails.

Usually the dance was held in the fall, when the ripe berries caused the bears to dance in the mountains. As with the Tobacco society, variations in dreams could give birth to a separate chapter. Once, a mourner discovered a nest of eggs, subsequently dreamt of them, and then displayed them during the next dance. Henceforth, his Wolverine chapter was renamed the Egg chapter.

SOON AFTER OUR BATTLE with the Flatheads we began moving from one place to another. Finally we stopped along the banks of Big River near the mouth of Elk River and a Bear Dance was held.

This dance was usually given by some man or woman who had dreamt a vision of the Bear Dance. The performers were people with special medicine powers, who could make objects come out of their mouths and disappear back in and do other things we cannot understand.

The people prepared for this dance by drying a lot of thinly sliced meat strips and pounding them into pemmican which they mixed with buffalo-leg-bone marrow and dried chokecherries. Then they rolled the mixture into different-sized balls which they spread on a buckskin and covered.

I was one of the spectators sitting in a large circle around a pole. A bearskin with red-painted claws was tied to the eastern side of this pole—but it could also be tied to the western. Six or seven singers walked into the circle carrying their drums, and sat on one side of the cleared area. At a signal they hit their drums, the bear songs began, and the dance leader came out of his tipi, his forehead painted red with two red stripes drawn from the corners of his eyes down his cheeks. He wore a buffalo robe with the fur side out. Four other men and a boy followed him, all painted and dressed in the same manner. They began dancing in the east, came around the pole to the west, and then turned back to the east. They imitated a bear's movements, holding their hands in front of them with the fingertips pressed against the palms, shaking their heads, and stepping like bears on their hind legs.

Now we were all standing, shouting, and clapping our hands to our mouths. I was watching the dancers so closely I did not see a young woman dance slowly up to the center pole. Suddenly she drew a deep breath and blew out a cloud of red paint. Rubbing her face against the bearskin she blew more red paint where she had rubbed, doing this until she was exhausted. Her relatives held her as she tried to dance. Then they made her kneel over some burning sweet grass. When she smelled the smoke she stopped blowing the paint. Even her hair was covered by paint the wind had blown back on her. Her relatives wrapped a blanket around her and led her away, giving her some of the balls of meat.

In the meantime the singers continued their songs and the dancers moved around the pole. A man came out of his tipi wearing an otter-skin headband and with a broad red stripe across his face. As he sang a Bear Dance song, he danced toward the pole. People yelled that this was Buffalo Lump, a powerful medicine man who could shoot a gun without a shell. Coming closer, he called for us to spread out robes.

96

We laid down several and crowded around as he walked up to the bearskin, rubbed his face against it, and returned to the robes. As he leaned forward a stream of bullets rolled out of his mouth, many more than any man could hold. He told us who liked hunting to take one, and four men did. Buffalo Lump said that was enough and picked up the rest, swallowing one after another. He asked for water and after drinking some poured a little on his head. Then he ate some of the meat balls.

The singers began again and everyone shouted when Flesh çame from the camp with a robe over his head. He was known to be so fond of horses that he spent most of his time with them. After dancing around the pole he rubbed his face against the bearskin and turned to us. Something seemed to be filling his open mouth. Hair appeared and we saw a colt's tail come out until it seemed full-length. His relatives quickly made a sweet-grass smudge, holding him over it and raising his arms above his head. Each time they did that the tail went back and finally it was gone. He drank some water, a little was spilled on his head, and he ate some of the special meat.

I could never understand all this and believe the Bear society members were great medicine people.

Then Small Sun had it announced that if all the war parties the next winter season returned successfully he would give a Bear Dance the following spring.

That next spring season a pole was planted where Chief Bell Rock now lives, and a bearskin was tied to it. When we were all gathered, Small Sun said that last snow season Rides The White Horse had brought in many horses and Cottonwood Tree had done the same. He said that Head Of A Man had returned successfully with his men and that Sits In The Middle Of The Land, robbed of his horses one night while camped along the Musselshell River, had followed the Piegans, bringing back the stolen horses and many more besides. He had also returned with the scalps of two men he had killed. Small Sun said that we had enjoyed good luck and that he was giving this Bear Dance as he had promised.

This ceremony was like the last with the four men and the boy coming in, dancing and singing as they circled the pole. Then the individual dancers entered and I remember Lots Of Bear throwing back his head and blowing out a bunch of bulrushes. Some fell among the crowd and people grabbed them for their medicine bundles.

One young man said he had nothing inside him but would do something else. He scraped up dirt from the ground, mixed it with water, and rolled it into small soft balls. After closing his hands over the balls and rubbing them he opened his palms to show beads which he gave to the women.

Not long after Small Sun's Bear Dance, time came for berry-picking and camp moved in slow stages toward the mountains. Scouts searched in all directions for chokecherry bushes and plum trees, finally finding both along Woody Creek. A camping place was selected and parties of men, women, and children set out each day. The older women pounded the berries into pulp which they formed into peglike shapes and placed on blankets to dry in the sun. Later these were stored in parfleches for the winter.

The warriors hunted for game and scouted to protect the berry-pickers. At night we kept guards around the camp, especially near our grazing horses.

Bull Does Not Fall Down usually joined me on these hunts and scouting duties. As game grew scarce because of the constant hunting we decided to take a longer hunt of a few days. Riding east, we crossed the Bighorn River, and began hunting in the broken country toward the Little Bighorn River.

In what the white people call Devils Pocket near the Little Bighorn we found a large deer with big antlers. We shot at the same time and it fell into a dead pine tree. Bull Does Not Fall Down told me to drag it out of the branches. When I grabbed a hind leg I saw it was only stunned by having a horn shot off. I had left my rifle with my horse so I sat on its back to stab its heart. Suddenly the deer got to its feet and began bucking down the slope. We rushed by Bull Does Not Fall Down but he was laughing too hard to hold his gun. At the foot of the hill the deer gave a long leap and I was thrown on some boulders, the wind knocked out of me. The deer turned on me but missed because one antler hit the ground before the broken one could stick me. Then it cut my face with its hooves and ran off. Bull Does Not Fall Down wanted to follow and finally we killed it, packing the meat home.

Around that time there was much dancing and celebrating in camp and we flirted a lot with the girls. Crooked Arm often advised me to marry and I felt that my own home would be a great advantage. I had been feeling close to one girl and sent Young Mountain with presents to her father. This time I was not refused and a few days later started life in my own tipi.

Two Leggings in 1919, wearing his pipeholder's war shirt hung with ermine skins and decorated with beaded strips over the shoulders and down the sleeves.

Above: Sees The Living Bull. After Two Leggings earned his trust, the famous medicine man adopted him and gave him dreams to guide his raids for horses and scalps.

Right, above: In 1871 William H. Jackson photographed the last of the Crow buffalo-hide tipis, pitched along the Yellowstone River.

Right: At the Crows' first agency near Livingston, Montana, Jackson photographed Sits In The Middle Of The Land (second from left), signer of the 1868 treaty and head chief of the Mountain Crows during much of Two Leggings' early life. With him are (left to right) Poor Elk, Long Ears, Shows His Face, and Old Onion.

Smithsonian Office of Anthropology, Bureau of American Ethnology Collection

Smithsonian Office of Anthropology, Bureau of American Ethnology Collection

Most concerned of the "Wise Ones" who tried to control Two Leggings' young ambition were Two Belly (left, top) and Crooked Arm (left, bottom). Photographed during an 1879 Crow delegation's Washington visit, Two Belly's hair style reveals that he was in mourning at the time.

Below: In 1872 the first Crow treaty delegation rode horseback from central Montana to Salt Lake City before taking the train to Washington. Among its members were Wolf Bear (far left, seated), who joined Two Leggings on a raid to uphold the honor of their warrior society, Long Horse (far left, top), Sits In The Middle Of The Land (seated, third from left), Iron Bull (seated, fourth from left), Old Dog (seated, fifth from left), and their Indian agent, Fellows D. Pease (standing, fifth from left).

As partners on his early, clandestine raids, Two Leggings chose Bull Does Not Fall Down (left) and Medicine Crow (center) because he trusted their courage and confidence. His brief term as a courier for the United States Government shortly after the Custer massacre was shared by Spotted Horse (right).

Two Leggings' first war medicine bundle was made by Weasel Moccasin, then passed to Two Leggings' brother, Wolf Chaser. It contained, left to right, (1) blue cloth meaning good luck, (2) herb bag to renew horse's wind, (3) eagle's head which tied to chest imparted that bird's powers of flight, vision, and noiseless approach, (4) eagle plume tied to horse meaning swiftness, (5) porcupine-quill-wrapped feathers meaning same as eagle's head, (6) swallow for power to evade enemies, (7) otter-skin and eagle-claw sash for eagle's ability to pounce on enemy, (8) bear's hair and claws to keep horse fat and prime.

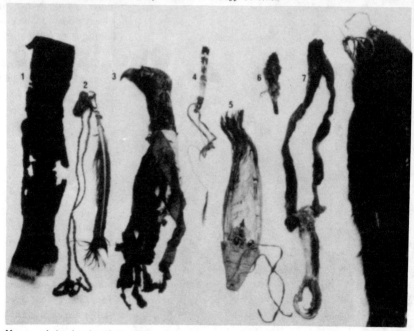

Girl on horse (above) is about to be initiated into the Crow Tobacco Society. The adoption procession, women forward and men drummers and singers behind, will halt its dancing four times before arriving at a special adoption lodge.

Frame of Tobacco Society adoption lodge. The original Crow Sun Dance lodge was of similar design but required twenty poles instead of ten. While the Tobacco Society lodge had a wide belt of hides for shade, the Sun Dance lodge was covered waist-high with brush.

Right: Anthropologist Robert Lowie purchased the very doll which Two Leggings saw White On The Neck tear down during his Sun Dance, the sacrilegious act with tragic consequences for the Crows.

American Museum of Natural History

Right below: Two Leggings bought the Sun Dance bundle, together with this doll, which had been used during his first Sun Dance. Lines under the doll's eyes imitate a screech owl's markings and represent visionary powers. Marks to one side of central blue stripe— the sky—mean old people's wrinkles, granting the owner long life. Those to the other side represent fog. Around the neck indistinguishable black dots mean hail and rain; the owner could call down a sudden shower between himself and enemy pursuers.

Museum of the American Indian, Heye Foundation

Two Leggings' Sun Dance bundle also contained (1) buffalo-hide rattle with its painted face representing the sacred being who had shown the bundle's originator a vision of the Sun Dance doll, (2) hair-lock attachment symbolizing fog which could magically descend to protect a raiding party, (3) whistle fashioned from eagle's wingbone, (4) deerskin kilt, (5) skunkskin necklace rubbed with white clay and hung with owl feathers, (6) rawhide container which held all these items.

Personal rivalries were not uncommon when young Crows were driven to excel in their earning of war honors. After Big Shoulder (top) neglected to give Two Leggings the honor of leading a revenge raid, the two kept a cool distance. On another war party, bristling under the overbearing commands of Hunts The Enemy (bottom), Two Leggings severed himself from the pipeholder's group but rejoined before returning home.

Smithsonian Office of Anthropology, Bureau of American Ethnology Collection

For special occasions the Crows constructed a medicine sweat lodge of 104 willows.

Before one door of this common sweat-lodge frame (below) waves a red blanket offering. In front of the rear door a buffalo skull lies on a mound. To one side of the frame stands a sacred miniature sweat lodge with incense-burning coals in its center.

Above: Unwrapped on pieces of trade cloth lie glass bead offerings to the Braided Tail medicine bundle, its central object the skull of a famous medicine man who lived during the first half of the nineteenth century.

After Sees The Living Bull returned from the fast, when he saw moccasins made of a coyote head and a fox head barking fire at him, he made a war medicine moccasin bundle from two coyote heads, each trimmed with scalp locks.

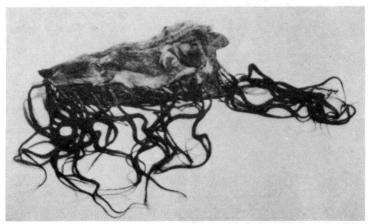

Hairy Wolf (top), an acclaimed Crow warrior, took on the responsibility of climbing to the top of White On The Neck's Sun Dance lodge to flap his arms like an eagle's wings and blow his whistle, one of the ceremony's important preliminary rituals. Another well-known Crow war leader, Long Otter (bottom), was the man chosen by Big Shoulder to lead his revenge raid instead of Two Leggings.

The "four inexperienced men" whom Two Leggings (far right) led on the last Crow war party in 1888 were (left to right) Other Bull, Old Horn, Old Coyote, and Old Jackrabbit.

Two Leggings just before his death, his arm displaying the horseshoe-shaped scars cut by a friend during an early fast.

Now I wanted to provide for my safety by making a medicine for future raids which would satisfy my companions. I asked Old Dog for help and while he performed the ceremony and sang his medicine songs, I tied a willow branch into a hoop. After wrapping it with buckskin strips painted yellow, blue, and black, I tied a hawkskin to its top, making a medicine representing everything in my dream.

I was anxious to test this medicine but already I had complete faith in it. I told Young Mountain that I had a proper medicine and that in my last dream many horses had come toward me from the north. We invited eight others and made ready to leave. My wife sewed several extra pairs of moccasins. Then I built a sweat lodge of forty-four willows and invited Crooked Arm and Two Belly. They were surprised and wanted to know how I had the right since they were supposed to teach the younger men these sacred things. This was make-believe, they said, and bad luck would come to those who joined in it.

I said I was not pretending and that on Where The Thunderbird Sits Down Mountain I had received a powerful vision showing me how to build this sweat lodge. They were not convinced but attended the ceremony and gave their blessing. Afterwards Crooked Arm said he still thought I was too young to have that powerful a vision and wanted me to buy the right to build the sweat lodge from some well-known medicine man. Their dreams had been proven true, he said, and their medicine had been tested. He liked me and hoped someday I would be a chief, but I must do things the right way.

I promised to follow all this, but I lied. I was stubborn because I had always had to make my own way.

Early the next morning we rode out of our village on Willow Creek toward the Piegan country. Now I carried my medicine as well as my pipe and felt like a real pipeholder.

After crossing the Musselshell River and riding in the direction of Bear Creek, we came upon a Piegan camp in a valley near Where The Bear Sits Down Mountain and waited until dark.

Leaving two men with the horses, eight of us walked toward the camp. That night the Piegans were careless. Far from their tipis we found an unguarded horse herd quietly grazing. We easily drove off over a hundred head, starting back immediately because I wanted no accidents. After picking up our own horses we galloped through the night, all the next day, and through the next night. Then we stopped long enough to feed and water the horses and eat something ourselves. We never knew if they followed us, but gave them no chance.

Right after our little rest we rode on, finally entering our village with eighty head running before us—the rest had played out and been abandoned. Then I divided the horses among my men. We received many honors and songs of praise during the dancing and feasting after our return. This trip was one of the most successful I ever made.

Crooked Arm still believed I should buy a medicine from some experienced medicine man and warned me not to let my luck make me forget the older people's valuable experience. But I felt my dreams were powerful and this last success made me very proud. The whole camp sang my praises and I was in no mood to listen to anyone. Now I am old and see the same things happen among white people. The young think they know everything and that we are no longer useful. But they learn, and for some it is too late.

Soon afterwards five friends and I left for the Sioux country. After stealing six horses we were discovered and chased for two days. We were lucky to find a hiding place and covered our tracks, so they gave up. But when I returned home I did not hold my head so high. This trip scared me and for some time I did not feel like going out.

After this Crooked Arm would not talk to me. Finally one day when many of our leading men were attending a sweat-lodge ceremony he called me over and reminded me of that last escape, saying that maybe I had pretended I had a medicine so my friends would think I had received some powerful vision. He asked me to relate all my dreams to him and said that if I followed his advice the Great Above Person would help me. I did not like his telling me this and answered that I had only had a vision of the sweat lodge.

I still could not listen. But if he and Two Belly had not shown such concern I would probably have been killed long ago. In time I realized the good example and valuable advice of these great men, and saw how stupid and reckless I had been.

Chapter Eighteen

*The Crow labels for rivers, mountain ranges, creeks, and other
geographical locations were drawn from the same sources
as their personal names: supernatural experiences, actual
events, and physical features.*

*Present-day Pryor Gap received its Crow name of Hits With
The Arrows from the legend about a boy who had been
befriended by dwarfs dwelling there. Crows passing through
these mountains were instructed to make offerings to these
dwarfs by shooting arrows into a certain crevice. Hence, the
gap was called Hits With The Arrows, Pryor Creek was named
Arrow Creek, and the Pryor Mountains were known as the
Arrowhead Mountains.*

*When White Man Runs Him, a Custer scout, fasted in the
Pryor Mountains they named his peak Where They See
The Rope, because the white clay-painted thongs attached
to skewers in his chest were visible to the villagers below.
A site near Lewistown, Montana, was known as Where The
Moccasin Hangs because war parties left their wet footwear
hanging there after crossing the river.*

*The Musselshell River was so named for the shells
found in its bed, the Powder River because along its arid banks
buffalo and riders churned up great clouds of dust, like ash
or powder. Near Forsyth, Montana, a jutting landmark for
returning war parties was called The Coyote's Penis.*

IT WAS LEAF-FALLING SEASON and time to cut new tipi poles so we
moved to Hits With The Arrows where there were many straight
pine trees.

While camped there I often noticed the three buttes along the eastern ridge of the canyon. We called these favorite fasting places the Medicine Dream or Dwarf Buttes from an old story our grandfathers told us in which they were the home of dwarfs. Only Skin On The Forehead had fasted on the most eastern butte but I decided to climb it, even though Crooked Arm warned me I could never reach the top.

After my preparations to meet the Great Above Person I started out, carrying my white-painted buffalo robe and a rawhide rope. At sundown I reached the butte's base. The sides rose straight up, but with my rope tied between two poles like a ladder I got to the top and kicked the poles away. My brother had promised to help me down in four days.

Looking over the edge I could see our tipis along Arrow Creek. I built my resting place, lay down, and prayed for a vision.

On the third day a strong wind with heavy hail blew over the mountains and I thought the butte shook under me. The following night I dreamt my vision of long ago. The spirit from before returned with the hawk sitting on the hoop on his head. Once again a voice sang three times, and when my vision person stood up the hawk whistled, flapped its wings, and streaks of lightning flashed from its eyes in many directions. A voice said those streaks were showing me where to travel. My vision man sang: "Everywhere I go, they will come to me."

This song became one of my medicine songs on future raids. My spirit man called me his son and asked if I saw a trail with horses. Early the next grass season, when the snow was almost gone, he said I would steal them. He pointed to the Sioux country and I saw a whole herd running toward me.

After the hawk had shown me several directions it shut its eyes, folded its wings, and hung its head. My dream person had appeared young but now he seemed like an old man. This meant I would also grow old. He carried a coyote over his arm and said that its name was Stays Among The Buffalo. This meant that I would act as scout on many raids to come. He sang again: "Go by here and thank you."

As he sang he pointed and I saw many horses' ears and then I was awake. My blanket lay some distance from me and I was too weak to stand. For a moment I thought about this wonderful vision, certain that now my ambition to become a pipeholder and a chief would come true. After thanking the Great Above Person I felt strong enough to stand. I picked up my blanket and went to the cliff edge. The sun was just rising and our women were building fires for the morning meal.

My brother would not come for another day. Since I had received my vision I walked to where I had kicked my ladder and found it snagged in a tree. When I threw my blanket down it also caught on a branch but I picked it up on my climb down. At home my wife made me a light meal and I lay down.

I had already asked my brother to build me a sweat lodge, and after resting awhile I asked Crooked Arm and Two Belly and some other old men to smoke with me. When they arrived Two Belly filled the pipe and passed it around. Then he said that for a long time he had been watching me try to make a name for myself. When he was gone, he said, he believed I would be a chief. He told me to smoke the pipe and tell everything I had seen on the butte.

I said that at the melting-snow time I was to head for the Sioux country and return with from fifty to seventy head of horses. My vision person had told me to go on these raids until we had many horses.

I said that for the second time I had seen a person standing at the eastern horizon with a hawk on a hoop and that I had already made a medicine of this dream for stealing those horses. Before I had only seen part of the man above the horizon but this time I had seen his chief's leggings, which meant that one day I would be a chief. Two Belly told me that I was a good man and did not doubt I would do all this. After our talk we entered the sweat lodge. I did not tell any of the younger men about my vision.

Spring season finally came and camp moved toward Elk River near the mouth of Arrow Creek, stopping just east of the present Billings Fairgrounds and on top of the rimrocks. The Elk River Valley was below us and in those days seemed covered with buffalo.

After a few days camp moved west to a big bend in the river. The women jerked and dried meat and tanned hides while we waited for the ice to leave the river. Then we crossed, traveling along Blue Creek and hunting for buffalo.

One day Young Mountain and I were hunting and stopped to smoke on a ridge. I said that the season had come to go out, but warned him not to tell Medicine Crow because he would tell his father, who would try to stop us. He said that Medicine Crow probably would not come anyhow because his new wife was so good looking he would be afraid some young men would try to visit her.

He asked about the horses in my vision and I said that I had only seen four clearly, two grays, a bay, and one with a split ear.

When we returned to camp I told my wife to make some extra moccasins. Young Mountain had just gotten married and told his wife to make some extra pairs also. When we were ready I built a sweat lodge, making an offering to the sun.

Somehow Medicine Crow heard because he came to invite us to his father's tipi for a smoke. Sees The Living Bull kept us there for a long time trying to convince me that my time had not come. I promised to put off my trip but I lied. Later, when Young Mountain and I were talking outside his tipi, Sees The Living Bull came out. He warned us again not to go until my medicine told me, which he said was not for another moon. He reminded me what had happened to men who disobeyed their visions. But Young Mountain and I arranged to start before dawn.

Just as we were leaving the next morning someone yelled Sioux had stolen horses during the night. The whole camp was quickly awake and search parties were formed. We joined them, since my last vision had showed my next trail heading east. We caught up with some more people on the banks of Elk River near the present east bridge of Billings. After crossing the river all of us followed the Sioux trail to Arrow Creek and from there south to the foot of the mountains. It had grown dark but we rode all night until we came to the Bighorn River close to where Fort C. F. Smith was later built. We saw where they had killed a buffalo and stopped to eat beside the river. We kept riding until Wolf Bear, the pipeholder, said that we could not catch them before they reached their village. After deciding to return home he ordered scouts to ride in the rear and on the flanks to prevent men from running away. If anyone was caught his weapons would be broken and he would have to travel back alone.

But I did not want to return without even seeing any Sioux. I told Young Mountain to ride slowly to the head of the column. Working our way up until only Wolf Bear was ahead, I whispered that at my signal he should ride off to one direction and I would go in the other. We arranged a place to meet.

We were riding fine horses and each carried a gun, ammunition, a buffalo robe, plenty of moccasins, and dried meat. My medicine was wrapped in its rawhide case and fastened to my belt. I pointed to it, telling Young Mountain that it said we would return safely.

We were on the highest hill east of the site of Fort C. F. Smith, about to descend its western slope, when I gave Young Mountain the signal. Someone yelled as he galloped off to the left and I to the right. When the scouts drove me to a high bank I slid down while they stopped at the edge. Although they could not catch me now I was careful as I rode to our meeting place at the foot of the Bighorn Mountains. There I rested, holding my horse's reins and wondering if Young Mountain had been caught. But soon he rode over a hill and said he too had been chased off a bank. We quickly located the Sioux trail, keeping careful watch as we rode. Then Young Mountain noticed someone following us. It was Old Woman, who rode up to ask where his friends were. When we broke away, he said, the scouts had divided to chase us and this allowed others to scatter. They had arranged to meet somewhere along the trail.

That night there was a full moon and we could see long distances. No one else arrived so we rode east along a creek bottom until I noticed horses ahead and stopped. They were Crows and I suggested to them that we all ride until daylight to find the Sioux camp. Then we could hide during the day and steal our horses back at night. I thought the main camp would be either on Rotten Grass Creek or the Little Bighorn River.

A boy named Tobacco riding a bad horse said that he was poor and wanted to come. When we had run away he had dismounted, pretending to tighten his cinch, and had been left behind. He knew we were chasing the Sioux and said it did not matter if he was killed.

I pitied him and made certain he carried a good gun and knife. Then I told my men that my last dream had promised me these horses. Even though the old men wanted me to wait I knew my time had come.

The Sioux had stolen about two hundred head and their trail was plain in the moonlight. We followed it to Rotten Grass Creek and then upstream, arriving at the mountains about sunrise.

I was so tired I must have fallen asleep on my horse. Suddenly a man appeared in the western sky pointing to something. Among a bunch of horses I saw a black, a gray, and one with a split ear.

Young Mountain and I climbed a hilltop to scout while the rest stayed in the thick trees. But I was too sleepy to see well. Then Young Mountain pointed out a Sioux scout standing on a little rise near some pine trees, a blanket wrapped around his gun and body. After noticing seven more driving our stolen horses eastward, we

105

crept back down. I told my men to mount, hoping to get around the next hill and surprise them from the front. Leading them out, I sang my medicine song: "Thank you. A long time. I am going to be a chief. Thank you."

I told my men not to be afraid and explained that this song had come to me in a dream, that we would have good luck, recover our horses, and kill some Sioux. I advised them to throw off their robes to ride faster.

A man slightly ahead suddenly pulled in, saying by signs that he saw tipi flaps. Around the bend I saw tipis and people cooking. We hurried out of sight and decided to hide in some nearby trees during the day since we could not return to the mountains without being discovered. Leading our horses into a deep coulee in the grove, we left two young men with them and returned to the edge of the trees.

I told my men to paint themselves and get their medicines. As we watched their camp we saw they were not Sioux but Cheyennes. The sun rose higher and I told the others that at dawn I had been told we would have horses tonight. Our luck had changed, and I told them to smoke with me and not to worry.

While we were in the trees we noticed Cheyennes scouting the country. I had the horses exercised deep in the trees. I also had some men try to find food and water. We were suffering from thirst and as the day wore on it grew worse. When the sun passed the middle some men and women walked toward the flat near our hiding place to play shinny. Several players came close that afternoon but none entered the trees.

Finally the sun went down and we thanked the Great Above Person for protecting us through the day and asked him to give us courage for the night.

We were lucky that clouds covered the moon, just as we had been lucky the night before when the clear moon showed us their trail. As soon as it was completely dark we quietly walked our horses to the river, allowing them to feed and drink so they would be fresh for the work ahead. We heard the Cheyennes singing and beating their drums and calling out the names of their men who had stolen horses. We waited until the singing died down and the camp was quiet. Then I told Young Mountain to choose two men and look for the black, the gray, and the horse with the split ear. After showing him the direction I told him to return if he did not find them.

For a while there was silence and then we heard horses. A large bunch galloped in with our men behind them. Young Mountain rode a spirited horse and was leading a black, a gray, and one with a split ear.

Each of us roped one, turning our own in with the rest. Then every man selected six to ten head to drive before him to make better time. We rode all night and when the sun rose we saw no Cheyennes behind us. For three days we had not eaten but I could not risk spoiling our luck.

After sunset we found a sheltered place and stayed long enough to water and feed our horses while we killed a buffalo and quickly broiled some meat. Then we rode through that night and at sunrise reached the top of the rimrocks along Elk River. In the valley below we saw our people taking down their tipis. After painting ourselves and unwrapping our medicines we drove the horses through camp, singing and shooting our guns into the air. I felt very happy because it was the second time I had been this lucky.

We rode past Wolf Bear but he was angry at having returned without horses or scalps and lacking men, and would not notice us.

Soon after this trip my wife left me and I married a girl named Medicine Porcupine. Although she was the daughter of Chief Shell On The Neck he did not make me give any presents for her. He must have thought well of me. She was a good woman and I was happy with her.

The camp moved and hunting began for fresh hides for tipi covers. When we had enough we moved to Arrowhead Mountains for more tipi poles.

Chapter Nineteen

*In his recollections Two Leggings mentions practically
every class of Crow medicine bundle. While their functions
often overlap, distinctions can be made.*

*Twice Two Leggings describes Sun Dance bundles.
They can be termed war medicines, but they were never
carried on raids. Two Leggings discounted the power of his
first proper war medicine bundle because it was
a gift from his non-warrior brother. When he manufactures
two unaccredited bundles, both are another
kind of war medicine—the hoop medicine bundle. One of the
prime ingredients in the bundle which will answer
Two Leggings' prayers is a small rock, a "child" of Sees
The Living Bull's famous rock medicine bundle.*

*Preparing for his raid, Hunts The Enemy is given the
choice of two bundles to take along, a skull medicine bundle
and an arrow medicine bundle. While the latter was
an ordinary war medicine, the former rivaled the Sun Dance
bundle in sacredness.*

*Other varieties were the love medicine bundle
described in this chapter, the witchcraft medicine of bear sinew
in the Bear White Child legend, the buffalo-hunting
medicine which Two Leggings fabricates and
then legitimately purchases, and the horse medicine which
he uses for a speedy escape from Sioux.*

WHILE OUR CAMP was at the joining of the Bighorn River and the
Stinking Water south of the Arrowhead Mountains, Wolf Bear led a

war party to stop people from talking about him. Poor Face and Fire Wing were among his warriors. They came upon Cheyennes during their Sun Dance while the Arapahoes and other tribes were camped with them. When they returned with many horses the celebration in their honor made me very anxious to go out.

I spoke to Half Yellow Face and Bear In The Water, both pipe-holders. They had also been excited by Wolf Bear's raid and soon we had a group of young men.

Half Yellow Face called us into his tipi after sundown. I sat to the right of Bear In The Water who was to the right of Half Yellow Face. The other warriors completed the circle around the fire. When Half Yellow Face's wife placed some glowing coals in front of him he lit his pipe and it was passed around. A closed medicine bundle lay before him on a buffalo robe. When the pipe returned he stood up, lifted his hands to the sky, and asked the Great Above Person to look down on us. He said that when the sun returned in the morning we would be on our way. He said that he was taking along the powerful medicine which the Great Above Person had given to Cold Wind, through his powerful servants, the elks. He promised to pray and sacrifice to it and asked the Great Above Person to protect us on this revenge trail.

After sitting down he laid sweet grass on the coals and purified his hands and the bundle in the smoke. Then he untied the thongs, slowly peeled off the wrappings, and spread the contents before him.

The medicine's main object was a flute, painted yellow and with two lines carved into it, one straight and the other zigzag. An elk's head and a bighorn sheep's head were also carved into the flute. A bunch of curlew and red woodpecker feathers was attached and an eagle feather hung from the end. Half Yellow Face addressed the bundle as his father and said that it had carried its child, Cold Wind, through many danger trails. Cold Wind had made him a duplicate medicine and now Half Yellow Face said he was also its child. Half Yellow Face prayed that the medicine would protect him and all who accompanied him. He asked its help in finding the Cheyennes so we could recapture our horses and return safely home.

After singing four medicine songs belonging to the bundle he laid the medicine back on the robe. He explained that Cold Wind had received it during a long fast on a high mountain top near the head of the Stillwater River. He had seen a flute with bark on the stem appearing above the horizon, as if a strong hand were pushing it from below. When the flute's full length was visible it sank out of sight. The second time the flute appeared the bark was peeled from the wood and the third time Cold Wind noticed carvings on it. The fourth time it came forward until it stood in front of him. Then it disappeared and before him a man on horseback was playing the flute. This man was surrounded by enemies; and each time he played, one enemy was killed. Four times he blew and each time he took their scalps. Cold Wind noticed that the man was himself. This vision went away and another man carrying a flute rode up from the horizon; he recognized himself again. When this man played his flute some women tried to take it away from him, but he held it too high. Half Yellow Face explained that it was also a love medicine but that we were using it only as a war medicine which was its strongest power. After the man had changed himself into a bighorn sheep, the vision disappeared.

Calling us his brothers, Half Yellow Face said that he was telling us all this so we would have faith in the medicine. He pointed to the curlew and woodpecker feathers and said that Cold Wind had seen those birds sitting on the flute as the man was holding it. The curlew had said it would stop him if he tried to lie. The woodpecker had said that no wood was too hard to penetrate. Half Yellow Face explained that we all knew the birds were divided into two clans and that along with some other birds the woodpecker belonged to the curlew's clan. The curlew was telling his clan members to help the dreamer and never to deceive him. Half Yellow Face explained that the woodpecker's words were like our saying, "I will eat that deed," which means that no matter how difficult or dangerous something is, it will be no harder than eating a meal. The woodpecker goes through the toughest wood with the same ease; Half Yellow Face said that with its help and this medicine's power we would overcome our trail's danger the same way.

Showing us the eagle feather he said that Cold Wind had been told his body and breath were in it. Whenever he took the medicine on the warpath it would be as hard for the enemy to shoot him as to hit this feather fluttering in the wind.

He said that the carved straight line was the vision man's voice which went straight out to an enemy and killed him. The green-painted zigzag line was the spirit of the medicine owner's voice which goes first to the earth and then to the enemies, confusing them so they can be easily killed. Half Yellow Face said that the carved heads were the two animals appearing to Cold Wind. They had also given the medicine songs he had just sung to us. Those animals were members of the medicine's clan along with the curlew, the woodpecker, the

110

swallow, the gum eater, the deer, the moose, the mule deer, the bear, and the chicken hawk. We were to watch out for those animals on our trail because they would tell us what to do. He said that if they appeared in our dreams we must tell him so we could be guided and return singing victory songs.

The flute was painted yellow, he said, because of the yellow flowers of spring and the yellow leaves of autumn. The medicine's power would last from season to season until forever, granting old age to its owner.[1]

Finally the medicine was passed around and we each prayed for it to give us strength and good luck. Then we began the medicine songs, singing them so often that I warned Half Yellow Face. But he would not listen. Our medicine fathers want us to pray, to sing the songs they have given us, and to go through the ceremony accompanying each medicine, but they do not want this overdone. Half Yellow Face would not stop and sang for most of the night.

We left camp just before dawn, crossed the Bighorn Mountains, and descended their eastern slopes. Three days later we located a large Cheyenne camp close to the present town of Sheridan. For the rest of that day we hid among the cottonwood groves that lined the river, but moved in with darkness. I was in the rear when I heard shouting and shots. Running back and mounting my horse I galloped toward the mountains. Everyone had scattered but it seemed as if all the Cheyennes were after me. They had enough moonlight to see and were still behind at daybreak. I reached the mountains and whipped my exhausted horse up the steep slopes. By the time we were on top it could hardly walk. I jumped off and ran, praying out loud. Behind me the Cheyennes were singing. I was sure they would torture me before killing me. Although the rough ground kept them from riding fast I could never escape on foot.

Then I saw Great Unmarried Man on a large black horse at the edge of a cliff. About sixty feet below, the ground was covered with big boulders. The Cheyennes were now within shooting range and bullets whistled over our heads. Yelling for the boy to jump I threw myself off, hit the rocks, and rolled to the bottom. I looked myself over; my legs and arms were only skinned. The boy had ridden off on his horse. His head was cut on top and one leg was gashed open. The horse was so badly hurt we had to abandon it. As the Cheyennes appeared at the cliff top, throwing rocks and shooting, we crawled down the canyon. Once out of sight I wanted to keep moving because they would probably run along the canyon ridge until they found a place to climb down.

I knew all this bad luck was because Half Yellow Face had angered his medicine father by singing too many songs.

The Cheyennes must have begun chasing the other men. We stopped hearing their shouts and saw them no more. The boy was vomiting because he was scared. When he told me to go home alone I said I would wait to bury him. Then he cried for water so I laid him in the shelter of a big rock and found a creek about half a mile away. I packed him there on my back and we went to sleep.

The next morning I discovered a spring and after he felt a little better I helped him walk. We drank cold water and I bathed his head wound. We only had our guns, my knife, and our shirts. As night fell we grew cold so I cut off leafy branches for cover. I woke up to the boy whispering for me not to move. Opening my eyes I saw a large rattlesnake sliding along my body. It raised its head and crawled across my chest. I have always been afraid of these snakes but I lay still. After it had slid away I could not move and sweat covered my body. When I finally tried to stand, my legs would not hold me.

It was bright and very hot so I told the boy we should start early. I had not eaten anything since the night before and was very hungry. The boy was still weak and asked for a stick to support himself. Then we began walking through the woods. We saw more rattlesnakes but felt too miserable to kill them. Before long the boy said he felt dried up and was dying.

When I said we would reach home together he asked me to tell his mother to come after him. But then he said that maybe it was better if I waited until he was dead so I could take his gun to her.

The worst part was our hunger, and I had seen no game. All the time the boy begged me to leave him, but I would not listen. About three bowshots away I saw some willows; in the mountains that always means water. Packing him on my shoulders I carried him to the spring and dipped water for him with my hands. He could not get enough. During the day it grew hotter. The boy kept calling me brother and saying that he was starving. He cried when he thought of his mother. He had always been her favorite because her other children had not treated her well. I became angry and started to weep also, making up this song: "We have no way to live anymore. Soon we will be dead."

The boy told me to stop because he was not dead yet. Then I told him to be quiet. But when I suggested killing a deer he begged me not

112

to leave him. I knocked off the horn from a buffalo skull and brushed out the inside with the chewed end of a willow twig. In this I mixed wild peppermint and water. He drank it and felt better. During the hottest part of the day we lay down. When I was asleep I saw a dead tree with frost on its bark. A voice said that horses were near this tree. A person appeared, showing me the horses and saying that on the other side of this hill was something to let me live. When I woke late in the afternoon Great Unmarried Man said he did not think he was sick anymore but complained that the rocks hurt his feet. Both our moccasins were in pieces and we stopped at some pine trees where I scraped off pitch and glued a piece of my breechcloth to the inside of his moccasins. We slowly made our way to some nearby woods and at nightfall I cut branches to cover us. Before the boy went to sleep I gave him sage to chew. He did not like its bitterness, but the next morning said that some more might help cure him. I said I was not giving it for a medicine but because fast animals eat sage and it might help him run.

He chewed some more but it made him thirsty and he spit it out. After he heard about my dream he was willing to find something that would help us to live. Finally we reached the other canyon wall. As we were resting I noticed something black moving in the trees. Before I went to look I told the boy that if he heard shooting to lie very still.

It turned out to be a horse drinking from a spring, a buffalo-hide rope fastened to its saddle. Immediately I fell to the ground. But I was ready to risk anything and when no one appeared I walked up. The horse was very tame and when I rode back to the boy I said that this was the Great Above Person's gift which had been shown to me.

I held the horse's lead while we faced the sun to pray. A buckskin bag was also tied to the saddle, holding three pairs of moccasins. They were too small for me but fit the boy.

He rode while I ran alongside holding on to the saddle. In those days I was a great runner and for a long time we traveled that way toward the northern valley. After crossing the divide we rode double and that afternoon entered the valley.

The boy felt well but hungry and I was also starved. But when I wanted to kill our horse he said it had saved our lives and we should take it home. There was no use staying at a creek we had just reached so we rode double again until we came upon a small buffalo herd. We were afraid to ride too near. As I dismounted I prayed to the sun to give us just one.

Crawling on the off-wind side to within a few feet of a young bull,

I killed it with one shot. Great Unmarried Man was anxious to eat but I reminded him of our older people's warning that if we have not eaten for a long time we should first drink some blood, then eat the tallow, and finally take just a little meat.

After drinking some blood we packed all the meat we could carry. In the woods I built a fire with my flint and steel which I always carried in a leather sack on my belt. Then we broiled and ate some tallow. Finally I cooked a rib, warning him that if he ate too much he would feel worse than after jumping off that cliff. We forgot our troubles and I stopped being so cautious. The whole country seemed friendly.

I told the boy not to be afraid because my dream had shown we would return home safely and would go out again this winter to capture many horses.

I cut out the sac holding the buffalo's heart, stretched it on a willow twig, and filled it with water. I also skinned the hide, burned off the hair, and cut a piece to cover my foot and meet on the instep and behind the heel. Then I sewed the pieces together with an awl and sinew from the buffalo's back muscles. When it dried it would fit tightly. We also loaded plenty of meat on our saddle.

We rode until sunset when we stopped to eat and then continued on through the night. Two days later, on the banks of Elk River near the Mountain Lion's Lodge, we found our camp.

Everyone thought we were long since dead and there was great excitement as our horse walked among the tipis. Those who had seen me outnumbered could not imagine how I had escaped. I had to tell our story many times. Even Sees The Living Bull wanted to know about it. I also told him of my dream and said that I expected to capture those horses as soon as the frost was on the trees. This did not make him happy. He said I had been given those horses for the snow season after this one and that earlier I would have bad luck.

But I could not understand my dream that way, and planned a raid for the coming snow season. Now I know he was right.

Chapter Twenty

Long after Big Crane was renamed Two Leggings, as told here, he received a third name, His Eyes Are Dreamy, probably relating to some visionary experience.

At birth, names were either conferred by a selected paternal clansman or taken from the first objects the mother saw after delivery, a white-hipped horse, the top of a moccasin, and so on.

A subsequent vision, a noteworthy battle exploit, or a personal peculiarity might yield a man more names. Old Dog, the maker of one of Two Leggings' hoop bundles, was so known because of his habit of leading an old dog to carry his spare moccasins. In adult life, a new name often announced a new personality and a luckier fortune.

Some nicknames expressed characteristic behavior of paternal clansmen. Both girls and boys received names this way. Once a woman hit herself over the head in a fit of anger; thereafter one of her brother's children was known as Hits Herself Over The Head.

SHORTLY AFTER OUR CLOSE ESCAPE, camp moved to the Arrowhead Mountains, stopping near Hits With The Arrows. Grass season had passed and leaf-falling season was nearly over. The mountains gave us wood and sheltered us from the cold eastern winds. There was plenty of game and we faced Arrow Creek, which gave us all the water we needed. Our camp site was so good that everyone was glad to hear we would stay for the snow season.

Two Belly asked me to be his neighbor and I had my wife pitch our tipi next to his. Then I visited him often and listened to his stories.

He told me that my past honors were not enough to make me a pipeholder whom the chiefs would allow to lead a war party. He said that if I kept acting recklessly someday they would mourn my death. He advised me to buy a medicine bundle from some well-known medicine man.

I answered that I was sure I would not die in battle. Although I had not enjoyed the luck I would have wanted, I said this would change. Already I had fasted several times and would keep doing it until I received a dream powerful enough to make me a chief. In the meantime, I said, I would join raiding parties.

Before the cold weather we made a few hunting trips as far as the Bull Mountains along the Musselshell River. Then the days began shortening and one morning we woke up in the middle of a freezing blizzard. Everything was covered with snow, but we were safe and warm. Those were the days when we visited each other's tipis and when the old men told tales of our grandfathers. I wanted to show myself as brave as those men. I wanted to make a name for myself which would be spoken by my grandchildren years after I had gone to the Other Side Camp.

Although we count the new year from the time the snow-turned-back [the first snowfall] it was still late leaf-falling season and a few days later a warm wind blew in. The snow began melting and some places were completely bare. About this time I heard that Bushy Head was going to the Sioux country. I was the first to ask to join.

In the early morning, after Bushy Head's preparations, thirteen of us set out on foot, leading two pack horses to carry our supplies. Bushy Head had dreamed of Sioux horses along Big River and some distance below Plum Creek. We followed Arrow Creek to Elk River, which we crossed at the Mountain Lion's Lodge, and walked through the hills toward the Musselshell River. Late one night we reached the southern spurs of the Bull Mountains and made camp in a thick pine grove. We had been traveling for some time and our supplies were gone. Two men went looking for buffalo and soon returned with two hides and meat. After cooking and eating the best parts we went to sleep. No guards were placed since we were still far from Sioux country. We slept past sunrise and while we washed in a creek a helper built our cooking fire. Then we ate, roasting some meat to pack with us, and continued north.

The wind was still west and by now almost all the snow was gone.

We hoped for colder weather since it was tiring to walk across the soft ground.

Toward evening we arrived at the Musselshell River. The younger men wanted to spend the night here but Bushy Head and I were for crossing and his word was law. Some did not like this but we were on the other side before sundown.

We camped a few miles north of the present town of Roundup at the base of a rimrock with pines on top. The weather was so fine that after eating we fell asleep without making a shelter. Again we placed no guard and the rimrocks protected us from the little wind now coming from the north.

Sometime past the middle of the night I felt that someone slapped my face. Waking up, I did not recognize the country. I felt very cold and noticed my blanket had been blown away. It was snowing hard with a strong east wind rushing around the rimrock edge.

I woke up the others, afraid they would freeze without enough covers. Some of the young men, tired from the long march, had not felt the change and were already numb. Weasel could not feel anything from the knees down and was unable to stand.

We moved about a mile west where a sharp curve in the rimrocks protected us from the wind. After rubbing Weasel's legs with snow we placed him next to a fire and wrapped a blanket around him.

We were afraid to fall asleep and huddled together with our backs to the rimrock. The fire reflected off the rocks and kept us a little warm. Although we were glad to see daylight, it grew colder. We roasted the remaining meat which made us feel better. The snow had stopped just before dawn and Bushy Head gave orders to move. But as we were packing the two horses it fell again and we decided to wait. The wind blew harder and soon there was a blizzard, the snow so thick you could not see an arm's length ahead. We fed that small fire through that day and that night and through the next day and the next night. On the morning of the third day the sun finally appeared, but the air was colder with the clear sky.

We had not eaten anything for two days and saw no game so we decided to try to reach the trader's store at the mouth of Plum Creek. The snow was higher than our knees and higher than a horse in the drifts along the coulees. It would take us about four days to walk to the store, but camp was even farther away and Bushy Head did not want to go back.

I was only wearing a torn pair of buckskin leggings and as we started out my legs grew numb. I took the red blanket from around my shoulders and cut it into leggings. The buffalo hide we had brought was frozen stiff and I cut off its long hair. Pulling the extra leggings over my old pair I tied them at the ankles and stuffed hair in between.

Someone had killed a deer. Bushy Head was roasting the meat and as I walked up he stared. My legs were like young pine trees. When he called me Lots Of Leggings the others laughed, telling me to eat or I would have only extra leggings for my meal.

They teased me for three more days, calling me that name until we reached the trader's store at the mouth of Plum Creek on Big River. In the store the trader saw my leggings and asked a man who spoke a little English my name. When he said Lots Of Leggings the trader did not understand and said Two Leggings; my friend said that was right.

The weather stayed cold and more snow fell. For many days we walked along Big River trying to find the Sioux camp, often camping to wait for the weather to improve. After traveling like this for two moons, the days began to lengthen. Finally we located the Sioux and stole about fifty horses. It snowed some more, but now we were glad to have it hide our tracks.

On our way back we passed the trader's store and again he called me Two Leggings. For the rest of the trip we had cold weather and I never took off those leggings. The snow became so heavy the horses wore out and in the early spring, when we walked into our camp, only one remained. There was great rejoicing as we had long since been given up for dead. Two Belly was the first to invite me for a smoke and asked about our trip. After I finished he smoked silently until his pipe was empty.

First he called me Big Crane but then he said Two Leggings. I had been on a dangerous journey, he said, and it was good this trail gave me a new name. He hoped it would also remind me of my foolishness. Every time I went on the warpath I seemed to meet worse dangers and one day I would not return. While I had not had to fight this time, he said, I had little to show for it. He thought this a warning from the Great Above Person. I told him that the next day I was building a sweat lodge and was going to invite him and a few other great men. I promised to make the medicine I had seen in my dream. Although I had made such a medicine before, with Old Dog's help, I said the

118

ceremony had been short and was not followed by the ceremonial sweat bath I thought necessary.

He answered that they would not enter my sweat lodge until I had shown them my medicine and told them about it.

I was disappointed because I knew they would never accept my first medicine. But I was sensing a change in my life and was willing to do as they said.

After inviting Bull Weasel, one of our oldest medicine men, to help me, I began to gather the materials. First I needed a big hawkskin and so I left early the next morning. After searching all day without any luck I returned to learn that I had been chosen leader of five scouts to search for buffalo on a mountain called High Peak In The Middle.

We left before dawn. The weather was mild and we reached the mountain by the middle of the second day. Standing on top and looking through my telescope, we located several large herds and some smaller ones grazing close to us. After sending three men back to camp, I had nothing to do while camp moved to the mountain's base so I hunted for the hawk and finally killed one. Our people arrived three days later. As soon as my tipi was set up Bull Weasel helped with my medicine.

I made a hoop from a red willow branch. Covering it with buckskin I painted it half blue and half black and tied the hawkskin and some red feathers to it. The black meant night and the blue the earth. The red feathers meant the clouds and the hawkskin was my vision. Bull Weasel and I took all day to complete it. Much singing and smudging and other ceremonies were necessary to make it powerful. Then I invited Two Belly and some other men to my sweat lodge. When they heard my medicine had been properly made they arrived. I was glad and began thinking about going out on raids again.

But when I met Crooked Arm he said that although I owned an accepted medicine I was not to act carelessly. He still thought I should stay in camp this coming snow season.

He made me angry and I did not answer. I stayed in camp for many days, thinking only of my medicine. The snow was melting fast, and each day I felt more like leaving.

Chapter Twenty-One

*When Two Leggings dreamt his wishful dreams, they
promised horses as well as scalps. The animals he saw were
descendants of horses which originated from Santa
Fe's stock-raising environs in the early seventeenth century.
Between 1730 and 1760 the Comanches, and their
cousins the Shoshonis, furnished the Crows with their
first mounts. This set in motion a trade which found the Crows
driving herds obtained from western transmontane tribes
into present-day North Dakota. At the Mandan
and Hidatsa villages they obtained twice the horses'
original value in such European-made articles as knives, axes,
kettles, gunpowder, and Northwest Company flintlocks.
Also they exchanged articles of their own manufacture—
dried meat, buffalo robes, and tipi covers—for squash,
pumpkins, smoking tobacco, and corn.*

*Horses quickly replaced dogs as the Crow index of
wealth. Before long the Crows were second only to
the Flatheads in their horse holdings. Accounts allot at least
fifteen head per tipi, with the number often soaring to a
hundred.*

*On July 21, 1806, the explorers Lewis and Clark
awoke to find twenty-four horses missing. All that remained
of the thieves was a cast-off moccasin and a piece
of robe. Their first theft of American mounts epitomized the
intent and extent of Crow concern with white interlopers.*

THAT HUNT WAS not very successful and everyone was hungry for
fresh meat after the long winter of eating only dried meat. Our chief de-

cided to move east and meet the herds that roamed south each spring season. After crossing the Bighorn River we camped near the Wolf Mountains where we got most of the robes and fresh meat we needed. Then we left for the joining of the Little Bighorn and Bighorn rivers where Two Belly wanted to camp briefly before moving into the Arrowhead Mountains. When I told him of large herds which I had heard were grazing in the Pine Ridge Hills he announced camp would head there after some more hunting along the Elk River bottom lands.

Two days later we left and at dusk arrived at a camping place. We hunted again for several days and then one morning left for Elk River, spending the first night at the Mountain Lion's Lodge. That night I had a dream. My medicine bird flew to earth with a man in its claws, dropping the body near the Musselshell River on a ridge in the Bull Mountains. Then four enemies heading toward this same ridge fell dead, and a beautiful buckskin horse came to me.

When I woke up I lay still, wondering what it meant. I remembered my dream during my escape from the Cheyennes and the Wise Ones' advice not to go out. But they could not know how clear and strong my dreams had been. I would go out this coming snow season for the things my medicine fathers had promised.

That day I built a sweat lodge for the Great Above Person and said prayers for success, gave thanks for my dream, and offered red feathers instead of the usual red blanket. People heard that I was preparing for a raid. Young Mountain rode over from the Many Lodges and several other warriors asked to join.

Two Belly and Crooked Arm invited Young Mountain and me to Crooked Arm's tipi. After our smoke Two Belly said that if I took those other men with me camp would be unprotected. He said Crooked Arm had dreamt that if I left now someone would be killed. Two Belly wanted to move camp to the mouth of Arrow Creek and from there through Hits With The Arrows to the Buffalo Heart Mountain. Enemy signs had been found and he thought we would be safe there. He said we had killed enough buffalo and now the women needed new tipi poles which we could cut in the mountains. Two Belly asked why I wanted to bring sorrow to the people.

I promised to tell him the next day whether I was going. But I described the four bodies and the beautiful horse which had come to me. A successful raid, I said, would give our people more reason to be happy and to dance.

I lied when I said I might give up my trip. I could not forget what my medicine bird had given me. When we were outside I told Young Mountain that we would remain with the camp through the next day but would leave early the following morning.

On one of his last hunts north of the Elk River and close to the Bull Mountains Young Mountain had seen enemies, but being alone he had turned back. That was my dream's direction, and I told him of the bodies and the beautiful buckskin.

Early the next morning the tipis were taken down, the pack horses and travois loaded, and our camp leader led us to the mouth of the Arrow Creek. From the Mountain Lion's Lodge to here was not far and our tipis were up long before sunset. The chief wanted to stay for a few days while our people traded at the new white man's store built by Long Beard [Thomas McGirl].[1]

Telling Young Mountain and the others to keep their horses in camp that night, I also warned them not to mention our plans. But someone must have talked because late in the evening I was called to Two Belly's tipi. On the way I met Young Mountain and said that whatever happened we would leave as soon as I left the tipi.

After we smoked I was given a good meal and then Two Belly said that he had heard I was taking away many of his best warriors. He told me it was not safe to leave camp without protection and to re-member Crooked Arm's advice.

As I was promising not to go a horse galloped up to the tipi and One Blue Bead ran in, covered with sweat. We had been raided dur-ing the night and all of his and Shot In The Arm's horses were gone along with many more. He had found one of the thieves' ropes and they were Sioux.

Outside I joined Young Mountain and we ran for the horses. Camp was wide awake with most men jumping on the first horse they found. The women and children were crying over their stolen horses; the men were singing war songs.

Riding up to my tipi I dashed inside for my gun and medicine and ran out. When I jumped on my horse to catch up with the others, Young Mountain was close behind. Everyone seemed to be spreading out. I noticed someone near the river bank calling to us. It was Black Head, who had discovered where the Sioux had crossed.

He told me to lead since I had been planning a raid and had said my dream was good. But he said that the earth does not move and by travel-ing steadily we could overtake them. He wanted to be sure our horses would not lose their strength.

After fording the river and picking up their tracks on the other side I made them stop so I could make medicine. Kneeling on the Sioux tracks which headed north over a group of ridges toward the Bull Mountains, I drew a straight line across their trail with my finger. Then I formed a dirt bank along the line's far side and made a smudge of white pine needles. Sitting on the trail I faced where the Sioux had gone and smoked my pipe. I pointed the stem and told the Sioux to smoke this and wait until I caught up with them. Now their trail would be rough and they would grow sleepy.

After I stood up I unwrapped my medicine and prayed to the Great Above Person through whom I had received it, saying that I had acted as he had said and asking him to have pity on the women and children crying over their horses.

As I finished a stolen horse walked out of the brush toward us. Here I said was the sign of my medicine's power. We were eight but Black Head asked me to wait for others. Whenever we were about to leave, men would call to us from the opposite bank.

About the middle of the day we finally left. It grew very hot and I prayed this would make the Sioux sleepy. Their trail led east and north, directly toward the spot where I had seen the four bodies. Now I knew that everything would come true.

Late that afternoon we came to where they had killed a buffalo and made a fire. I would never have stopped for a meal the first day out; already they were growing careless.

Young Mountain, Hawk High Up, and I rode ahead to a nearby hill. If we saw anything we were to ride our horses back and forth. But when we searched through my telescope there was no sign of Sioux, and we signaled for the others to join us. After doing the same thing on the next ridge my men killed a deer and cooked some meat. We rode to a third hill, picketed our horses near the top, and crawled to the cover of some tall bushes. A big basin lay before us and at the far end I could see the Bull Mountains covered with pine trees. By the time the rest had caught up the shadows were long. But we had ridden slowly during the day and our horses were still fresh. I told my friends we would travel the shortest route to the pine-covered ridge in my dream, close to the Musselshell River.

The moon shone brightly enough for us to ride apart from the Sioux tracks. I did not want to come upon them in the night. Soon after the first streaks of dawn showed in the east we reached the ridge. Black Head had noticed a big buffalo herd to the east. The Sioux had not yet passed.

After picketing our horses we took off our saddles and rested.

Young Mountain, One Blue Bead, Paints His Body Red, and I kept a careful lookout from behind the trees on top.

Noticing movement on the hills several rifle-shot distances to the south, I picked up my telescope. Horses broke out of some timber with men riding behind, all heading for us. I counted five Sioux and recognized our horses.

I left One Blue Bead and ran down to the others. We painted our faces and unwrapped our medicines, tying them where we had been told in our dreams. Bobtail Wolf painted seven red spots on his face running from one side of his jawbone over his forehead to the other and representing the dipper. He tied his foretop with a piece of otter skin, fastened some feathers to the back of his head, and sang a medicine song: "My son is coming."

Boils His Leggings sang a medicine song for Young Mountain, painted a red bar over his mouth, and fastened a red-painted eagle feather in his hair. Making him face the Sioux, he pointed to the sun and said that he wanted Young Mountain to do some brave thing so the people would know him. He called him his son and told him to look into the sky.

Bobtail Wolf sang a medicine song for his brother Goes First. Then he fastened an otter-skin strip to his brother's forehead and gave him a shield painted with the thunderbird. He sang another medicine song, repeating it until Black Head and Few warned him to stop.

Black Head asked me to sing a medicine song for the whole party. Seeing that the Sioux were still far away, I sang one. Bobtail Wolf was singing another medicine song for his brother: "My child, I am coming toward you."

He told his brother that it was strong medicine and would protect him. He sang again: "I am coming toward you today."

Telling my men to stand close together, I rode around them four times, praying for the Great Above Person to help us recover our horses and kill some Sioux. Then I sang my medicine song: "Anywhere I go I will always thank you. Thank long ago. I will be a chief."

Bobtail Wolf was still singing for his brother. When we tried to stop him he said we meant nothing to him. We felt sorry for his brother.

Taking my eagle-tail medicine out of its wrappings, I whistled seven times and looked under the hoop. Four enemies lay on the ground and a number of horses ran toward me. Black Head had watched and asked what would happen. I told him not to be afraid, that I had seen my true dream again.

124

One Blue Bead ran down to say they were getting close. When he had first looked through my telescope he had recognized a pinto, a roan, a baldface, and a black horse. These were among our fastest horses; it would have been difficult to catch them. A Sioux was leading the pinto as if he meant to ride it and another man was on the black. But just before One Blue Bead had left, this man on the black had changed mounts to chase a small buffalo herd to the north.

I sent Young Mountain up the ridge, telling him to signal when they were within rifle shot. I told my men to shoot straight because One Blue Bead had reported that they all carried good guns and one also had a bow. The younger men were very excited and I had trouble holding them back.

Then Young Mountain made signs and jumped on his horse. Yelling our war cries, we whipped our horses over the ridge. When the Sioux heard us they dropped the stolen horses and raced to a nearby hill, dismounting and shooting from behind rocks.

Some of us rounded up our horses while the rest surrounded the Sioux. When we had driven them a safe distance I left some younger men as guards and rode back. Our men were riding in fast circles around the Sioux, hanging over their horses' sides and shooting from under their necks.

One of their horses broke loose and galloped in front of me. When I caught its reins I saw the beautiful buckskin of my dream. Now I was sure we would kill the four men. We had seen the fifth Sioux return from his hunting and run off when he saw his friends surrounded.

We were not hitting anyone so I told my men to dismount and crawl up. A Sioux called to us, waving his knife over his head. Loud Hawk said that he was calling us women and asking us to come near so he could stab us. I told my men to close in and not let the yelling make them nervous.

Big Lake was lying in front behind a boulder. As he lifted his rifle he fell back. We thought he was dead but his forehead had only been grazed. We dragged him out of the shooting. After a quick council we decided to charge. The first time we were thrown back but then we drove them out of the rocks and into a coulee. The one who had called us women had run first. Big Lake recovered and now crawled to the coulee's edge and shot into it. A Sioux stumbled out with blood pouring from his forehead, threw out his arms, and fell on his back.

As Goes First ran to join Big Lake, singing his medicine song, he was shot through the heart. This was because his brother had sung too many songs over him.

125

We were all angry and charged the three remaining men. One was killed immediately but we did not know who did it, he was hit so many times. Young Mountain was in front of me running down the coulee with his head bent forward. A bullet struck him in the neck, coming out his spine. Another bullet cut a hole in my shirt but I kept running and shot into the head of the man who had killed Young Mountain. Pulling out my knife, I slashed at his scalp. Then I began crying and shot him again and again. I forgot everything until I heard sounds like animals growling and turned to see Old Tobacco holding the last Sioux's rifle barrel. We could not aim because they were jumping around so much. Old Tobacco gave a wrench and the Sioux slipped on a stone. As he fell he pulled the trigger and the bullet hit Old Tobacco in the forearm, coming out the middle of his upper arm. Before the Sioux could get to his feet two bullets knocked him on his back. He was still trying to stand when Bobtail Wolf ran up and stabbed him twice in the neck. Blood poured out and he fell dead.

We scalped only three because the last man's hair was short and dirty. We let that fifth man get away. After carrying my partner and Goes First to the top of a high bluff we covered their bodies with rocks.

My dream had come true, but our homecoming was sad. Crooked Arm's dream had also come true. Young Mountain's death was a great sorrow for me. I could not be content with our success and made up my mind to take revenge.

When we returned Two Belly called me to his tipi and reminded me that he had wanted to go to the Arrowhead Mountains. Now I had lost my best friend and another man also. He said that my dream might have been true but that if I had listened to the older men's advice I could have found another opportunity. Their dreams, he said, had more truth than those of young men.

He was right and I kept silent. Immediately we broke camp and moved to Arrow Creek, traveling through Hits With The Arrows towards the Buffalo Heart Mountain. As our camp moved from place to place, following the buffalo, I would often walk into the hills to weep over Young Mountain.

Chapter Twenty-Two

*Two Leggings hoped he would regain the
goodwill of Sees The Living Bull through a ceremony of the
Tobacco society. This group's activities revolved
around the cultivation of a holy plant—never smoked
—and the adoption rites for new members.*

*Two Leggings ascribed the plant's origin to the
time of creation. Another story calls it the personal medicine
of No Vitals, the chief who led the Crows away from
the Hidatsa. In turn new chapters were formed by men
receiving visions with variations on the Tobacco
theme: Breath dreamt of a blackbird; when his newly organized
Blackbirds danced they wore blankets to imitate wings and
attached blackbird skins to their backs.*

*The annual planting ceremony occurred when the
chokecherries ripen—around May. The Crow word for the
society, "soaking," referred to the preparation
given the seeds prior to planting. A procession, led by "He That
Mixes," the rite's official, walked to that season's plot,
which was fenced in with a brush barricade. There
the seeds were planted, with each couple allowed two rows.
Another ritual occurred during the harvest when the
chokecherries are ripe, sometime in late summer.*

YOUNG MOUNTAIN HAD DIED because I had not followed the medicine
men's advice. It was hard to have to learn this way. In the past I had
met with some good luck and had also experienced many close escapes,
but now I had lost my best friend. I began to see how reckless and
foolish I had been.

One day when we were camped near the Buffalo Heart Mountain I noticed some well-known men talking together on a hillside, Two Belly, Sees Under, Crooked Arm, Old Dog, and No Fears. After Crooked Arm had called me over he told me to wait before going on another raid because he had had another bad dream. He said that he had given the same advice to Man Who Can Talk English, but he would not listen. Man Who Can Talk English's medicine was made by some other tribe [1] and if he kept on he would be killed. He said that Man Who Can Talk English would kill any Indian or white man he met. Crooked Arm wanted me to buy a medicine from Sees The Living Bull so that my luck would change and I could become an accepted pipeholder. He did not make me concerned for my own safety, but I grew afraid I might have more bad luck and lose more men. Then all my hopes would be ruined.

I watched Man Who Can Talk English lead his men out of our village and waited for his return. But they never came back and we learned later they had all been killed. Our camp moved to the present site of the Mission of St. Xavier but so many bad things happened there our chiefs moved us back to the Buffalo Heart Mountain.

I could also have asked Red Bear to make me a medicine. He was one of our greatest medicine men and could stop the sun, darkening the earth for several days.[2] But Sees The Living Bull was my friend Medicine Crow's father, and perhaps he was a greater medicine man since he had made a medicine for Red Bear. Before I could ask for his help, however, he would have to adopt me as his son during the Tobacco Dance.

Some days later I rode to the Mountain Crow camp and found his tipi. He was at the back and invited me to sit down. When he asked why I had come I said that I wanted him to adopt me and to make my medicine. His medicine was stronger than mine, I said, and I needed better luck on my raids.

He said I was wrong, that it was the Great Above Person who gives us what we need. I begged him to adopt me, promising a good roan, a buckskin, and one other horse, all three well-known racers. I also offered other things, but he refused. He was angry with me for going against their advice so often. I cried all the way back to the River Crow camp.

Three moons later I heard that a Tobacco Dance was to be held in the Mountain Crow camp. Immediately I rode over. On the dance day I wore my best war shirt and a pair of newly tanned buckskin leggings. To my hair I attached my long false-hair attachment and around my neck I hung a silver wampum necklace.

I thought that now Sees The Living Bull would adopt me and waited for his invitation. The ceremony began and I saw people gathering but no one came. I waited until the sun had traveled half through the day and finally I walked into the ceremonial lodge and joined the dancing. I do not know whether this had ever been done, but I was trying to follow Crooked Arm's advice. Sees The Living Bull sat in the dance lodge and talked with Iron Bull,[3] who was asking for my adoption. But he shook his head and would not look at me. When I walked up and asked myself he said he had heard a great deal about me and thought I was a medicine man already. I realized how foolish I had been not to listen to these men before. Now they distrusted me. I would never become a leader and a chief as I had longed since childhood.

When the next Tobacco Dance was held I was not invited but joined in anyway and again asked Sees The Living Bull to adopt me. Finally he forbade me to enter the dance lodge. Before I could be adopted I had to be invited four times. Now he would not even allow me to dance.

One day in his tipi I pleaded that he was our father and we his children and that if he made me a medicine I would avenge the five River Crows who had been killed since the last snow. When I returned, I said, the women would dance and the warriors would have their faces painted black. When I said that if he loved his children he would help me it was the strongest thing I could say, but he sat like a stone.

Camp was broken and Sees The Living Bull and some of his people moved north where they spent some time before returning to the Arrowhead Mountains. I joined the Mountain Crows there, and although Sees The Living Bull was no relative I followed him everywhere. I had my wife pitch my tipi close to his and did everything to make him feel kindly towards me, inviting him often to eat with us and saving the choicest pieces of meat to leave at his tipi. When I killed a deer I would have my wife tan the hide very softly for his wife. I also carried firewood and water for her. When the cold winds blew from the east I hunted for the buffalo with the heaviest fur and had my wife make robes for his wife. Many moons passed and nothing happened, but I never left camp except to hunt for him.

Then one morning his wife came to invite me to a meal. I was very excited when I entered their tipi. Sees The Living Bull did not speak while we were eating. But that did not bother me; older people often behave that way. After the meal his wife told him that I had been following them for a long time, selecting choice meats, making robes, and doing little tasks. She told him that he should give me what I desired so much.

I thought my time had come. I can still see him sitting across from me, his hair parted in the middle like a woman's and cut short at the shoulders. But his lips did not move and his expression did not change.

I returned to my tipi and lay on my robes, crying and praying for the Great Above Person and my sacred helper to soften his heart.

The next morning I was woken by Sees The Living Bull calling me outside. When I met him he asked me to have a meal with him. Once again I was hopeful and walked behind him to his tipi. We did not talk while eating. After we had smoked a pipe he said he had been testing me for a long time because of the way I had acted before. I was poor, he said, and he would pity me now because he admired the way I had been following him; it proved I had learned. He told me to come to his tipi the following morning with seven straight willows and one forked one.

The next morning I sat beside him and watched him make a miniature sweat lodge inside his tipi. When he asked how many willows he had used I said eight. He told me to remember that and also to remember that there is a Great Above Person who gives certain things to us people of the earth. I had gone to war on my own and Sees The Living Bull had refused to help me, but now he had decided to pity me. He said we are not great but that the Great Above Person can make us great. From now on, he said, the Great Above Person would know what I was doing.

Then Sees The Living Bull placed buffalo grease and charcoal in front of him. While rubbing the grease over the branches he explained this meant plenty of food would be given to whoever received his medicine and that this could happen in camp or on a raid. He prayed to the Great Above Person to grant me this power, saying that he was giving me the lodge to build whenever I needed help.

After I powdered the charcoal he rubbed it over the branches and sharpened their ends. Clearing a space and smoothening it over with more powered charcoal, he dug a little pit in the middle and dropped in small live coals. Then he drew a number of bottle-shaped tracks around the hole with his finger. Each track's opening pointed to where

130

the little lodge's entrance would be. Bending the first willow, he pushed the sharpened ends into the ground a foot apart, running east and west. The second willow he placed a little apart but parallel to the first. Then he bent the five remaining willows across these so that the lodge frame faced east. Holding some bear root he moved his hand around the frame from right to left, stopping at the entrance. He did this three more times before finally laying the root on the coals.

He explained that these were the lodges that softened the heart of the sun. We sacrificed to the sun, he said, and I should make this ceremony whenever necessary. When Sees The Living Bull asked if I knew how to make the lodges I thought he meant their construction and how to perform the ceremony. But he also meant the little patterns he had traced on the charcoal floor. I did not ask about them and never learned their meaning.

For some time I stayed in his tipi, listening to stories of our people. Before I left he told me to bring twenty-four willow branches the next morning. I had been hoping he would make my medicine that day, but was not discouraged by the delay. That evening, as Sees The Living Bull had suggested, I invited several older men to a sweat bath for the following day.

I had the twenty-four willows cut early the next morning and helped Sees The Living Bull build a regular-sized sweat lodge. I was to be the door raiser and Sees The Living Bull told me I would probably be given certain dreams.

After the lodge was made we sat and waited for our guests. Sees The Living Bull's dream forbade him to enter a sweat lodge. Soon our guests arrived and prepared themselves.

When Neck Bone walked up I pretended three times to raise the door flap. The fourth time I really held it aside. As he stooped to enter he told me he had seen a vision of horses. He called me his child and gave me those horses.

Then Small Face went in and said he had dreamt of the new grass coming up. Calling me his child, he wished I would live until then.

When I raised the flap for Burns Himself he also called me his child and said that his vision of a successful war party was now mine.

The fourth man called me his child and said his vision had shown him several scalps and that in the coming seasons he hoped I would take them.

Other guests came after these men had entered, but a person can only receive four visions at a time so they sat down without speaking.

After the sweat bath I gave everyone a meal. When they were gone Sees The Living Bull said that these fathers of mine had made wishes for me as they had entered and had offered prayers for my success inside. He wanted me to go home and return early in the grass-growing season. Then he would do something for me. Although I was disappointed not to have received a medicine I knew he would stop everything if I tried to interfere.

On my way back to the River Crows I remembered Neck Bone's vision. Before I went back the next grass-growing season I decided to go on one more raid. A little later I joined some men to Dirt Creek, returning with a few enemy horses. But they were strays and I did not think much of our trip. When I got back I received word from Sees The Living Bull that he did not want me to leave anymore without his consent.

Piegan had joined me on this trip. When I told him that although I had been shown many things I had not yet received a medicine he said that Sees The Living Bull owned a very powerful rock medicine. Its large rock had a smaller rock child in the same bundle. He suggested I ask for that because it would give me much good luck.

Chapter Twenty-Three

Two Leggings had good reason for wanting to accompany well-known pipeholders like Hunts The Enemy. The chances for success and survival were greater when one was protected by proven dreams.

Like Two Leggings, Hunts The Enemy was born a River Crow and a member of the Not Mixed clan. However, he had been able to secure his own medicine without outside assistance. This, and his membership in the rival warrior society, may account for part of their mutual antipathy. During his lifetime Hunts The Enemy led thirty successful raids in which he cut a tethered horse, took three guns—one from a Pend d'Orielle chief when the latter's firearm was pressed against his mouth—and cut eight Piegan scalps. He died in 1907.

Twice, Two Leggings joined war parties led by Half Yellow Face, another famous pipeholder who gained renown as one of six who scouted for Son Of The Morning Star—Custer's Crow name—just before the massacre. Along with all the Arikara scouts, he and White Swan were assigned by mistake to the Little Soldier Chief —Reno's Crow name. At first it was thought they had also been killed, but during the butchering of Reno's forces they hid in a cave for two days and nights.

TIME PASSED SLOWLY while I waited for grass-growing season and my visit to Sees The Living Bull. During the days I hunted and in the evenings I listened to the old men's stories.

But when I heard that Hunts The Enemy was leading a raid to the

Piegans I could remain in camp no longer. In his two years as a pipe-holder he had always been successful. Although younger warriors were always anxious to join him he never took more than ten men. Sees The Living Bull had told me to stay home but I wanted to ask him to let me go just this once. Riding over to his camp I noticed snow clouds moving fast across the sky.

Sees The Living Bull listened and when I finished he looked straight ahead for a long time. Then he put his pipe down and said he still thought it would be better if I stayed at home. But he knew how I felt and if I really wanted to go he said I must leave my pipe and medicine and join as a helper. I was very happy.

Snow was falling as I rode back. In camp a friend told me that Piegans had raided our horses and that Hunts The Enemy was going to recover those and steal some more.

Hunts The Enemy always hid somewhere so the younger warriors would not bother him, but I asked Bull Eye, his brother, to speak for me, telling him that my medicine father had allowed me to go as a helper. Bull Eye promised to try and I waited in my tipi for the answer. After dark, as my wife and I were finishing our meal, Bull Eye came in and I offered him the pipe. He sat down and we smoked in silence. Then he emptied the ashes and said that Hunts The Enemy had remembered my bravery on other raids and wanted me to prepare myself and come to his tipi. There he would open the powerful medicine of Braided Tail and wanted all his men present. After that we were to meet on Porcupine Hill before sunrise.

I was glad and thanked Bull Eye. When he was gone my wife put her arms around my neck and cried for me not to go. I asked if she wanted a coward for a husband. She said I had shown my courage many times and that if camp were attacked I could prove myself. I told her that if I stayed I would get fat and lazy like Wolf Tail and Bear Grease. Once they had been warriors but now they were women. Their wives had wanted them at home and now they did not have enough winter clothes and would not even hunt. But she put her arms around me again and spoke about a bad dream. I told her to stop talking since her dreams were only women's dreams. I asked what would Hunts The Enemy think if I sent word I could not go because my wife wanted me home. I told her to hurry and gather my moccasins because we were leaving soon after the ceremony.

She was unhappy but quiet. While I prepared my weapons she collected several pairs of moccasins, strips of sinew, and awl, and some pemmican. After wrapping everything in a bundle to pick up later I

134

picketed a horse for the trip—one of the best runners I ever owned. Then I joined Hunts The Enemy who had returned to his brother's tipi.

When I walked in I saw Hunts The Enemy, Bull Eye, Ten Bear, Head, Plenty Bear, Willow Top, Little Heart, Never Dies, and a boy whose name I have forgotten. Never Dies was the bundle's owner and sat at the back with two unopened medicine bundles before him.

They passed the pipe and we smoked in silence. When it came to Never Dies again he emptied the ashes and laid it beside the bundle. Calling Hunts The Enemy his brother, he said that he had been invited to bring this powerful medicine to aid Hunts The Enemy on his coming raid. He said it was good that Hunts The Enemy had done this and that he had brought two medicine bundles so Hunts The Enemy could have his choice. One was the powerful arrow medicine which he had received from his father, the other the powerful skull medicine of his father's father's father who was Braided Tail.[1]

Hunts The Enemy chose the skull medicine and Never Dies wrapped the arrow medicine in a blanket and laid it aside. Then he smoothed the earth floor, and asked for coals, which were quickly brought by Hunts The Enemy's wife. As he scattered a small handful of bear root on them, sweet smoke filled the tipi.

He purified his hands and face in the smoke, held the skull bundle in it, and began unwrapping the deerskin coverings. As we watched he prayed and sang four medicine songs belonging to the bundle.

Finally the skull was uncovered on a wrapping of soft buffalo calf-skin. Hundreds of presents, given to the bundle by the many people who had consulted it, were tied to this inner wrapping. The skull and wrappings were smeared with red paint. Red feathers and eagle plumes were also inside.

Never Dies laid seven red feathers in front of the skull and asked someone to fill and light his pipe. After smoking in silence he pointed the stem at the skull and asked the Great Above Person to guide us and warn us in case of danger.

He told Hunts The Enemy that this bundle was too heavy so he would give him the seven feathers which carried the same powers. The day before, he said, he had made a smudge and sung a song. Under the skull he had seen that Hunts The Enemy would return with many horses and that two enemies would be killed. He told Hunts The Enemy that when he saw the enemy he must fasten these seven feathers to his hair and pray to them.

Then Never Dies sang a medicine song and we all joined in until we knew it. Another pipe was passed around and when its ashes were emptied Never Dies wrapped up his bundle. Before we left everyone gave Never Dies a gift and Hunts The Enemy presented him with one of his best horses.

I did not want to be late and told my wife good-bye long before dawn. She did not speak but there were tears in her eyes. After everyone had gathered at Porcupine Hill we headed north toward the Musselshell River.

That first night we camped at the head of Yellow Willow Creek. Then we rode to Trout Creek where we found another Crow camp. Crooked Arm was its chief and he asked if I was carrying Sees The Living Bull's pipe. When I explained that I was going as a helper he said I should have stayed home but to do my best.

We left the boy behind because his horse went lame, and we began to ride toward the northwest. For the next two days we all rode together, but as we neared Piegan country Plenty Bear and I were sent to scout. Early each morning we had to gallop long distances ahead of the others. The country was rugged and our work very tiring. When we approached a high hill Plenty Bear would gallop around to scout the southern side while I covered the northern side. We were approaching the Great Falls of Big River and expected Piegans at any time.

I felt like a coward. I was acting as a helper only because I had left my medicine at home, but the men treated me like a child, ordering me to carry their wood and build their fires. When Hunts The Enemy told me I had been wrong to leave my medicine I said I was following an important medicine man's advice. But I lacked protection and worried all the time that I might do something wrong and get killed. Then I would think how fast the days went by, while in camp time would have passed so slowly, and I would forget my fears.

For the last two days snow had fallen hard and riding was difficult. Plenty Bear and I were waiting for the men to meet us at a site we had chosen for the night. When they arrived we began building shelters against the wind and snow. While we were collecting brush, Hunts The Enemy asked me to kill a buffalo from a small herd we had spotted in a nearby valley.

This made me angry. First he had appointed me his scout and now he wanted me as his hunter. I had brought my horse to chase enemies, I said. If he wanted me to kill buffalo he should give me another horse. I told him that he had plenty of men who had not had to ride as hard as I. One of them could do his hunting.

136

Without answering me he sent someone else. But about the middle of the next day, when they had joined us again, he asked me to kill a buffalo. When I refused once more he said they could not fight if they were starving. He pointed out a hilltop and told me to scout the country from there until they brought me something to eat. Before I rode out I asked Little Heart to cut some meat with plenty of fat to bring to me later.

The sun had fallen halfway toward the west when I reached the hill. Nothing was in sight so I sat down to wait. When they arrived it was still a while before sunset but I was very hungry.

Once again Hunts The Enemy asked me to kill one of the many buffalo in the lower valleys. After I refused he told me to stay at another hill all night so I could scout at sunrise.

While we were sitting and talking Little Heart had walked my horse around. When I mounted up I noticed meat tied to the saddle. On my ride I ate buffalo roast and was glad Hunts The Enemy could not enjoy his little revenge.

The sun was almost down when I reached the hill. Nothing was in sight to the west. Looking back I saw that our men had killed another buffalo and were making camp along a little stream hidden by cottonwood trees. When it was dark I rode into the valley, picketed my horse, and slowly walked to camp until I saw my friends sitting around their fire. Someone stood up and I recognized Little Heart by his walk. After I whispered for more meat he waited until the others were asleep and brought me a large loin piece. I returned to my hilltop and slept until daylight. Then I signalled to Hunts The Enemy with my blanket that I would scout the country ahead and he signalled back to go on. I rode until I was far enough away to make a cooking fire.

After tying the leftover cooked meat to my saddle I rode slowly until I located a well-hidden place. It was still early in the day when they arrived. Hunts The Enemy approved of the site and we built shelters. Again he wanted me to hunt and again I refused, saying I had not eaten for two days. Although I offered to go if he gave me food, he sent Little Heart who quickly returned with a two-year-old cow. Hunts The Enemy was in the trees when Little Heart rode in and I tied some choice parts to my saddle. Then I led my horse a little distance from camp. As soon as Hunts The Enemy came back he pointed out another hill where I was to stand guard until nightfall.

When I was out of sight I gathered dry snake brush and roasted my meat, leaving what was left in the hot coals to pick up on my return. For the remainder of the day I watched from that hilltop but saw

137

nothing. It had snowed about two days, then it had cleared and grown warm, but now I saw clouds gathering in the west and moving eastward. By the time I rode back it was raining. On my way I stopped to take my meat out of the coals. When I reached camp it was pouring down. The other men had hobbled their horses but I tied mine to a tree and joined them in a brush shelter.

The next morning I was awakened by shouting. I thought the Piegans were upon us and grabbed my gun. Dawn was just breaking and it was still raining. As I ran into the fog I saw Ten Bear untying my horse, Hunts The Enemy and the others around him. Their hobbled horses had run off during the storm. I told them that they had known about the storm. If the Piegans attacked I wanted my horse fresh. I told him to send men on foot to find their horses.

While two men left we waited in our shelter. From the way they ran back into camp we could tell something was wrong. Ten Bear said they had followed the horse tracks along the river but when the fog had lifted a large Piegan camp appeared around a bend. Our horses had joined their herd. When the Piegans noticed those hobbled horses they would start a search. He said we would have to kill as many as possible before we died.

I told Hunts The Enemy that I had not lent him my horse because he had not treated me right. But I said now I could save him. When the Piegans came I would pretend to escape in one direction while they got away in another.

He thanked me and after we arranged a meeting place they left immediately. Then I rode to see if the Piegans had discovered our horses.

About the middle of the day I noticed excitement around their camp, men saddling horses and people running everywhere. About twenty Piegan warriors began riding along the river and more were trying to catch up with them.

Hunts The Enemy had a good start and he was good at covering trails. I also knew my own horse. Riding as if I were trying to keep out of their sight, I soon heard a cry. The Piegans left the trees along the river and raced for me.

I pretended to signal to men ahead and occasionally turned to shoot, but my arrows always fell short. They were singing war songs. As they came almost within bowshot I would top a ridge and whip my horse. When they appeared I was out of range again. Then I would ride slowly up the next ridge to rest my horse. But they were so eager they raced up and down and wore theirs out.

138

One Piegan, riding a good horse, was far ahead of his friends. I could outrun him but decided to trick him. We were galloping through coulees and over hills, keeping an even distance between us. But he kept pulling away from his men. Then I entered the course of a dry creek. After passing many half bends I noticed a rocky point that made the bed turn sharply. Reining in on the other side, I tied my horse to a tree and crouched behind some bushes. As I strung my bow and pulled an arrow back I could hear his horse running on the dry stones.

His eyes were searching for me as he came around. I hit him lower than I intended, my arrow going through his groin and pinning him to his horse, which screamed and fell. I ran down with my knife and he shouted something I did not understand. He tried to grab my arm as I stuck my knife into his stomach. While I was cutting his scalp I heard the other Piegans and had no time to pick up his weapons. Running to my horse I sang a victory song and waved the scalp so they could see. The rest had done my horse good and it jumped up the coulee rim. By the time they discovered the body I was safely away, but still in sight. As I waved the scalp and sang, they shook their weapons and a few started after me.

Then I decided to take no more chances. About sunset I lost sight of them in the distance. Long after dark I allowed my horse a little grass and water. After riding another day and another night I finally made a large half circle to our meeting place. Three days later, when I arrived, no one was there. I built a shelter, killed a fat buffalo, and waited. When they showed up two days later Hunts The Enemy treated me differently and gave me credit for the escape. I had to tell many times how I had killed the Piegan. They cut up the scalp, each man tied his piece to a long willow pole, and we danced the scalp dance around the fire.

Then we talked over what to do. Some wanted to go home but Hunts The Enemy knew that I, his helper, would get the honors while he would be laughed at. He decided to return for our horses and to kill some Piegans.

Mine was the only horse so I scouted again. We traveled carefully because the Piegans might still be out. During the night we walked along the river bottoms, sheltered by the big cottonwoods along the banks. In the daytime we hid. Finally, at dawn many days later, we arrived at the big bend in the river and hid in some willows in a coulee. Their tipis seemed to have moved across the river. Then we noticed we were between two camps, one on either side of the big bend. All day long people walked between them, using the path on their side of the river.

Night came and no one had seen us. Walking from my hiding place I thought of the older men's advice not to go out before the right time. I made a vow that if I was not killed tonight I would do as they said.

While we were eating dried pemmican Hunts The Enemy told us that since we were so few we would all enter the camp. Just as we were about to swim across he said my horse would make too much noise; he wanted me to cross above the camp and wait. Although I also wanted to capture horses he would not listen. They crossed with poles under their arms to avoid making noise. When I was far enough away I crossed on my horse and sat down to wait.

Soon I saw many horses coming toward me. But when Hunts The Enemy divided them up he did not give me one. They had passed another herd which they were returning for. When I asked Hunts The Enemy to let me come he answered that I had no medicine and was only a helper.

I said my medicine must have been with me when I drew the Piegans away and killed that man, but he ignored me. He took three men and they returned with more horses. When I asked for some he promised me two the next day. We quietly walked them away, but once out of hearing galloped them hard. As we were driving them home I grew angry and could not stop thinking that I was bringing no horses for my relatives. Finally I turned out of the group and rode back to the Piegan camp.

I would pull up to listen whether they had discovered our raid, but heard nothing until I approached their camp. Then dogs began barking and I grew afraid. Dismounting, I prayed to the Great Above Person that I was poor and wanted horses. I said that I hoped to be a leader again and asked him to prevent the Piegans from hearing or seeing me. Even though I was not carrying my medicine, I sang my medicine song: "I want something good."

The barking dogs did not seem to bother the Piegans. The night was clear and the stars very bright. After telling myself that my songs and prayers would help to bring me safely home I felt better. As I moved forward I saw dark shapes ahead. Horses were staring at me. Making sure they were unguarded, I rode slowly up, tied my belt to my horse, and led it into the Piegan herd. I noticed a big sorrel pinto mare and tied my rope around its mouth. Then I mounted it and turned

140

my own horse into the herd. First I quietly walked them out and soon was far enough away to trot them. A little later I drove them into a hard gallop. Clouds began to cover the stars and I felt snow flurries in my face. Now I was not ashamed to be heading home.

All through the night I kept them going fast and by morning I was far away, our tracks covered with snow. But I still did not head straight back; the Piegans would probably send men that way. Then the snow stopped, the sky cleared, and the sun was shining. I rode one horse until it played out, then turned it in with the rest and chose another. For the rest of that day and through that night I rode like that. Two horses were unable to keep up and I left them. I rode through the following day and at sunset, when I dismounted to look through my telescope, Hunts The Enemy and his men were ahead of me, driving their herd before them. But when I caught up I passed apart.

Little Heart rode over and said a roan in my bunch belonged to his grandfather and if I returned it he would give me ten good things. I told him that two days before they had treated me like a stranger. I had gone back alone and now they were strangers to me.

Little Heart called out my name and asked if I loved my children. He promised to give me ten tanned buffalo robes with the heads left on for the horses. Then I had to give in because when someone asks if you love your children or your brother's children it is a sacred expression.

The others had joined us and I told Hunts The Enemy to take the gray mare. Then everyone wanted a horse but I gave away no more.

Little Heart thought it would not look right if we returned separately. After some talking I put my horses with their bunch and joined them. If I had reached camp first I would have been considered the pipeholder.

We did not stop that night nor the next night. For three days we had not eaten and were very hungry. When we finally discovered buffalo I told Hunts The Enemy that before I was going to be a pipeholder and they had talked me out of it. Now, I said, I would be their helper and kill their meat.

Running close to one small herd, I picked out a fat cow and shot it. I cut out both rib pieces and started a fire. The men ate and I roasted some extra meat to pack with us. When we mounted the sun was down. After riding all night we ate again at dawn, rested a little, and reached the prairie country about the middle of the day. Then we traveled a little easier and at dusk stopped to sleep above Crooked Arm's camp on Yellow Willow Creek.

As the sun was rising we drove our stolen horses into the camp, shooting our rifles into the air and singing: "We are here. We went by there. The last one was better than the first."

Everyone greeted us with singing. That night a great victory celebration was held and we all dressed in our finest clothes. Then we had a scalp dance for the man I had killed. My name was mentioned in the songs, but Hunts The Enemy received most of the praise.

My brother was staying there and I gave him ten horses. He kept some and gave the rest to his friends. My own tipi was in Two Belly's camp on the Bighorn River, and after a few days' rest I returned there and gave a good black horse to Sees The Living Bull, leaving about ten for my own herd.

After I had told my medicine father everything he called me his son and told me not to pretend to be a helper or a boy if I wanted to become a chief. He said that everyone would hear Hunts The Enemy's name even though I had done braver things.

This was true, and I had already made that vow. Besides, green-grass season was not far off. I waited in camp for the time when I hoped Sees The Living Bull would give me his most powerful medicine.

Chapter Twenty-Four

*During the winter Sees The Living Bull had devoted four
consecutive nights to introducing Two Leggings and his wife
to the members of his Tobacco society chapter.*

*Months later, on the morning after the tobacco planting, an
adoption lodge was erected of ten large pine trunks in tipi shape.
Within a preparatory lodge Sees The Living Bull painted
and dressed Two Leggings; his wife did the same for Two
Leggings' wife. Separated from them by a line of sacred tobacco
seed bags, a dozen drummers were beating to imitate the
thunder. Other society members jammed into the remaining area.*

*The painting completed, the women began to shuffle out
in single file. Sees The Living Bull and his wife brought up
the rear, escorting Two Leggings and his wife. The procession
moved slowly, stopping four times while the participants danced
in place. After all were sitting within the adoption lodge,
a famous warrior ran out and shortly returned with water,
representing the report of a returning war party. Then relays
of dancers began to perform. At a noon intermission Two
Leggings' fellow Lumpwoods piled up the initiation fee of
blankets and war shirts. Since Two Leggings had joined to obtain
Sees The Living Bull's medicine, he did not exercise his right
to any of the other members' medicines. Later that afternoon,
when the dancing was over, the drummers raised their sticks,
everyone else little willow sprigs, to encourage the growth
of the sacred tobacco.*

THE MELTING SNOW CAME, followed by the grass-growing season.
My wife and I packed our belongings and traveled to the Mountain

Crows where Sees The Living Bull had moved. After waiting one day I picketed my white horse, loaded with presents, by my tipi door. Then I invited my medicine father for a smoke. When he came I told him that the presents and horse were his. I asked him to adopt me during a Tobacco Dance which I had heard would be held in three days. Calling him father, I said that although he had showed me many things I still had not received what I wanted most. I asked him to give me or make me one of his medicines so I could bring back more horses and scalps.

For a long time he would not answer. Finally he said that if I had patience he would give me a pipe so I could be a pipeholder. He reminded me that he was not medicine himself, that it was the Great Above Person who gave all medicines. But he promised to give me some of the Great Above Person's medicine and to teach me many things. In seven days there would be a full moon. I was to visit him then and he would build a sweat lodge and do something for me.

The next morning the Mountain Crows broke camp and went down Elk River to meet the River Crows for the planting of the tobacco. On the way Sees The Living Bull and I struck camp with them in the mountains. We traveled no farther because the River Crows joined us there. During the celebration of the tobacco planting Sees The Living Bull adopted me. I was very happy. Now he could not refuse me.

On the sixth day I brought Sees The Living Bull a beautiful Hudson Bay blanket, a buckskin shirt, leggings, moccasins, and a buckskin-colored horse. I was poor, I said, and asked him to have pity on me. I promised him everything I owned if only he would give me his powerful medicine.

He answered that since I wanted this so badly he would give me all he had. The following morning I was to cut one hundred and four willows and he would teach me how to make a sweat lodge. Then I was to bring twenty-four more for a separate sweat lodge. He also wanted seven stones, a long cottonwood pole, seven buffalo chips, red paint, charcoal, sweet grass, bear root, and a red blanket. He told me to begin the sweat lodge by digging a hole elbow-deep for the hot stones. Then I was to plant the first willow in the ground one full step from this hole and continue the other hundred and three in a circle around the hole. Finally he told me its location.

By dawn I had cut all the willows and had collected the other things at the lodge site. I dug the center hole and piled dirt around the edge so it looked like a prairie-dog mound. With my fingers I traced little trails in the pile to represent prairie-dog paths and covered them with powdered charcoal which meant success in war. Sees The Living Bull arrived in time to help me plant the willows in the ground. Then I intertwined their branches to form the roof frame and left a door space facing east. We covered the entire frame with buffalo hides, the last being a large robe with the head on, which faced the east. Finally I dug a hole west of the lodge for the long cottonwood pole.

Sees The Living Bull had me invite seven medicine men to assist in the ceremony: Little Face, Burns Himself, Face Turned Round, Bird Has A Shirt, Tobacco, Neck Bone, and Little Belt, because they had dreamt many dreams. After I had visited their tipis they walked up to our sweat lodge. Neck Bone was just about to enter when Cuts The Turnip arrived and told Sees The Living Bull that if he loved his children he would let him enter this sweat lodge.

Sees The Living Bull gave his consent but told me later that he had invited seven men because the number represented the dipper, one of his medicines. He had hoped that while they were inside he would receive a vision. By spoiling that number Cuts The Turnip had disturbed his medicine spirit. Cut The Turnip should have known better but Sees The Living Bull could not turn him away.

As I raised the door a fourth time for Neck Bone he called me his child and said that he had seen a snow-covered ground showing many tracks. He hoped I would live until then and bring home many horses.

When I raised the door for Burns Himself he called me his child and said he had seen the leaves turn yellow and hoped I would live until then.

Then Face Turned Round said he had seen a returning war party driving four captured horses. One was a fine bay and he wished me to have it before the leaf-turning season.

Bird Has A Shirt was last and his dream showed a war party returning from the Sioux country. Leading it was a fine warrior carrying a scalp from the end of a long pole. This man was singing and rode a beautiful captured roan horse. Bird Has A Shirt called me his son and hoped I would be that warrior.

The other three men and Cuts The Turnip entered without a word. During their sweat bath Sees The Living Bull and I waited outside. After a while I filled a pipe and passed it in. As each man smoked he pointed the stem to the sky and then to the ground, asking the Great Above Person to give me success on the warpath, plenty of game,

145

good health, and a long life. When they came out some younger men took baths in the same lodge.

I had already given Sees The Living Bull the red blanket. Now he spread it on the ground and with charcoal painted a black circle in the middle and a disc above that, representing the sun and moon. Holding the blanket up to the sun he told the White Man Above In The Sky, the moon, and all the stars that I was giving them this red blanket. Again he called to the sun, his father, and said that he was giving me this sweat lodge and asked him to help me if I needed anything.

After his prayers he had it announced in camp that he wished to see all the children. When they arrived each child rubbed himself with the blanket. Then it was tied to the top of the pole I had planted on the west side of the lodge. Sees The Living Bull told the sun that now the blanket belonged to him.

Sees The Living Bull invited me to his tipi early the next morning to receive a medicine he would make. The other sweat lodge of twenty-four willows which I had built close to the larger one was left for the following day.

In the morning some medicine men were already in his tipi: Two Belly, Crazy Wolf, Sees Under, Crooked Arm, Scar On The Mouth, Face Turned Round, Burns Himself, Hesitates, and Neck Bone.

When I sat down Sees The Living Bull began to tell us about his own medicine dream and his first raid. This was his story.

I fasted in the same place four times, staying four days each time. But it was not until the last of these fasts that I met my medicine father. Early the fifth morning a person rose above the horizon until I saw his entire body. As he walked toward me, fires burst out where he stepped. At last he stood next to me and delivered the message that Bird Going Up was coming to me.

He was wearing strange moccasins, the left upper made from a silver fox's head, the right from a coyote's head. The ears had been left and scalp locks were tied around the moccasins' edges. The right heel was painted black and the left red. The man wore a beautiful war shirt trimmed with scalp locks along the arms, and his leggings were decorated with horsehair scalp locks from the manes of different-colored horses.

A little rain woke me and my dream became a real vision. My dream person was standing next to me when I heard the little coyote head on his moccasin howling. When the fox on the other moccasin barked, flames blew from its mouth. I kept trying to see if this man's face was painted but it was hidden. He carried a coup stick with a raven sitting on it. This raven tried to teach me the language of the birds but the man stopped it. Suddenly I heard a loud thunderclap. I seemed to be picked up and dropped while my blanket was thrown in the opposite direction. Landing unhurt on the mountain slope with my head downhill, I saw a bird's big tail and large claws, but could not see the body. Red streaks of lightning shot from each claw, leaving trails on the rocks. I noticed hailstones on the bird's spread-out tail. As the rain turned into fog I tried to see the bird's head but lightning flashes crossed in front of it. My dream person told me that this bird was great, that the noise from its throat sounded like thunder. The raven on the coup stick said that I was to have had many visions but that the messenger prevented him from giving them. It meant my dream person, the real messenger from Bird Going Up who was giving me all these visions. Then the raven disappeared and I looked again at my dream person. A large red circle was painted on his face, broken by two other circles scratched into the red paint. The raven returned to its perch on the coup stick and my dream person told me that Bird Going Up had told him not to let the raven teach me the language of the birds. Instead, he said, he would teach me some of his medicine songs and sang the first one: "The bird is saying this: Wherever we are, nothing may be in our way."

After each song he blew several times on an eagle-bone whistle. The second song was: "The bird is gone. I will let him return and watch over you."

The third song went: "I am letting him stay. I am letting him stay."

He sang the fourth song: "I am going toward human beings and they are weak."

His fifth song was: "The bird from the sky will take care of you."

He sang his sixth song: "Wherever I am going, I say this: I am the Bird of the world."

His last song went: "My child, I am living among the clouds and there is nothing impossible for me."

When my dream man finished the seven songs he pointed east, saying that people there would make me suffer. Whatever direction I looked he said he could tell me what was there.

Pointing west he asked if I saw a burning mountain. I saw it but did not understand its meaning. My dream person told me never to go to the Flathead or Shoshoni country.

A strong wind came up and I watched my blanket blow away. When I turned back my dream man was gone. I was wide awake and the sun was already high in the sky. As I started home my feet were very sore and I felt weak. More than two days later I came upon White Mouth near the village. He said many people thought I had been killed by a bear and were mourning my death. He was my relative and as we walked back together asked why I tortured myself so much. He said I knew I would not live forever. There were many like myself who were poor and had large families, but he said they did not torture themselves. He kept talking that way but I made no answer. The hunters had just returned with fresh meat and he told me to eat some in my grandmother's tipi.

The news spread that I was back and many came to visit. After talking to them I greased the soles of my feet and slept. The following morning White Mouth invited me to eat in his tipi. After our meal he told me again not to starve or torture myself. Still I did not answer. He agreed to pass on my request that everyone bring a willow branch until I had forty-four and that they should also collect firewood. He went outside and soon I could hear the camp crier speaking to the people. When I had the willows and firewood I was asked if I had any further instructions. I told the people to build four sweat lodges in a row with openings to the east and west. In front of the first lodge they were to pile firewood because we would take our bath there. I had them plant a long pole near that lodge's eastern opening.

Everyone helped me build those sweat lodges. When they were made I told the people to follow me and led the men, women, and children into the eastern opening of the first lodge and out the western opening. As I led them through the second, third, and fourth lodges the people laid presents on the sweat lodge frames and also tied a piece of cloth and other presents to the long pole. Coming out of the fourth lodge I turned right, walked back to the eastern entrance of the first lodge, and announced for anyone wanting a sweat bath to prepare himself.

Has A Red Feather On The Side Of His Head,[1] our chief, told me that he had been watching over our people for many years and now was growing old. He said he had seen these lodges and believed I had received a powerful vision. I did not tell him what I had seen. He

148

hoped that sometime I would be able to look after our people but advised me to marry and make a home for myself.

I still did not reply but thought I should do as he said. A few days later we broke camp and moved down Powder River where we pitched our tipis again. There I heard that Not Dangerous was going on a raid and decided to try out my medicine. It was the moon when the leaves turn yellow and I had seen my vision in the moon when the chokecherries ripen. Not Dangerous asked if I had made my medicine bundle and I told him no. But I also told him that before my last fast I had dreamt of a gray horse near Red River (in the Black Hills country) and the time had been when the leaves turn yellow.

He had seen me build the four sweat lodges and make the ceremony for the whole camp to share. He had faith in my medicine and said that we would travel toward the horse in my dream.

He appointed me chief scout. After traveling for several days I had a dream. Before sunrise the next morning I told the five other scouts that we would bring good news to our leader. By the time the sun was a man's height above the horizon we had discovered some Sioux chasing buffalo in a valley. We knew they could not move before their animals had been skinned so we raced back to Not Dangerous. He was so pleased he offered me his title as pipeholder, but I could not accept. While we waited for the sun to rise higher our men prepared their medicines and sang their medicine songs. I was the only one without medicine and just carried a buffalo-hide rope. When Not Dangerous asked what I was going to do with it I answered that I was going to capture many horses. His expression showed he thought I was a powerful man. Everyone was ready but we traveled slowly and did not reach the hilltop until after sunset. In the distance we could see their fires.

Saying I was looking for my horse, I began to follow a coulee not far from their camp, keeping in the shadows. Around a bend I saw a dark shape and thought first it was a guard. But it was a horse and I tied my rope around its mouth.

As I led it up the coulee I discovered another horse which I mounted, leading the gray closer to the Sioux camp. Soon I came upon a large bunch, grazing quietly and unguarded. Riding around until I was between them and the campfires I began to walk them out. When I was far enough away I drove them into a run. As I met our men I told Not Dangerous to divide the bunch up, but that I would keep the gray.

149

We left immediately and arrived safely in our village above the present Crow Agency.

Everyone believed I had some great medicine. But in dreams later on I was given an even greater medicine. It is the rock with many faces which my wife found and which has given me powerful visions.[2]

Sees The Living Bull then taught me those seven songs and I never forgot them. When he finished he said he wanted me to take his horse and ride east until I had reached the top of Bushy Pine Hill. If I did not find a dead eagle there I should turn right and ride to the top of Red Top Hill south of camp. If I found nothing there I was to ride to West Hill west of camp. If I still had no luck I should ride north to Cherry Hill. If my entire search was unsuccessful he said I would not become a pipeholder or a medicine man.

It was a beautiful day. When I reached the top of Bushy Pine Hill I looked into the valley with our tipis and lines of smoke rising to the sky. Soon I would do things to make me a great warrior and a chief. My medicine father had also said that I might become a medicine man. I made a prayer for success to the Great Above Person and to the sun. Somehow I never thought I might fail. Galloping down the slope I rode through a little stream and into the valley. As I searched the ground for the eagle I saw six men sitting and smoking on the side of West Hill, Yellow Crane, Three Wolves, Shot In The Hand, Nursing, Chicken Hawk Cap, and Bucket Leg. I rode up and noticed a spotted eagle dead on the ground and immediately told them that I had come for it. When Three Wolves asked if I had left it there I explained that Sees The Living Bull was going to make me a medicine and had sent me for an eagle. I asked if they had shot it or touched it, but they had just arrived. When they allowed me to take whatever part I needed I was very happy. I dismounted, pulled out the two middle feathers of the tail, and rode to my medicine father's tipi.

When I handed them to him he said he had expected the whole bird. I described the six men sitting nearby and said that I was glad they let me have a part.

Sees The Living Bull said he would make a great medicine that would permit me to go out as a war leader. He told me to walk around camp and bring him a raven, or a small red fox, or a coyote. He gave me my choice, saying that a raven medicine would mean any bird could tell me where to find the enemy. A red fox medicine would not be very powerful but would give me that animal's cunning. A coyote medicine would bark and bite, and those noises would become a human voice leading me to horses. But if I wanted to be a powerful chief he advised me to take the eagle-tail medicine.

Another man asked Sees The Living Bull what medicine he had made for Red Bear and he answered an eagle medicine. They all agreed I had been going on raids without much luck and that if I continued without a proper medicine I might lose some men. If I took this eagle-tail medicine which my medicine father was willing to make, they would feel I was going to be successful.

Sees The Living Bull asked if I wanted a red circle on my face or a half circle painted over my forehead with the ends reaching from jawbone to jawbone. He also asked if I wanted my eyelids and lips painted red. When I narrowed my eyes the red lids would mean lightning, the power to see the enemy before they saw me. The red lips meant that my medicine songs would be more powerful. I wanted the red circle for the sun and also the red eyelids and red lips.

Then Sees The Living Bull lit a sweet-grass smudge and purified his hands and face. After painting them he reached for his medicine and opened it. On one side of the rock was a human head and under it a buffalo head. On the other side were the heads of an eagle and a horse. When it was completely opened he told me that he was my father but that this rock was my grandfather to whom I should pray.

When I finished praying he took a small rock from the bundle and said it was the large rock's child. He picked up a small tobacco medicine bag and told his wife to tie a small buckskin wrapper around the rock child. After tying it to the medicine bag he placed the bag on different-colored pieces of cloth which he said were the clouds. He sewed a weasel skin and a horse tail to the eagle tail and laid this before him together with an eagle claw.

Sees The Living Bull said that I thought I was now a chief but I was not. However, he said he would give me something to make me a chief. When he had finished he said I could go anywhere and not be afraid.

Laying each medicine down, he sang the song belonging to it. Then he painted a red circle on his face and a red streak on his eyelids and lips. He said if I chose the eagle medicine I must paint a red streak over my eyes. For the rock medicine I was to paint my mouth red and for the tobacco medicine I must paint a red circle on my face. The streak over my eyes meant I could always see the enemy; the red over my mouth, good luck and plenty to eat. The red circle on my face was the red clouds. If I saw a ring around the sun or moon or stars I should paint myself like that because it represented all three. The paint had been given to him by the star which always stands close to the moon. After I had my medicine, he said, I would never fear bad dreams. I could go my way and bring back horses and give him his share.

He wrapped some red paint in a paint bag. He told me that the earth was everlasting but that things on this earth do not last long. However, I would live to be an old man. Then he painted the rest of his face and body with red paint.

He promised to give me the eagle tail for a medicine and also an eagle head. Whenever I saw this kind of eagle flying high in the sky I would notice smaller birds flying around it. He promised to include one in my medicine.

After showing me a blackbird, a redheaded woodpecker, and a sparrow, he asked which I wanted on top of my medicine. I chose the blackbird since these birds are usually found with horses. A man with their medicine always takes the lead on a horse raid.

I walked to a place where blackbirds were swarming and killed one with a stone. When I returned Face Turned Round took the bird, skinned it, and gave the skin to Sees The Living Bull, who then told me to bring him three hairs from a horse's tail or mane. Again I walked out and when I met Fox driving some horses I asked for a few mane hairs. He told me to come with him to the river and there I recognized a mouse-colored horse, one of the fastest of the tribal-owned horses.[3] Fox gave me permission to cut a few mane and tail hairs. In the tipi Sees The Living Bull asked if they had been taken from a mare or a stallion. After I described the horse he approved and sent me out for different-colored beads. When I returned he asked if I wanted my wife to string them. But I said that I would do it since she might not always be mine, while this medicine would stay with me always.

Stuffing the blackbird's head with bighorn sheep hair, he mixed in some sweet grass and a little horsehair. He placed the rest of the horsehair in the beak, painting two pink spots on each end to represent different-colored horses. Between two strips of weasel skin which he had tied to the eagle-tail feathers, he wrapped my string of black, white, and yellow beads, representing the clouds.

When Sees The Living Bull finished these preparations he undressed to his breechcloth and moccasins and told me to do likewise. We knelt facing east in the middle of the tipi, I on his right and the old men sitting around us. Handing me his famous rock medicine, he told me to press it to my heart. He mixed some pink paint with water and sweet grass and rubbed it all over his body and smeared it on my hair. Then he painted a red circle on my face and painted my eyes and lips red. Finally he fastened the eagle tail to my hair and gave me an eagle-bone whistle.

When he had fasted on that high mountain peak he said his vision person had been painted as he had painted me now. What he had seen was better than my vision which had caused my bad luck. But though my dreams had not been powerful, he said now they would change. Before I had only seen shadows, but now I would see real things. He said that when a spirit person appeared in my dream I would notice how he had painted himself. He said he was almost finished. After singing me a song he was going to raise the eagle tail to my eyes and under it I might see a horse or a body.

After blowing his eagle-bone whistle he asked how many times he had blown it and I answered seven. He told me to remember that number. On the warpath I was to blow my whistle seven times before singing. Then he sang: "Whenever I go, I shall see them."

Whistling four times he raised the eagle tail and looked under it. He held it before my eyes and I saw hair hanging down which disappeared when I looked closer.

When I told him this he said I should go to Musselshell River when the leaves turn yellow and continue to Where The Lightning Strikes on the other side of Big River. There I would kill an enemy and would see another lying on his back whom I was also to kill.

Giving me some dried pine needles, he taught me more songs to sing during my raid. He also gave me his pipe and told me to put away my own. Whenever I went on a raid he said one of my men should carry this pipe before me. Then the enemy would think it was night and not see us.

My medicine father said he had shown me real things. I was to fast again, leaving my medicine behind and waiting on a high hill for my spirit man. My first war party would be to the Musselshell River and there I would find the scalps he had described. Before I left he promised to tell me where to camp each night. If I wanted to be successful and justify his trust, he said, I must follow all this.

Finally he taught me one more song which gave me the power to make rain. While I escaped ahead of the downpour an enemy would be slowed down.

It was dark when I returned to my tipi. At last I had received a medicine. At last I was a real pipeholder, known to everyone. Now I had to show I could hold the respect of these sacred men. Although it would be awhile before I could test my powers, this time the waiting was not so hard.

Chapter Twenty-Five

Calculating from Two Leggings' occasionally broken sequence of seasons, the hunts described in this chapter probably took place around 1869–70. In 1871 Agent F. D. Pease's report listed 2,700 Mountain Crows and 1,400 River Crows, many mouths to feed from the already thinning herds. At this time the Government was still permitting the Crows to hunt at will, though pressuring them to return to the reservation once the summer's kills were over.

One early record of a Crow camp's summer roaming after the herds describes them on the move forty-seven out of seventy-six days and covering a median distance of nine and a half miles per day. Following the courses of streams, they halted because of rain, because of serious illness, to pasture horses, to hunt and prepare hides and meat, and to settle disagreements over routes to follow.

During the winter, when the bands probably broke up into smaller residential groups, men often hunted in small parties or alone, as Two Leggings has done earlier. Even after the Crows had horses they used the old method of the buffalo drive. Having surrounded a herd, they either drove the animals into a corral at the foot of a bank and shot them at leisure or stampeded them off a cliff. An early nineteenth-century account numbers seven hundred buffalo killed in one such drive. But most communal hunts from horseback netted several hundred animals.

SOON AFTER RECEIVING my medicine I returned to the River Crow camp and waited to go on a raid. One day Two Belly invited eleven of us to his tipi. He lit the pipe and passed it around and after we had smoked we talked. He wanted to move to our winter quarters and had chosen Little Tipi Creek close to the Buffalo Heart Mountain. I thought it a little early and Big Lake and Red Hail agreed. But most of the men wanted to go and the move was planned for the new moon.

After our meeting I visited Big Lake and Red Hail. We decided that when camp moved we would hunt in another direction. Everyone was short of supplies and I thought we should collect sufficient provisions before leaving for winter camp.

Five days later I woke to the camp crier ordering the people to pull down their tipis. Women began packing their robes and household goods on horses which the men were bringing in from the pastures. The remaining supplies were stored in parfleches and loaded on travois drawn by horses or dogs.[1] Finally the tipis were taken down and packed and the poles tied in equal bundles on either side of a horse.

The morning was bright and clear. The camp leader, whose name I have forgotten, sang his medicine song and prayed for success on the march and for plenty of game in the new location. As he rode with his camp leader's medicine unwrapped and tied to his shoulder, the people fell in line behind him, all singing.

It made me a little sorry to leave, but then I thought of the hunting ahead and forgot about it. As planned, I branched off at a little creek. Red Hail and Big Lake followed with their households, while the main party continued along the river.

We were heading for the hilly southern country where we had discovered a large buffalo herd some days before. In the clear air the Bighorn Mountains seemed only a short ride away. The first winter snows already showed on their upper slopes, and the cottonwood trees along the creek bottoms were starting to lose their leaves. No birds sang in the air, and the sagebrush and grass had turned the colors of leaf-falling season. But the weather was still warm.

Then we noticed three men riding to catch up with us. Before they got close I recognized Two Belly and could tell he was angry. He began scolding us right away.

I explained that because of the lack of supplies and the early season I wanted to store enough meat before leaving for winter camp. Close by, I said, were enough buffalo to feed everyone.

Two Belly said I should have told him before. I had been selfish and had not thought of our hungry women and children. If we returned

156

with him, he said, they would prepare for a hunt the next day in which I would be leader.

Later that afternoon, after the three of us had rejoined the camp, the men met in a large circle. Several pipes were lit and passed around. Two Belly asked me to tell his people where I had discovered the large herd.

When I finished he stood up again and suggested we leave the older men, women, and children with enough warriors for their protection while we led the rest on one or two big hunts.

Everyone agreed and the women were told to set up camp along the creek bottom. Before sundown we arrived at the place where I had seen the herds. After telling them where to camp I sent scouts to locate the animals, warning them to stay far enough away as they watched through the night. Two Belly had ridden with us and now he asked if I was going to make a buffalo-hunting medicine. I had no right to make such a medicine and should have asked a real medicine man for help, but I was too proud.

I told them to bring me seven buffalo chips which I laid in a row. Facing east, I asked for a pipe. After it was handed to me I lit it and prayed for success. Then I stuck an eagle feather upright in my hair, telling the hunters I was making medicine for a good wind the next day. As I held my forelock I said they could decide. If I bent it left the wind would blow from there, and if I pointed it forward or backward the wind would blow from those directions. I said that if I blew pipe smoke behind me there would be a strong wind. If the wind blew toward the buffalo as we approached I promised to make medicine again, but if it blew toward us I would not do anything.

Two Belly said he would rather not have any wind and told me to put my forelock straight up if I thought that would make us successful.

After doing this I drew a mouthful of smoke and blew slowly into the hollow of my hands. I told the men to be ready the next morning and said there would be little or no wind.

Long before dawn everyone was awake and we brought in the horses. We led our saddle horses and buffalo runners so they would be fresh, and rode the pack horses. Two Belly warned the hunters to ride slowly or the buffalo would hear them. During the night, riders had kept in contact with the scouts.

There were about a hundred and fifty of us. I was supposed to be the leader and rode ahead. No one knew how worried I was. The wind was behind us from the south and the buffalo were reported straight north. I overheard some men talking about my kind of medicine man. When Two Belly rode alongside and asked what I intended doing I grew scared. But I told him that as soon as we reached a certain ridge he would be satisfied.

I did not have the power to say the wind would change. I only hoped the buffalo had strayed so we could change direction.

As we approached the hill I thought how wrongly I had acted. I knew it would be the end to my future if I let anyone suspect me. But I made a vow to the Great Above Person that if my make-believe medicine worked I would buy a proper buffalo medicine and sacrifice to him. Men rode up to ask me things but I ignored them, praying that something would change.

When we were within gunshot of the rimrock base the wind suddenly died down. Finally we reached the foot and I led my horse up the narrow trail that curved to the top where a scout waited. Still there was no wind. I looked back and saw the line of our men like a snake behind me. Nearing the top, I noticed a little dust cloud blown toward us by a northern breeze.

I thanked the Great Above Person, repeating my vow and promising never to do such a thing again.

A scout ran down to report the buffalo grazing quietly on the northern side of a rimrock a little distance away. Now it was safe to ride to another rimrock. Two Belly was beside me and said that I was a powerful medicine man and that when he died I would take his place. He had doubted my power in the morning, he said, but now he was sure of me. I nodded my head and rode on.

On the flat top we got off our pack horses and mounted our buffalo runners. A sloping prairie led to the foot of the next rimrock. The buffalo were grazing on the other side. I told my men to follow me at a slow trot and then everyone could hunt as he wanted. From the next rimrock we saw the huge herd grazing only two rifle shots away.

Riding into the middle of them I was quickly alongside a fat two-year-old cow and about to shoot when my horse stepped into a badger hole. I did a complete turn in the air and rolled away as three buffalo raced by. If I had not been on the herd's edge I would have been killed. My horse had also landed on its back but managed to get to its feet. It was frightened and when I grabbed for the bridle it jerked away and chased the buffalo.

The men passed me, some asking about my horse and others just
158

laughing. Then I was alone with the buffalo carcasses. Soon the hunters returned and began skinning and butchering their animals. I recognized Two Belly and Big Lake with about five other men. There was nothing to do but walk up.

As I was explaining why I was on foot Curley rode by, calling out that my horse was running wild among the buffalo. I thanked him but could do nothing. Big Lake offered one of his four buffalo and I thanked him and started skinning. I had no horse to carry the meat and asked Big Lake if he could bring my pack horse. All the time I had to listen to people talking about this medicine man who was hunting and skinning without a horse. I paid no attention when they asked how many more buffalo I intended to kill. Big Lake finally returned and I loaded my meat.

My wife wanted to know why I had returned without the hide and where I had left my horse. Her sister was living with us, and although they did not say anything I knew what they thought about so little meat. A cousin of mine returned late in the evening with my horse. He had seen my fall and had caught it in the herd. He started saying unpleasant things because he had lost the chance to hunt himself. I had to give him a present for recovering the horse. I felt properly punished.

Soon afterward I completed my vow and bought a powerful buffalo-hunting medicine from one of our medicine men, explaining that my last hunt had brought me such bad luck I was afraid my own medicine was not powerful enough.

Then I felt ready to make my name good again. Although I was still being teased I told no one about my new hunting medicine.

About six days after that unlucky hunt the meat and hides had dried and we traveled along the foothills of the Bighorn Mountains, camping at the Black Buttes. Scouts were sent in different directions and returned in two days with news of many buffalo close by. Then I told my friends that I would be leader again, built a sweat lodge, and invited the older people.

My medicine was an eagle feather painted with six white spots giving me the power to direct the wind. After the proper ceremony the wind would blow from the direction pointed by the feather in my hair. The six spots meant that the owner could cause a sudden hailstorm between himself and a pursuing enemy. Later I used the feather many times and it always worked.

Two Belly had announced that we would stay there long enough to dry the meat and hides. Now we hoped to kill enough to last us through the winter. This time I did not worry.

Long before the sun rose we set out. The skin tipis were still lit up from the fires inside. The morning was frosty and the leaves made noise under our horses' hooves. We rode silently and at sunup arrived on a hilltop with a wide view of the prairie. Four or five gunshots ahead a small group of buffalo bulls were grazing quietly along a little creek, and farther on the country was black with them. A strong wind blew into our faces. We would be able to ride right among them before they smelled us. I heard many approving words about the medicine I had made for this hunt. A few friends told me to hold on to my horse, but I did not mind.

We changed to our buffalo horses and I tied my bridle to my belt with an extra piece of thong. When we all raced into the herd I chased a young bull. As I was aiming my gun the bull ran into my horse. The thong broke and I was on the ground, my eyes and mouth filled with dust. My friends behind had trouble avoiding me. I felt miserable and realized I was still being punished.

Someone caught my horse and even before I could clean the dirt from my eyes I was riding after buffalo again. I killed several and my wife was happy when she saw the hides and meat.

The following day Two Belly invited me and some other friends to his tipi. During our smoke they made fun of me, wondering whether I had asked my horse if it had been hurt and if it had asked me the same question. They said that at the next hunt I should make medicine and then stay home while hired boys killed my animals. But the hunt had been successful and although I was teased they felt my medicine had been powerful.

Soon after that Stands Among Them, Clear On The Forehead, Female Face, and I were hunting and located a group of old bulls and two younger ones. We decided to let the old bulls escape because their meat would be too tough. But before we had circled them one old bull smelled us, stopped grazing, and stared in our direction. Then it kicked dirt back with its front hooves and led the others racing down a coulee toward Elk River. We were right behind as they followed a flat bordering the river. The bank grew into a steep mud bluff and they could not escape into the hills. Female Face rode between the river and the buffalo, driving them against these banks. When they passed a small ravine the old bull thought he had found an opening and led his herd into it. But the ravine was a dead end with dirt walls on three sides. The old bull began tearing out great chunks of earth with his horns. The others milled around while we closed in.

Suddenly a young bull broke away. One man shot and missed as it made for the river. I was a little in the rear and jumped off my horse, kneeling to shoot. When it rushed me I tried to reach my horse but the bull had scared it off. Then I stumbled over a rock and fell, my rifle landing out of reach. The buffalo snorted and came at me. I prayed to my medicine and the Great Above Person and thought how much better it would have been to die fighting. As I caught sight of its red eyes, its head lowered onto me. My wind was knocked out and I thought I was dead. I felt my soul start on the journey to the Other Side Camp.

When I came back to myself I thought I was riding a bucking horse and was confused. Sweat seemed to cover me. Then I woke. The buffalo's horn had only hooked under my belt. When it raised its head to gore me again it had felt my weight and had run for the river. Now it stood in shallow water, swinging me up and down and ducking me each time. The water had woken me but I was kept under so long I felt I was drowning. Each time the buffalo shook its head the curve of its horn mashed my insides like berries. When I tried to call my friends the buffalo held me under and soon I grew too exhausted to care. After fainting again I heard what seemed to be thunder. I felt myself falling, my soul left me, and everything went black.

Some time later I heard a mumbling which turned into voices. For a moment I wondered if they were my spirit ancestors welcoming me into the world beyond. But soon I recognized my friends' voices calling my name. My soul returned and I woke. I thought I was badly hurt and kept calling for them to take me away. But except for being cut on my face when the buffalo had bounced me on its run to the river, I was unhurt.

My friends had thought the horn went through me. They had followed us, killing the bull in the shallows. I never again dismounted during a buffalo hunt.

Chapter Twenty-Six

*The game-stocked Yellowstone Valley was sufficiently
tempting to other tribes that Crow raiding parties rarely had
to travel far to encounter enemies. But some of their forays
did cover long distances and last many months.*

*Around 1825–30 a war party led by Twists His Tail returned
to its River Crow camp after an absence of two and a half
years. Part of their booty was a pregnant woman dressed in a
deerskin dress fringed with pleasantly tinkling ornaments. She
was probably Apache, evidence of a journey which had seen
the Crows enter a country "where prickly-pear cactus grew
as tall as a man and its leaves the size of a shield."*

*But they also went east, walking as far as the middle course
of the Missouri to raid the Sioux, or north into Canada to steal
from the Blackfeet, and across the continental divide for
Nez Percé horses.*

*When they rode it was as mounted infantry; the skirmishing
took place on the ground. Of such stretches in their hide saddles
the Crow comment was, "buttocks were worn out."*

IT WAS STILL the moon when the leaves turn yellow. One day a war
party led by Arapaho returned with news of Coyote Howls' death. I
told Two Belly that I wanted revenge but that first I would visit Sees
The Living Bull who was camped in the Hits With The Arrows
country. That evening I made a sweat lodge and the next morning
rode to his tipi.

When I told him my plans he asked the direction I intended to go.
I answered Where The Lightning Strikes, the place I had seen when

he had made my medicine. He approved and told me where to camp each night.

I sang many songs as I followed the winding Arrow Creek home, arriving long after sunset at the joining of the two rivers.

That night in my tipi I sang my medicine songs. After purifying my body in a smudge of white pine needles I fell asleep and had a medicine dream. A big hawk flying high in the sky fell to earth and rose again with a man in its claws. It dropped the body at the place in my earlier dream. When I woke I knew that my medicine was with me and prepared to leave. I had told friends that I expected to go out as soon as I returned from Sees The Living Bull's. Eleven joined me; Woman Face, Clear On The Forehead, and High Hawk were about my age but the others were younger.

Before sunrise we headed toward the Musselshell River. There was plenty of game so we carried no provisions. But that day we could not get within shooting distance of anything. After making camp in the bottom of the Musselshell Valley we went to sleep hungry.

By dawn we were already riding and before the sun was a man's height above the horizon had killed two buffalo. Now we jerked and packed some of the meat.

Just before sundown we arrived at the next camping place which Sees The Living Bull had described, Stone Pile, a day's travel north of the Musselshell River. After a night there we took the trail to Big River, opposite the eastern spur of the Little Rockies, where we camped the third night. At the end of the fourth day we came to the mouth of Dry Creek on the western shore of Big River. The next day we expected to reach Where The Lightning Strikes River. Now we had to be careful for across Big River was enemy country.

In the morning I sent men to scout the opposite banks. When they reported no enemy signs we made skin boats, weighted them with stones, and tied on our clothing and weapons and ammunition. We swam across with a piece of driftwood under one arm, pulling the boats with thongs in our teeth. For some time the nights had been frosty and the water was cold. On the other side we were so numbed we risked a fire. Some men gathered dry wood, especially dry bark when they could find it since it made little smoke. On the east we were well hidden by a high bank, and thick chokecherry bushes surrounded us. After we were warm we wiped out all traces of the fire. I sent four men ahead to scout the banks as we traveled among the big cottonwoods lining the valley bottom.

Toward evening we approached Where The Lightning Strikes where the river banks are cut by a creek bearing the same name. The scouts still reported no enemy signs, but knowing we would meet them here I had my men tie their horses and make camp.

Early the next morning we built a fire, careful again not to use smoking wood. After we ate I ordered my men on their horses, telling them that I was sure we would soon meet enemies. I posted a lookout on a nearby hill and rode carefully up the creek, the others far behind. As I drew near the location in my vision I turned a bend and hid in a willow grove to watch the creek bottom's upper reaches. I was still not certain enemies were in the vicinity, but I had faith in my medicine dream. Then buffalo spilled over the southern bank several rifle shots away, and behind them rode two Sioux.

Singing my medicine song I ran back and met the scout running down the hill. He reported ten more Sioux riding our way. Although we were twelve, two were boys carrying only knives. But I reminded my men that these Sioux were not brave and that as soon as we began shooting some would run off.

I told them to take out their medicines and sing their songs. I told them to be brave. Sees The Living Bull had said there was no reason to be afraid. After opening my medicine bundle I blew my eagle-bone whistle seven times. Then I knelt and held up my eagle medicine with my left hand. As I looked under it I sang: "The bird above is kind to me. There are some Indians. They are easy to me. I want to talk to them. They are easy."

Then I blew my whistle again. Swaying from side to side, I saw two falling enemies underneath my medicine. I was going to kill those Sioux.

The ten other Sioux were a few rifle shots away, but had not yet crossed the spot where I had seen the two men fall. Now the first two hunters disappeared behind the ridge in my vision and I led my men up the other side.

The other Sioux saw us and rushed to join their friends. As the first hunter rode over the ridge I shot him in the leg. Dismounting as soon as he fell I dodged his pistol bullet and killed him with another shot. After I scalped his beautiful hair I held one half up to the sun.

My men were spreading out along the ridge and firing. High Hawk wounded one who escaped. When the ten Sioux saw me kill that man they raced away until they were too far to chase. Also, we feared they might be part of a larger camp.

164

My first pipeholder's vision had been fulfilled. Although we had only killed one and wounded another I was anxious to bring my men safely back. We traveled all day and reached the river that night, pulling out the skin boats we had hidden under brush. Then I felt safe and, as I swam across, sang one of my medicine songs: "He was just going in front of us."

This time the cold water did not bother me. Once on the other side I remembered that other war parties were out and told my men to hurry. Our celebration would be even better if we were the first to return successfully.

All that night and through the next day we galloped along the Musselshell River. About sunset we came around a bend and saw a Crow camp and recognized several men returning from a buffalo hunt. I took out my new medicine which Sees The Living Bull had given me and we made charcoal and blackened our faces. After everyone had tied on their medicines and the scalp was attached to a long thin pole we rode toward camp, shooting our guns into the air. A moment later the drums began and the women ran out of their tipis singing a scalp song. On all sides people called out my name and pointed to my scalp. They sang my song: "Wherever he is staying, we are going where he is."

They also sang this song: "I want to have another song."

All night long we sang and danced. My ambition had come true and I was a real pipeholder. By dawn we were too tired to celebrate any more and finished by singing a love song: "The one I love, do not go home. You are the only one I love, do not go home."

I gave away half of the scalp and kept the other half to take to our home camp which I learned was on Porcupine Creek. Two days later we left and when we rode into our village, celebrated all over again. I sang this medicine song: "Whoever he is, I am going to him."

The whole camp joined in and everyone felt good. I had avenged Coyote Howls and my name was spoken through camp. I never tired of telling about this trip, and visitors returned to hear it again.

My medicine father was camped with the Mountain Crows along Elk River at a place now called Pease Bottom[1] and I was anxious to see him. Three men from my last war party rode with me and I led a horse for him. When we could see his camp we shot our guns and I sang a victory song: "I thank you. Go right by here. I thank you."

As Sees The Living Bull invited me into his tipi I said that here was some nice hair for him. He seemed pleased as he took the scalp out of the buckskin cover I had made. I told him that everything he had predicted had come true but that instead of two men I had killed one and wounded another who escaped. I had been afraid of telling this but he called me his son and said that everything was all right. While I should have chased them until one more was dead, he said, the wounded man would die before reaching home. He wanted me to stay in camp this winter, and next spring when the water rose to go to Bear Creek. There I would kill an enemy and in the moon when the grass is high I would kill another.

And it happened as Sees The Living Bull said. The events he foretold always came true. He had given me his medicine and now he gave me his dreams and visions which brought me many victories as the summers and winters passed.

Chapter Twenty-Seven

*In Two Leggings' boyhood there were eight
warrior societies whose duties were to guard the camp against
nocturnal raids and to police the hunts. A member might
order an anxious hunter back into line; disobedience
brought a swift whipping. Returning from a clandestine
raid, the Crow hotblood might find his tipi in ribbons; the society
chosen by the head chief the previous spring had
discovered his unauthorized mission and delivered punishment.*

*The Foxes and Lumpwoods, which emerged
as the dominant societies when Two Leggings was reaching
manhood, were very similar in insignia and
organization. In each two officials, elected for one
summer season, bore otter-skin-wrapped crooked staffs,
while two other officers carried straight staffs.
These positions were often regretted; the straight-staff bearer
must plant his emblem into the ground during a
fight. If no fellow member passed between him and the enemy
he was duty bound to stand until he "dropped his robe."*

*The fierce rivalry between the Foxes and Lumpwoods
displayed itself on the battlefield and at home. On raids each
would try to outdo the other in accumulating honors;
in the spring each would attempt to abduct former mistresses
who had in the meantime married members of the opposing
society.*

WE WERE CAMPED along the Bighorn River close to the mouth of the
Little Bighorn River, but game grew scarce so we moved to Rotten
Grass Creek and then to Mud Creek, near the foot of the Bighorn
Mountains.

Sees The Living Bull told me that if I wanted he would give me his vision of the killing of a Sioux east of Wolf Mountains. But it was snow-melting season and I was lazy. I did not want to go on the war-path and put it off. Also, the Foxes had gone on a raid and I was waiting for their return.

One day Wolf Bear, I, and some friends were sitting in the shade of my tipi. It was warmer than usual and we did not feel like doing much. Camp had plenty of meat and there were no reports of enemies. It was still early in the day when we heard shooting and saw a party of Foxes riding over a hill, carrying long poles with scalps tied to the ends and singing victory songs. The women rushed out of their tipis and began the scalp dance song as soon as they saw their husbands and lovers.

The war party rode through camp. When they saw us Lumpwoods they sang and one song was about me: "Two Leggings poor man, Two Leggings poor man."

I walked away with the other society members, but the Foxes followed: "Those Lumpwoods are running away. They are afraid."

They called us all kinds of names because we had not gone to war. Some of their songs were about our wives. I told the others that I was leaving the next day and whoever wanted could join me. On our return I promised we would make songs against them.

The others were ready so I went to see Sees The Living Bull, who seemed glad. The following morning, after the proper preparations, I rode toward the Wolf Mountains with Plain Face, Black Hair, Little Heart, and Bobtail Wolf, all Lumpwoods and my companions since Young Mountain's death.

When we noticed some men leaving camp to catch up with us we waited and then all rode to a meadow just before the foothills of the Wolf Mountains. After our evening meal we sat and smoked. The full moon threw deep shadows over the country. All night Lumpwood members rode in and we heard that Wolf Bear was bringing his friends. Toward morning he rode into our camp, looking very fine on a lively horse, his pipeholder's war pipe hanging from a wide otter-skin strip over his shoulder. He was singing: "Our enemies just passed in front of us."

We moved into the Wolf Mountains but did not travel far because the trail was steep and we wanted our horses fresh.

Now there were several pipeholders and that evening they met together. I wanted to finish eating but they kept calling so I put on my

168

war shirt and leggings of softly tanned mountain-sheep skin trimmed with weasel skins and scalp locks. Around my neck I wore a good wampum necklace and attached long pieces of false hair to my head. In my own hair I wore a red plume tied to a brass ring. Then I rode my beautiful bay horse to their meeting ground.

After all the pipeholders had smoked, each spoke about the direction we should take. Old White Man had planned to go to a place called Where The White Clay Is. Hillside stood up and said he had dreamed that enemies were at Where The Lightning Strikes on the other side of Big River. Bobtail Wolf wanted to go to Where The Dog Bites. Hunts The Enemy said we should ride to Where The Gros Ventre Sun Dance Tipi Stands. Then Wolf Bear said that I had started this, that none of them had gotten angry. Many of the warriors had come, he said, because they knew I would lead them. He asked if I was going after horses or if I just wanted scalps.

When I stood up I told them of my medicine father's dream to cross the Wolf Mountains to the east and follow the mountains north where I would meet two enemies, one on a bay and the other on a gray. In his dream he had been told to kill the first, but to let the other escape because he was too dangerous. I said that I wanted to follow this trail which was short while the others required many days. I reminded them of the bad names we had been called and said that this way we could bring back scalps as proof of our bravery. When we made songs about the Foxes they would be silent.

As I sat down I could see they liked my words. Wolf Bear stood up and said that I was right to be angry. The trail I described was short so we would return soon to our tipis and wives and women. He said that with the help of the Great Above Person we would silence those Foxes.

They all agreed and I was now leader. The next morning we rode northeast over the rough trail through the Wolf Mountains. As we descended the eastern slopes we came upon buffalo as thick as grass. Camping by a creek a few men rode out to kill a fat cow. Soon we were roasting buffalo ribs. There were many of us and game might not be so plentiful north so we heated up the fire, laid down green willows, and spread enough meat strips for two days' travel.

That evening we chose four scouts, Sits Toward The Mountain, Kind Hearted Old Man, Bird On The Prairie, and another whose name I have forgotten, telling them to set out before daybreak toward Snake Hill, a high mountain at the northeastern end of the Wolf Mountains.

The next morning, after a quick meal, we traveled along the eastern slopes. It was good to be out again and the early spring air made me happy. I was sure we would be successful. That evening we camped at the foot of Snake Hill while our scouts spent the night on top, watching the northern country. In the morning I sent a boy to bring in the horses while we ate dried meat. He rushed back, saying that our scouts were howling like wolves. When the scouts rode in, waving their guns over their heads and howling, we all stood up. If they had only howled it would have meant buffalo, but the waving of their guns meant enemies.

They had spotted two Sioux chasing buffalo on the other side of the mountain and had left a man to keep watch. They were very excited and wanted us to leave right away. Wolf Bear took the lead, singing his medicine song: "There is somebody just going in front of us."

At the base of Snake Hill we left our horses and crawled up. The scout pointed them out, butchering their buffalo. We went down for our horses and began painting ourselves and unwrapping our medicines.

I was on one of the fastest horses I ever owned. It was well known to our people. Around its neck I fastened a necklace of rock-swallow feathers, small bells, and a stuffed hawk. When you watch rock swallows flying in a tight bunch you never see them touch. This necklace gave my horse that same power to dodge if I was chased. The bells meant a coming storm. If I was followed by enemies I would pray for a sudden storm to come between us, slowing them down. The hawk was a fast, high-flying kind that had long endurance; I wanted those qualities for my horse.

Paints His Head Red, next to me on a beautiful bay, painted his face with black stripes under the eyes. On his head he tied a stuffed eagle. He was singing his medicine song: "I am going to strike the enemy. I want to have the body."

If we rode straight down they could escape into the thickly wooded coulees. We descended on our side, carefully circled the base of the hill, and came upon them skinning their animals apart from each other. A bay stood beside the man nearest us. The other had a gray and I told my men to let him escape as I had been advised.

As we whipped our horses, Pale Face, Young Curlew, High Hawk, and I took the lead. The bay jerked its rope from the Sioux's arms where it had been loosely wrapped and began running in circles. The man fell behind the buffalo carcass and started shooting. We all fired and then I saw his gun on the ground and blood running from his nose and mouth. High Hawk and I were the first to ride up. As I leaned over to pick up his gun High Hawk shoved me away and grabbed it. Then I dismounted, scalped him as he was dying, and mounted again. Two men had chased his horse and both wanted it so badly they finally shot it.

The others were chasing the remaining Sioux toward the creek at the lower end of the flat. Straight Calf shot his horse. As it fell the man lay on the ground and shot back. He was brave and even shot a man in the leg. I yelled to them to leave him alone, that we had an enemy scalp and should return to make up songs against the Foxes. But they wanted to kill him.

Then we heard war cries and shooting. Many Sioux burst out of the trees where this man had been riding. We had not noticed a large camp pitched in the timber along the river bottom. I yelled to my men to head toward the mountains, but most were already on their way.

Six of us on long-winded horses covered for our friends, shooting back and riding slowly as long as they could see us, but whipping our horses when we were out of sight. By the time they topped a ridge, we were again out of rifle range.

When I noticed my horse tiring I shouted to the rest to keep riding while I made medicine. At the next ridge I dismounted and untied a little medicine bag which was always fastened to my shirt. With a small bone spoon I took out some powdered herbs and rubbed them into my horse's mouth and nostrils and on its jaw. After mounting again I sang my horse a medicine song: "My horse is fast. My horse is faster."

Although I was supposed to sing this song to each of the earth's four corners, east, south, west, and north, the Sioux were very close. When I was about to sing my last song I noticed two other groups of Sioux racing toward me from right and left, and heard the men in front singing. Bullets whistled by and kicked up dirt around my horse. I galloped down the ridge. By the time the first Sioux reached the place where I had made medicine I could laugh when they shot at me. For a long time my horse did not tire and I played with them again. Reaching the mountains I rode up a steep slope. Wolf Bear made signs from the top for me to walk my horse up. Then we watched the few remaining Sioux start the climb.

He asked if I had killed another but I said that I had just escaped. When he warned me that our trail would be useless if I was killed I explained about my horse. He agreed that the medicine had saved my life. Some Sioux were still behind us as we joined the others on the next mountain. For the rest of that day and through that night we did not stop. I switched to a pack horse, turning my own in with the extras we had brought. The sun was rising as we descended the last ridges.

The Bighorn Mountains were still covered with snow almost to their foothills and further west the snow on the Beartooth Mountains and Rockies shone in the sun. The sky was clear and first green was showing everywhere. Our horses kept trying to eat the new grass, but we pushed them on because the Sioux might still be behind. Also I was eager to reach camp so we could dance another scalp dance while the women sang for us. We rode all that day, stopping at dust to eat some dried meat and to give our horses grass and water from a creek. The moon was above the eastern horizon as we rode through the night. Just before dawn we came out of the breaks and entered Elk River Valley, soon finding our village near the Mountain Lion's Lodge.

We stopped to put on the war shirts, medicines, warbonnets, and leggings we had brought, and painted our faces to show we had been successful. I led six men galloping into camp. When we reached the center of the tipis we circled around, pretending to fight each other. Then we dashed back out, joined the others, and all galloped into camp, five abreast, firing our guns into the air. From the top of a long willow pole I carried my scalp. It was scraped thin, dyed with a mixture of blood and charcoal, and stretched on a willow hoop. Everyone was singing; this was my song: "I shall travel to some place. I shall be glad."

Our wives and girl friends rushed out of their tipis and people who had recently lost relatives took the scalp pole and danced with it and sang. The women also painted their faces with charcoal. We used the blood and charcoal mixture to paint the older women's and widows' robes solid black, and painted black stripes on the robes of the younger women and girls. Several men brought drums out of their tipis and sat down inside the camp circle. As the women danced the scalp dance we fell in behind them.

My name was praised by everyone and I forgot about the Foxes. We danced through the day and late into the night. Early in the morning the women came to the tipis calling for the men who had gone with us and we began the scalp dance again. The following day the men woke the women and we danced some more. For several days we feasted like this and were happy. Then I remembered the Foxes. They had not expected us so soon and were quiet during our celebrating.

172

I began one my scalp dance songs: "I went by here. The last one was better than the first."

Riding by a group of Foxes I said that now we would call them names. I collected the Lumpwood members still celebrating and we rode double with our wives and girl friends who always joined in this. We were singing: "Where they stop, I shall go straight there to where they stop. I thank you."

Boils His Leggings was the Foxes' leader. As we rode by his fine tipi I made a funny song about the Foxes. Boils His Leggings' wife rushed out with a club and began beating my horse. We left and after riding around camp once more I planned something. But I warned my men not to touch Boils His Leggings or his family. We all dismounted, hid our guns under our blankets, and sang as we walked through the camp: "We are going. We are going into the northern country."

When we arrived at his tipi Boils His Leggings was sitting outside, a magpie feather in the long braids coiled on his head. Red spots were painted on his forehead to represent stars. I think he had expected us back and wanted to make us afraid of his medicine power.

What happened next was not the way to treat a great warrior. But the same thing had happened to me and could again. We pretended to surround him and I talked loudly to my men, saying that this man was so powerful they could only shout at him.

Everyone yelled and clapped their hands over their mouths. When they had quieted down I said they should not shoot because their bullets could not kill him. If they touched this great medicine man, I said, he would do something to them.

My friends shouted once more and uncovered their guns, shooting off the tips of many of his tipi poles. Several bullets also tore holes in the smoke flaps. I had brought a drum and began singing: "Lump all over him. Lump all over him."

Then we were all singing and laughing and shouting. Boils His Leggings had rheumatism; his legs and hands were swollen and this was what I meant. Again his wife ran out, crying that I had ruined their tipi. She said I had never owned one as nice and called me a bad man. She was so angry she could hardly talk. Although Boils His Leggings could not show his anger, I saw in his eyes that we had hurt him as badly as he had hurt me.

We would have kept it up if Crooked Arm, the camp chief, had not appeared, carrying his medicine pipe uncovered. He invited us to smoke, saying we were all his children, especially me, and asked us to have pity.

I would only take the pipe if Boils His Leggings took it, since he had started this. Then Boils His Leggings said that I was foolish and not even a medicine man. From now on, he said, I would never sing victory songs or kill any enemies.

I told him that he had never received a dream and had had to buy his medicine from White Fox. I promised to show him that his power was nothing to me.

Crooked Arm told us to stop this, but Boils His Leggings kept talking. Then Crooked Arm told me that Boils His Leggings was older and not to listen. He asked us again to smoke and said that if I wanted to become a chief I must control myself.

When I took the pipe our revenge on the Foxes was over. But Boils His Leggings still would not smoke. After that he never went on a raid or killed any more enemies, while I went out many times and became an even greater warrior than before.

Soon afterward the Foxes took revenge on me. Returning from a short raid, I found my tipi empty and learned that a young Fox member had stolen my wife. During the early spring season this often went on between the Foxes and Lumpwoods. It had begun in the long ago when we were taught to endure all kinds of things without complaining. It would have been a disgrace for me to take her back. Although I had been very fond of her I could not show my unhappiness and did not try to see her.

Medicine Crow tried to cheer me, saying that there were many good women in camp. When I finally realized she was lost forever I asked for his help. Two Stars was still young, pretty, and a hard worker. Before she married Knows His Ground she had been my girl friend. Now he was away on the warpath. But I said that he would return to an empty tipi.

Medicine Crow and I rode to Knows His Ground's tipi early the next morning. When I opened the door flap Two Stars was alone inside. I told her to come with me because I was going to marry her. She knew I could have taken her by force. Without a word, she threw her buffalo robe over her shoulders and walked out behind me. I lifted her on my horse and took her to my tipi. We did not talk much the first few days, but she began her duties right away. She was a good tanner of robes, clean and good to look at, and I was happy.

For the year she remained my wife I stayed in camp. Then, early the following spring season, I went on a raid. First we went to Fort Benton and then northwest to the Piegans and the Blackfeet, discovering them along Badger Creek where the old Blackfeet agency stands. The seven of us were able to run off many horses and return safely to our camp on Plum Creek. On this trip we met a group of white trappers who had recently come into our country.

When I walked into my tipi my wife was not there. I asked around and was told she had returned to her relatives who were camped with the Many Lodges on the Bighorn River.

I was still young and wild. As soon as I learned this I ran off with another girl. But Two Stars was not happy with her family. When she returned within a moon she was surprised and angry I had married again.

I liked her and took her back. But my two wives were jealous and quarreled from the first day. Although I lived with them I saw other women, and this made more fighting as each blamed the other. I could do nothing with them and moved to my brother's camp.

One day there I dressed up in all my best clothes to watch a dance. A woman in the circle of dancers seemed glad that I noticed her. I must have looked good because that evening I heard a footstep outside my brother's tipi and a voice calling me. When I went behind the tipi I told her that as long as she stayed with her husband I could not marry her. I said I loved her and wanted her to be my wife. She threw her arms around me, kissed me, and wanted to go inside so no one could see us.

My brother's family was away so we sat down. Soon the door flap was raised; her husband looked first at me and then at his wife. After I had walked out I heard him ask about me, but did not hear her reply. I watched the tipi until they left and then went back in.

The next day there was a big Tobacco Dance and Medicine Crow and I were watching on our best horses. I was looking out for the girl's husband since he had the right to give me a beating, which I would have to take without complaining. But the dance was exciting and I forgot. Then people around me yelled and something hit my back, knocking me off my horse. He had come up behind me with a stick hidden under his robe. The people held him while Medicine Crow and I rode away. It had been my fault and I would have made a fool of myself if I had said something in anger. When the people asked why he had done it he described finding me the night before with his wife in my brother's tipi. Later my brother told me that I was on my way to becoming a chief and that a chief's first duties were to respect our customs. He said I should know that I was not supposed to be alone with someone else's wife inside a tipi. If I was looking for a wife, he said, there were many unmarried women of the right age in camp. I knew that he was right.

Soon after this I became fond of a young woman named Gets A Shield and married her. But she turned out to have a quick temper and I grew tired of her. One day she caught me with another girl and hit me. I did not strike back but walked to my tipi. She followed behind, asking why I did not go to that other woman. Without answering I packed up my few belongings and went to live with my brother. Later she became the wife of Curley, one of Custer's scouts.

After that I decided to obey our tribal rules. When I broke them I never had any luck. During these years I looked for the woman whose name I had heard in my vision. I married several times but my happiness never lasted. Then one day, when I was married to a woman who was bad-tempered and lazy, I entered a tipi and saw a young girl with a child in her lap. Something inside me said that this was she. Her eyes and beautiful hair were just as I had seen them and the parting was also painted yellow. She was bashful and would not look at me. She belonged to a large family, her parents and another family living together in three tipis. Her father was a chief. She would not answer when I asked her name. Then I told her that the Great Above Person had given her to me to marry.

When I learned her name it meant something different from the one in my dream, but there was little change in sound. I married her and she has been my faithful woman for more than forty years. I am raising a little orphan girl whose mother died a few years ago, and have named her Comes Out Of The Water.

After marrying this woman I seemed to be more successful and gained the respect of our people.

Then eleven of us went on a raid, riding down the Bighorn River until we found a Sioux camp where we captured many horses. As we were coming back we discovered another enemy camp near Dirt River where it runs into Big River, and stole more horses. When we finally rode into our village on the Musselshell River we drove over fifty head before us. There was a big celebration over our success. Among my six head was a fine black horse with which I won many races in later years.

Chapter Twenty-Eight

*About a year after the Crows signed the Fort Laramie treaty
of 1868, construction began on a sawmill, the new agency's
first building, near a mountain called Hide Flesher by the
Crows—close to today's Livingston, Montana. Distribution of
such presents as yellow blankets was organized through
Fort Ellis, a few miles west. Soldiers escorted wagons to the
Yellowstone and the goods were issued on the river's
north bank. But by September 1869, Superintendent A. Sully
was lamenting the new agent's delay and the absence of nearly
2,000 Mountain Crows who were south
on their winter hunt.*

*When Agent E. M. Camp and his steamboat-load of annuity
goods—clothing, food, and agricultural supplies—finally did
arrive from Fort Benton, the new man found problems on
his hands. The River Crows, whom he tried to persuade to
leave their temporary residence with the Atsina and
Assiniboines and move south permanently, were being
taunted by the Sioux: "We are rich and ride fat horses and
have plenty, while you are friends to the whites and are poor
and have no horses." And at home the Mountain Crows showed
little inclination for the "arts of civilization."*

AFTER RETURNING from that raid when we stole horses from the two
camps we stayed along the Musselshell and Elk rivers, and all the
time I remained in camp. Chokecherry-ripening time was coming
and one day I visited my medicine father. We did not talk while
smoking, but afterward he called me his son and told me not to
leave camp until another war party returned with a man killed. Its

177

warriors would ask me a favor which I must do. He advised me to alert my friends about this.

A few days later a war party with Big Shoulder as pipeholder rode quietly into camp and soon we heard wailing. As I left my tipi I saw Weasel Sits Down's wife sticking a knife into her head and gashing her arms and legs, leaving a trail of blood wherever she walked. When she tried to cut off her finger end her relatives took away the knife. Her husband had been Big Shoulder's brother. But the pipeholder had not acted properly and Weasel Sits Down had been killed.[1] Now Big Shoulder went into the hills to mourn.

An agency had already been built near the present town of Livingston and it was time to pick up our annuity goods. While on our way Sees The Living Bull told me that the night before he had dreamt of a blanket rising into the air and falling in a coulee. He had also heard a woman crying. If something happened in camp, he said, I was not to go because there would be fighting.

We reached the agency, received our annuity goods, and enjoyed many dances and feasts. A few days later we moved downriver and camped near a creek. The next morning as I went for my horses I noticed someone galloping toward camp. Upon returning I learned that Sioux had stolen horses the night before and two men who had chased the thieves had been killed.

Until now I had acted as I had wanted. But I had met with such bad luck that now I followed my medicine father's advice and did not go out. Some men returned late that night and said that after they had seen their friends killed they had surrounded the Sioux, killing two before they escaped.

The following morning I did something foolish and looked at the bodies of our men. Rawhide had tried to strike a man with his coup stick but was shot down before he got close. Coyote had been killed when he rode too near. Both were well liked and our camp mourned again.

I was invited to my medicine father's tipi the next morning along with Crooked Arm, Two Belly, and some older men. When I arrived Sees The Living Bull motioned for me to sit and, after our smoke, said that the time was near for what he had seen, that soon we would be painting our faces black. He told me to have my wife sew some extra moccasins, to get my horse ready, and to check my gun and ammunition. I was to be ready to start the morning after the pipe had been

178

offered to me. In the meantime he would build me another sweat lodge from one hundred and four willows.

Then he took a willow twig, bent it into a hoop, and tied on seven eagle feathers in a fan shape. After painting them black he offered this to the sky, praying to the Great Above Person that I would meet the enemy and have good luck.

Once I had accepted the pipe from Big Shoulder he said I would have to do whatever he asked. There was more talking during that gathering, most of it about the recent bad happenings.

Each day I expected Big Shoulder but ten days later he offered his pipe to Long Otter. He accepted and moved his followers some distance from the main camp to perform his medicine ceremony in private. When Sees The Living Bull heard of this he said that if Big Shoulder approached me with the same offer I should refuse, but to prepare my own raid.

Soon we heard that Long Otter and some men and even women were leaving. When I told my medicine father he said there was no hurry, that when the time came he would tell me. After Long Otter's party had left, he said, I would kill a man and return safely. He had dreamt of enemies moving along the lower reaches of the Mussel-shell River and promised to tell me when they got close. Now he located them camped among the first pine trees close to the Bull Mountains.

The next day Sees The Living Bull said that he had dreamt of shining light near Elk River, where Park City now stands. I was to go beyond that place. My war party would have to be small because so many had joined Long Otter. He said that today I should announce I was ready.

A number of men asked to join. Before sunrise the following day Sees The Living Bull and his wife came singing to my tipi. She carried a flannel blanket. I remember their song: "It is getting spring now. Thank you."

While they waited outside Sees The Living Bull called my name and asked if I saw that big scalp. He had dreamt again and had seen a long black scalp falling from the sky. I sang my medicine father's song which I loved to hear. It was very powerful and I had often used it to help me out of dangerous situations. This way Sees The Living Bull had given me his dream and I had thanked him with his song.

179

When they entered my tipi I gave him the seat at the back, across from the entrance. After we had smoked he told me not to worry that the pipe had not been offered to me. Now, he said, we would have to be satisfied with a smaller success, but would still paint our faces black.

He told me to start at dawn the next day, to travel on the river's other side, and to stop for the first night at a place he would indicate later. Then I was to cross Where They Ran Away From Camp Creek where I would have a vision of a big eagle carrying a long-haired man in its claws. When I had traveled to Painted Blanket Creek I would see the eagle drop the body. As I neared Flat Butte, close to the present site of Park City, I should take the blanket he had brought and spread it out. Then I was to place a necklace he would give me around my neck, open my medicine, and sing the songs he had taught me. After that I should hold the medicine up to my eyes and look under it for a further vision. Before reaching this place I would see some deer running through the brush and was to kill one and skin it. He said that when I performed this medicine ceremony I should also spread that deer hide before me.

Then he handed me his straight medicine pipe [2] and his own insignia which he had carried on raids in his younger days. For some time I had been a pipeholder, but I had never been trusted with such powerful things and felt too proud to speak. I promised myself not to shame him in any way. Holding the pipe in my hand I prayed to the Great Above Person that all my future trails would be successful.

Over seventy men, more than I had expected, rode out with me at first light. I sang as I led them, certain that we would return with our faces painted black. Following my medicine father's instructions I crossed to the northern bank of Elk River and traveled slowly through the valley. Since the first day's ride was short we would stop and smoke. As we approached our camping place I sent men ahead to kill a few buffalo, start a fire, and make a brush shelter. Upon arriving we ate, smoked, and slept until dawn.

Everything happened as Sees The Living Bull had said. The next day we arrived at the place where he had told me to open my medicine bundle, so I prepared a temporary camp. When we discovered that Long Otter and his party were camped within sight I forbade anyone to visit them. Big Shoulder was in that band and I told my men that if he came around he was to be told that I did not want to see him or speak to him. Some of Long Otter's men visited us that evening and I tried to learn their leader's plans, but they said they knew nothing.

I told my men to sit in a circle and took my place at the western end. One Blue Bead was on my right and I asked him to light my pipe. After smoking I gave it to the man on my left. No one talked while it passed around.

I spread out the blanket Sees The Living Bull had given me. Earlier in the day we had seen some deer and I had sent two men to kill one. Now I spread its skin over the blanket. Laying my war medicine bundle on it I built a little smudge. After everyone had smoked I purified my hands in the sweet-grass smoke and began unwrapping my bundle. When I had finished I picked up a little paint bag filled with sacred red paint and painted a red circle around my face with my right index finger. Then I reddened my eyelids and painted a red streak across my mouth. I told my men that I wanted them all to shout after my war medicine song: "When the geese come back, I know the country where I am going."

They shouted and clapped their hands to their mouths. I blew my eagle-bone whistle and raised my medicine to my eyes. When someone asked what I saw I said an enemy track leading into tall pine trees and a large flying eagle with a man's body in its claws. The man's feet dangled in the air and a robe which had been wrapped around his body fell among the pines on Painted Blanket Creek. After a day's travel, I said, we would head for that place.

Then I had camp moved to Where They Ran Away From Camp Creek not far away. Early the following morning I opened the medicine-pipe bundle Sees The Living Bull had given me and told all the warriors to sit in another circle. The man on my right lit the pipe, and after I smoked it was passed around until it was smoked out. I chose scouts and made them promise to report only what they actually saw. They replied that they had smoked with me, meaning they could not lie. Then they rode ahead, each wearing the wolfskin cap which was his badge.

I had told them to wait at a certain place if they saw no enemies. But about the middle of the day we heard their howls and soon saw them, waving their guns over their heads. I quickly ordered my men to pile dried buffalo chips in front of me and then we sat in a circle.

The scouts jumped off their ponies, kicked over the chips, and waved their guns again. The kicking meant they would tell the truth and the waving of their guns meant enemies. After sitting on my left, where a place had been kept, they asked for a smoke. I lit the filled pipe and passed it to the scout on my left. While it went around the chief scout told me that they had spotted a Sioux on horseback looking for game on a hillside. They thought this meant a large war party was camped nearby. After their report the scouts returned to keep watch through the night.

The next morning we ate dried meat because we did not want to light a fire, then joined the scouts. One met us at the foot of some hills to say that Sioux were camped on the other side. The night before they had not rested until they had counted the tipis. Leaving our extra horses tied to some branches with helpers to guard them, we followed him up to a wooded ridge.

The other scouts were lying at different points, hidden by sage bushes held in front of them. I dismounted and crawled to the chief scout. Just then four hunters left the Sioux tipis, riding straight for our ridge. Crawling back to my horse, I told my men to prepare their medicines and unwrapped my own. After singing my medicine song I blew the war whistle which was part of my bundle. When One Blue Bead told me not to whistle too loudly I said that my medicine father had told me the enemy would look up for a bird and not see us coming.

I whistled again, prayed to the Great Above Person, and sang a medicine song: "Big Bird Above is kind to us. I am watching toward the enemy. All enemies will easily be influenced. It is easy."

Then I raised my medicine to my eyes. Under it an enemy body hung in the sky. Our scouts made signs that the hunters were within gunshot. My men had tied on their medicines and had painted their faces with their personal sacred colors. We dismounted and crawled to watch them ride closer. I wore only my breechcloth and moccasins and carried my medicine pipe and bundle on my back. As I began running forward with my gun I bent low. Looking up, I saw the four Sioux about twenty steps away. One carried a robe over his gun; I recognized the man who had fallen from the sky. As I shot him I called to my men to attack. The other Sioux tried to get away when they saw him fall. He bent down to pick up his gun but did not have enough strength. High Hawk was a step behind me and ran up. Blood pouring out of his mouth and nose, the Sioux tried to draw his knife. But High Hawk clubbed him to death with his gun butt and scalped his whole hair. Cutting it into three pieces, he gave one to me and one to Pretty Tail who had joined us.

The rest mounted to chase the other three Sioux and quickly returned with one scalp. During a short council some suggested keeping after them but I said we did not have enough fast horses to risk approaching their camp. Besides, we did not know how many men were in their tipis. I told them that I wanted to return singing victory songs and have the women dance for us so our last defeat would be forgotten.

A few days later we drew near our village. Long Otter and his band also seemed to have come back successfully because we heard drums and singing as we stopped for the night. But I was proud of our raid and this did not bother me.

At dawn I led the men into camp, carrying a pole with my piece of scalp waving from the end. Those who had counted coup came first, the ones with pieces of the two scalps followed, and the rest rode behind.

Some of us were singing our medicine songs and the people received us with shouting. Then there were days full of feasting and singing and dancing. Everywhere I heard my name called out as a successful pipeholder. I had achieved what I had fought for, and I was proud.

Chapter Twenty-Nine

Except for an incident in autumn, 1887, the Crows were well known for their peaceable demeanor toward whites. Accounts describe white men raising their guns at the approach of mounted Indians, and lowering them in relief when the warriors formed their palms into flapping wings—sign language for Crows.

While the Government never heeded the repeated suggestions of its agents to arm the Crows, for their own good and to protect settlers from Sioux hostiles, it did hire them to perform scouting and courier duties. Crows accompanied General George Crook on the Rosebud River, General Nelson Miles against the Sioux and Bannocks, General John Gibbon against the Sioux, and General Oliver Howard in his pursuit of the Nez Percés.

The one exception began with the return of a successful war party led by a half-Crow, half-Bannock upstart named Wraps Up His Tail, or Swordbearer. When Agent H. Williamson burst into the celebrating crowd surrounding his government domicile, a wild shot passed over his head. Before his order to arrest the boistrous warriors could be carried out, the insurgents had fled to the mountains. A month later, after the group had surrendered, the twenty-four-year-old rebel, three followers, and one Army corporal were killed in a small melee.

SHORTLY AFTER THE CUSTER BATTLE we were camped above the present town of Forsyth. One day I noticed a soldier in buckskins ride up to Two Belly's tipi and a little later the crier rode through the village, announcing that scouts were wanted for the army chasing the Sioux

184

and Cheyennes. Two Belly sent a messenger asking me to his tipi. When I arrived some younger men were already there. Two Belly said that the Sioux and Cheyennes were all over our hunting places and that we should help the soldiers drive them back to their own country. Some of us might be killed, but he said that would not be as bad as having our land taken, losing our horses, or living in constant danger. I was doing nothing and told him I could leave any time. About thirty of us offered to join the soldiers. The soldier in buckskins wanted us to come with him immediately, so Two Belly had the crier tell us to bring in our horses.

The sun was down by the time we left. About the middle of the night we rode into the soldiers' camp and were given a good meal of buffalo meat. It was the first time I tasted coffee and I liked it. We ate fast and mounted again, accompanying the soldiers up Elk River to the mouth of the Rosebud River. On the other side the main soldiers' camp looked like a gathering of several large tribes.[1] A soldier rode toward us and handed a note to our guide, who then told us to follow him. Riding into the middle of that big camp I wondered if all the United States soldiers were there. It was dawn and we were tired and hungry. After being given some meat, crackers, and more coffee, we spent the remainder of the day resting. I was lying on the ground half asleep when a strange noise made us all jump up. We had never heard a bugle before.

A few moments later two soldiers with marks on their sleeves asked for two scouts to ride up the Rosebud River toward the hills and deliver a note to another group of soldiers. They explained that since our horses were tired they would give us fresh mounts. I was standing close to these soldiers and understood what they meant. Although I hoped they would not call me they must have already decided because after asking for Spotted Horse they spoke my name. I pretended to be asleep. The soldier waited a moment, looked at his paper, and spoke my name again. I stood up and walked over.

Spotted Horse and I were told that the soldiers were a day's ride up the river. A big brown horse and a bay were led out to us and Spotted Horse chose the brown. Both were beautiful and in the best condition and I did not care which I rode. When we left at sunset a few soldiers accompanied us but soon turned back. It quickly grew dark and since we had been told not to stop we rode until dawn, when we spotted a soldier on a hilltop. He rode down and after we gave him the note he led us to his camp.

Then we ate a good meal and rested until the middle of the day, when three more scouts rode in from different directions. There was no interpreter, so we did not find out what was happening. The officer in charge called us to his tent and made us understand that we could return to the other camp at sunset. We slept until the bugle made us jump again and a soldier handed us another note to take back. Once more some soldiers escorted us a little distance.

Then we were riding alone in the night. When the moon rose there was enough light to gallop. Although no enemies had been reported we were still careful. Before dawn, as we came close to the camp, I noticed that my horse did not seem to feel my quirt and told Spotted Horse that we should rest. After picketing our horses in some thick grass along the river bottom we slept until sunup.

I woke first and went for the horses. The bay seemed fine but the big brown horse was dead. Spotted Horse could hardly believe it. It must have been too fat. We ate some of the soldiers' food we had been given and rode double slowly. As we approached the camp a soldier lookout rode down the hill and accompanied us.

We were taken to the commanding officer and through an interpreter I told him that we had been ordered to ride hard and that one horse had died. We were afraid he might be angry but he said that horses and men must die sometime and since it was dead to forget it.

Spotted Horse and I felt better and thanked him. We stayed there that night and the next morning the bugle frightened me again. We built a cooking fire and, while we were eating, a soldier came over to explain that there was no more danger from the enemy and that we could go. He gave us a large quantity of meat for the trip back. We were glad to be going home and started singing as soon as we were out of the camp. On the trail we killed two deer and arrived at our tipis on the banks of Tullock Creek long after dark with plenty of meat.

I rested a day before riding over to Two Belly's camp, which had moved to the mouth of the Bighorn River. After I told him what had happened he said that whenever possible I should help the soldiers kill Sioux. If they were not driven off, the land we wanted for our children would be stolen. He said that long ago, when the Sioux had come from the south, we had moved to the Big River country. When other enemies had threatened us from the north we had moved west. All we wanted, he said, was to be left alone. But we must always be on our guard and always carry guns.

We helped the white man so we could own our land in peace. Our blood is mixed in the ground with the blood of white soldiers. We did not know they were going to take our land. That is what they gave us for our friendship.

Chapter Thirty

*Although by 1875 all the River Crows were at the Livingston
agency and had promised to remain through the following
winter, the tribe never felt at home there. The site was too far
from hunting grounds and sources of timber, too vulnerable
to enemy attack. That same year the agency was removed
to fifteen miles south of the Yellowstone River on Rosebud Creek.
Despite heavy Sioux raiding, twelve buildings were erected. Yet
this area also did not satisfy the Crows. They considered the
land unsuitable for farming and complained of the huge cattle
drives heading for the Union Pacific Railroad in southern
Wyoming. And the agents themselves were worried about
the proximity of whiskey peddlers.*

*In 1880, when the Crows yielded to the Government a
1,300,000-acre slice of their reservation, the remaining land
was allotted to individuals. Payment for the partition was to be
through yearly amounts earmarked for domestic improvements.
Then the Crows entered into another treaty granting right
of way along the Yellowstone to the Northern Pacific Railroad.
But it was not until April 1884 that the shift began to the third
and final agency on the Little Bighorn River, the first of the
new inhabitants being those Crows who had made
some gains in farming.*

ABOUT THREE YEARS after the battle of the Little Bighorn River we
were camped on the banks of the Bighorn River just south of the present site of Hardin. Already there were fewer buffalo on the plains and
we had to move frequently to feed ourselves. From there we traveled
to Elk River, camped briefly close to the Mountain Lion's Lodge,
and then moved slowly to Arrow Creek. Soon we moved to Fly Creek

and then into the Bighorn Valley. We needed hides for our tipis and a returning war party told of more herds near the Bighorn Mountains. After hunting there the chiefs announced that the men were to cut tipi poles in the mountains and no one could leave camp for any other reason. When we cut enough we returned to Arrow Creek, and then Two Belly, Goes Around, and their followers decided to head toward Big River while the main camp wintered near the Arrowhead Mountains. I followed Two Belly and on our way we pitched our tipis along the Musselshell River for a few days.

My medicine father was in Two Belly's camp and invited me to his tipi. After our usual smoke and talking about different things he said he had made me another medicine. Then he unwrapped a bundle, smudged it, sang a song, and told me to look under it. When I did this he pointed, asking if I saw about a hundred head of horses. I said I could not see them. He said he had been given those horses in a dream and told me where to find them once winter set in.

Medicine Crow and ten others said that when the time came they wanted to join me. For some reason our camp did not make the move to Big River but traveled farther west along the Musselshell. Every day I visited Sees The Living Bull and he promised to tell me when to leave. Then the first snows fell and one day he said he had dreamt again. I told my friends to be ready at sunup, but wanted them first to help me build a large sweat lodge of one hundred and four willows. Along with Sees The Living Bull I invited several chiefs and medicine men. While we took our bath they prayed for us at the entrance.

At dawn we rode out of camp. The snow was ankle deep and the weather very cold. Reaching Big River we rode along its southern shore, building brush shelters each night. Once I dreamt of a man standing beside my bed. As I stared he asked if I saw a black horse and a gray with some blood marks on its side. He told me to hurry because the enemy had left the gray behind and it was mine.

When I woke it was still dark. I told my companions about the horses and had them prepare a meal. As we started to ride, black clouds were rushing across the sky and the air was filled with little bits of snow which cut our faces. The snowfall grew heavier and we stopped to build a brush shelter near Where The Bear Sits Down Mountain.

Then a full blizzard was blowing and we stayed in that shelter for two days. The morning of the third day broke cold and clear, but before leaving I sent a scout to the mountaintop. When the sun was in the middle he returned to report a large Sioux camp just across Big River. Leading my men around the mountain to the south I found both banks of the river solid sheets of ice. Towards the middle, big ice blocks tumbled downstream. I told my men that if we stole the horses my medicine had promised they could never follow us back across. Tonight, I said, we would hide in the thick woods and tomorrow we would cross.

It was cold and quiet as we sat around a low fire listening to the Sioux drums. Early the next morning I was looking for a place to cross. After leading my men around a bend, Medicine Crow and I cut two long poles and built a raft big enough to carry our clothes, weapons, and medicines. Then we attached two thongs, broke the ice along the bank, and pushed it in. When I jumped into the water it was so cold I could hardly breathe. Someone handed me a rope and I tried to pull my horse while the men on shore whipped it. It reared and tugged back but finally we got it in. Medicine Crow followed and we each pulled on his horse until it reared backward into the river. Then we were suddenly going with the current and struggling for the other side. Medicine Crow called out for me to hang onto my rope or we would both drown. But the water made me too numb to answer.

Then one huge ice cake seemed about to hit us or cut us off from our raft. The Great Above Person and my medicine must have heard my prayers because a current turned it from the raft. We had to push smaller blocks out of our way but finally reached the northern shore. The ice was too thick to break and the water here seemed more powerful, almost pulling us, the raft, and our horses under the sheets lining the bank. But as we were carried along I felt gravel, and when I walked up, the water was to my waist. Medicine Crow and I climbed onto the ice, still holding the raft's thongs. When we got the horses' forefeet on the edge their weight broke it and we repeated this until they had cut a way for themselves to the bank.

We were too cold to feel anything and our horses were shivering. Leading them into the thick trees we built a fire and put on the dry clothes we had wrapped up on the raft. Then we brought the horses close to the fire and rubbed them with dry hay. After eating some of the meat we had brought, we mounted. The river had carried us a little distance down from the Sioux camp. Finally we tied our horses to some trees at the base of a high hill and climbed up to judge its size. No Sioux were riding in our direction. When we returned to our fire it was the middle of the day and the sun felt warm. Our

190

men had built two rafts and now they floated across while Medicine Crow and I took turns watching the camp.

When we were all together I told them to take out their medicines and paint themselves. I unwrapped the medicine Sees The Living Bull had given me of a big hawk's head and tail. Then I made another smudge of white pine needles and sang my medicine song: "There is another thing I am going to get."

Holding the hawk's head in my left hand and the tail in my right I raised and lowered them over the smudge. As I looked under them I said that my medicine had shown me those horses and asked it to help me get them tonight.

Someone asked me to lend him the hawk's head, promising me a good horse if he captured any. I tied it to his hair and wore the hawk tail fastened to the back of my own head.

The sun was down by the time we began riding toward their camp. As I led them north of the camp, where the land was cut with deep coulees, the snow was up to our horses' knees. Coming upon a bunch of horses we rounded them up and I left two guards. We ran into another bunch and when we had them surrounded I chose seven men to drive all the horses toward the Wolf Mountains without waiting for us.

Then I heard a Sioux crier announcing something and was sure they had discovered us. But when drums began and women started singing we knew it was only a celebration. Medicine Crow and I and a man whose name I have forgotten rode toward the village to cut horses picketed in front of the tipis. As we crossed a path worn down by horses going to their feeding grounds we saw a small group of horses ahead. While I rode on, Medicine Crow and the other man rounded them up. But I ran into more and drove them back without any trouble.

We had captured over a hundred head, the night was still early, and we had a good chance to get away. It would bring me greater honors to lead them safely back without having killed a man, and I did not want to spoil this. I felt that my medicine had kept the Sioux's attention off their horses.

We did not return to our morning camp site, but turned north into the hills and made a wide circle westward, leaving a good distance between us and the village. We galloped all that night, reaching the Wolf Mountains just before daybreak. Coming over a high ridge, we saw in the distance the rest of our men with the other horses.

Then all of us rode through the next day and night, changing mounts often. We did not eat or sleep until we reached Big River early in the morning and immediately built rafts for our clothes, weapons, and two men too tired to swim. Medicine Crow and I waited until last, keeping the horses from climbing back up the bank. When everything was on the other side we crossed. Then I was not so afraid the Sioux would catch us and built a fire to warm ourselves and dry our clothes. Later we came upon a small buffalo herd and I sent four men on good buffalo runners to kill four. That night we ate roasted ribs, and cooked enough for the trip back.

Now there was no danger of being overtaken and we all felt good. As I rode I thought of the celebration waiting for us and of the praise I would receive for being leader. I pictured the older men leading me through camp, singing songs about me, and calling out my name. I was so happy I sang my medicine song: "Anywhere I go, I thank you."

The bunch of horses running before us looked so fine I could not help myself and sang my song again.

We found our camp on the other side of Heart Mountain on Plum Creek. As we came into sight and fired our guns everyone came out to greet us. We rode into the center of camp, the women started to dance and sing, and some men pulled out their drums. Thirty-three horses were mine and each man also had a good bunch. When our story was told I received more praise than ever before.

Years later I learned that we had captured those horses from Sitting Bull's camp on its way to Canada.[1]

Chapter Thirty-One

Although the Crows were starting to live in permanent homes, till their fields, and send their children to schools, they continued raiding. Wrote Agent H. Williamson in 1886, "With the Crows much trouble is occasioned. They desire to pursue the thieves and retaliate in kind, which is very natural. . . ."

A year later, the Swordbearer incident occurred. In 1888, Two Leggings undertook this revenge trail against the Sioux, supposedly the last Crow war party. A letter from the Commissioner of Indian Affairs in 1887 to all his agents had done much to halt these raids by prohibiting intertribal visits and outlawing absences from the reservation without government permission.

Crows did not like to speak of the following years. As Two Leggings recalled his people's feelings during the thirty-five-year interval until his death, "their hearts were on the ground." By 1923 the reservation was roughly a third its original acreage and the Crow population had dropped to 1,772. The scarred warriors tried to farm their allotted lands, but they lived in their memories. Two Leggings welcomed his approaching death and told Wildschut, "Soon I shall live again those days of which I now only dream, soon I shall hunt the buffalo."

THREE YEARS BEFORE THIS HAPPENED the Government forbade our raids, but sometimes a man gathered a party and sneaked away. I was already living in a more permanent camp on the Bighorn River where I later built my house. The buffalo were gone and we received weekly annuities from Fort Custer, built on a ridge top across the river from my tipi. It was early summer and the rivers were swollen, but the soldiers had made a ferry.[1]

One ration day Pretty Old Man, who was camped with us, and I arranged to cross the ferry and then ride to the ration house. I went to choose a horse from my herd grazing along the timbered bottom that lines the Bighorn River. After catching one I rode toward the low ridge bordering the western valley wall, wondering if Pretty Old Man's horse had strayed. Usually it did not take him this long.

Reaching the crest of a coulee I saw him sitting on the ground not far away. As he made signs for me to stop he shouted that someone had stolen his horses and that their tracks led north.

My wife had followed behind me. When she caught up I told her to ride to the ferry and tell our friends that I was leading a raid, even if I had to go into Piegan country.

After she left, Pretty Old Man and I rode double back to my horses. I caught a fast, long-winded horse for him and we returned to my home to collect our medicines and weapons. Pretty Old Man's wife and children were crying inside his tipi. It had become almost impossible to replace horses.

On the way to the ferry we met One Leg, White Clay On The Forehead, and Eagle riding to meet us. Four inexperienced men with them were very eager to chase the enemy. All lived close by and went for their weapons and medicines. When they returned we found enemy tracks on a ridge leading into the Pine Ridge Hills. Farther on we stopped so I could scan the country with my telescope and see if any more were joining us, but I saw no one. When we stopped again to rest our horses and dry our saddlecloths Pretty Old Man, who had hung behind, rode up crying over his horses. Putting his arms around my neck he asked me to make medicine so we could catch them. I said I would try to cut them off, but promised that if I could not locate them we would keep on their trail.

I had Pretty Old Man fill and light my pipe while I unwrapped my medicine. Then I took it from him and drew several times, pointing the stem towards the enemy each time and asking it to smoke them to sleep so I could prepare my ambush. I spoke to the One Up There In The Sky and said he had taught me to do this. I asked him to help as he had many times before.

When I asked White Clay On The Forehead which earth creatures move very slowly he said that one of the slowest was the beetle that rolls manure into little balls and pushes them along the ground.

I said he was right and had a man find me one. Making a smudge and building a little earth bank across the enemy trail, I took the beetle and waited for it to crawl over. I showed Pretty Old Man how it fell backward each time it tried.

Then I made another smudge of white pine needles and held my medicine in it. After singing my medicine song and blowing my whistle I lifted the medicine to my eyes. The second time I blew my whistle I moved the medicine up and down. Something white was thrown into the air and fell into some rose bushes which grew in a certain place along Elk River. I told my men the enemy was sleeping in Elk River Valley and we would take a shorter route.

One Leg asked me to let them rest a little longer. While I was making medicine he had noticed three more friends racing to meet us. Pretty Old Man was still walking around crying and I told him that he had seen me make medicine, that we would find his horses in Elk River Valley not far from the Mountain Lion's Lodge.

When Buffalo Calf, Fence, and Bird Fire joined us we left the northern trail and rode west toward the present town of Toluca. From there we went to Fly Creek, which we followed to Elk River, keeping away from the rough Pine Ridge Hills.

The railroad had already been built and a section house stood where we finally came out of a creek bottom, close to the present town of Ballantine.[2] I halted the men to point out the grove where I had seen the blanket fall, about four miles away. We were hidden by the trees around the section house.

Then an eagle rose from the grove, dropped to the ground near us, and sat for a moment before heading toward the mountains. I told my men the eagle had told me Piegans were in those trees and now it was flying home. We rode quietly until someone spotted horses tied to bushes. But the three men I sent after them woke the Piegans, who burst out as if crazy. One took his gun but left his cartridge belt and knife behind; the other two stumbled into the undergrowth along the river. I noticed one wore a white blanket like the man in my vision.

After all our stolen horses were rounded up we mounted fresh. One Leg started ahead, yelling that since he was a cripple he might as well die now. I called him back to wait until I had gathered all the men in a tight bunch and ridden around them singing my medicine song. Then I unwrapped my medicine and saw under it another vision of the falling white blanket. The other men had also unwrapped their bundles and now each fastened his to his hair or wherever it was required to go.

Thunder sounded from the west and I knew they might escape if we did not kill them before the rain. Just as in my vision, we saw them trying to hide in the bushes. We dismounted when we were within gunshot, covering all three sides, the river at their backs. Buffalo Calf remounted to ride over to me but was shot off his horse. When One Leg ran from his tree the man with the white blanket shot but missed. The second time I fired back I broke his gunstock and wounded him. As he tried to run away I shot him in the back and he fell.

Then the rain poured so heavily we could hardly see the bushes. The thunder was very loud and there was much lightning. We found shelter, but when the storm was over it was too dark to follow.

The night grew so cold we went to the section house and asked the man in charge if we could stay, making him understand that we were Crows. He said it was all right if we carried in some firewood. We tied our horses, leaving Pretty Old Man outside to guard them, built a fire, brought in some firewood, and went to sleep. We were all very hungry but had brought no food. During the night Pretty Old Man woke me to say that two men were riding toward the section house. I joined him outside, telling him to shoot if they approached our horses. As they came onto the flat I saw they were two white men wearing hats. We shared their hot tea, canned beef and tongue, and crackers, and slept until dawn.

There was no need to be careful as we rode down river; whoever had been left alive would be far away. Riding over to the bushes, I found the Piegan's body. After scalping his whole head I cut it into four parts, giving one to White Eye, one to Short Bull, and keeping the other two. Also I carried away his rifle. We discovered that they were Sioux and not Piegans. (Years later, after peace was made between all tribes, I learned that this man had been a chief's son.)

When we returned to our camp we drove the captured horses through the tipis and I carried my scalp pieces tied to the end of a long pole. Soon the camp was alive, men brought out their drums, and the women began the scalp dance. I led the singing: "Across the river in those rough hills there is a scalp."

Everyone joined in. For several days there was feasting and dancing. I was invited everywhere and told the story over and over again.

We were happy. Now it seems so long ago. It all changed. The Government would not let us leave the reservation. We even had to have special permission to hunt.

Shortly after this raid the commander at Fort Custer, whom we called Lump Nose, sent for me.[3] I expected him to put me in prison, but I still went. When I entered his room he stood up to shake my hand and I felt better. He asked what had happened and after I had finished he said that enemies had stolen my horses and I had got them back, killing one of the thieves. He said I had done well. When he asked if I wanted something to eat I said yes and he went to a bureau and took out a coin. Saying he was my friend he told me to get something I liked. Again he shook my hand and I thanked him. When I got outside I looked at the strange gift. But when I went to the store and found all the things I could buy with the five-dollar gold piece, I understood.

Nothing happened after that. We just lived. There were no more war parties, no capturing of horses from the Piegans and the Sioux, no buffalo to hunt. There is nothing more to tell.

Selected Bibliography

CURTIS, EDWARD S. *The North American Indian.* 20 vols. Norwood, Massachusetts: 1907–1930.

DENIG, EDWIN THOMPSON. *Five Indian Tribes of the Upper Missouri.* Edited and with an Introduction by John C. Ewers. Norman: University of Oklahoma Press, 1961.

LINDERMAN, FRANK BIRD. *Old Man Coyote.* New York: The John Day Co., 1931.

———. *Plenty Coups, Chief of the Crows.* Lincoln: University of Nebraska Press, 1962.

———. *Red Mother.* New York: The John Day Co., 1932.

LOWIE, ROBERT H. *The Crow Indians.* New York: Holt, Rinehart and Winston, Inc., 1956.

———. *Crow Texts.* Berkeley and Los Angeles: University of California, 1960.

———. *Indians of the Plains.* Garden City, New York: The Natural History Press, 1963.

———. Anthropological Papers, American Museum of Natural History, New York:

    The Material Culture of the Crow Indians. Vol. XXI, Part III, 1922.

    Religion of the Crow Indians. Vol. XXV, Part II, 1922.

    Social Life of the Crow Indians. Vol. IX, Part II, 1912.

MARQUIS, THOMAS H. *Memoirs of a White Crow Indian.* New York: The Century Company, 1928.

WILDSCHUT, WILLIAM; and EWERS, JOHN C. *Crow Indian Medicine Bundles.* (Contributions, Vol. XVII.) New York: Museum of the American Indian, Heye Foundation, 1960.

Notes

Chapter One

1. Wildschut originally used "sleeps" for days, "moons" for months, and "snows" for years. According to Crow informants Joseph Medicine Crow and Roger Stops, only "moons" is accurate. If one wanted to say how long it took to travel somewhere or to do something one would use *ba-ko-a*, a short word referring to how many times the sun came up. These present-day informants agree with Lowie's names for the four seasons: winter, *bǎ're*; spring, *bǐ'awukase'*; summer, *bǐ'awakee'*; and autumn, *basé*. Lowie adds that years were designated as "winters." He corroborates Two Leggings' use of colorful phrases identifying seasons: when the ice breaks, when the leaves sprout, when the berries are ripe, when the leaves turn yellow, when the leaves fall, and when the first snow falls. Specific years were remembered by some significant event attached to them (*Social Life of the Crow Indians*, p. 242).

2. Since clans were exogamous—one had to marry into a clan other than one's own—they could never be purely separate residential groups. While Two Leggings or Wildschut would seem to mean here the coming together of the three tribal divisions, Curtis does note the independence of certain clans, specifically the numerically strong Whistling Waters, who around 1850 would absent themselves from the main body for long hunting expeditions and were probably an incipient fourth tribal division (*The North American Indian*, Vol. IV, 1909, p. 43).

Chapter Two

1. No major figure in a Crow orphan myth bears the name of Bear White Child. However, Wildschut obtained the skull medicine bundle of one White Child (*Crow Indian Medicine Bundles*, pp. 79–80). Lowie mentioned the tooth from a White Cub, "the greatest of Crow Shamans" (*Religion of the Crow Indians*, p. 420). Finally, Plenty Coups told

Wildschut of a famous skull medicine bundle of Bear White Child which he had seen opened by Bear in The Water and Yellow Bull (Wildschut, Unpublished Papers). Quite possibly an historical personage is being placed in the murky realm of Crow quasi-historical legend.

Chapter Three

1. The Blackfeet nation consisted of three bands. Ewers writes: "They are the Pikuni or Piegan (pronounced Pay-gan'), the Kainah or Blood, and the Siksika or Blackfoot proper, often referred to as the Northern Blackfeet to distinguish it from the other two tribes. The three tribes were politically independent. But they spoke the same language, shared the same customs (with the exception of a few ceremonial rituals), intermarried, and made war upon common enemies" (John C. Ewers, *The Blackfeet, Raiders of the Northwestern Plains* [Norman: University of Oklahoma Press, 1958], p. 5).

2. When the Crows smoked to sanctify a get-together and assure the speaking of truth, they usually filled the red-stone pipe bowls with traders' tobacco mixed with the leaf of a certain ground vine called *ópicè*. In recent times red willow bark is smoked (Lowie, *The Material Culture of the Crow Indians*, p. 234).

    However, I found the old mixture still used, with Bull Durham substituted for traders' tobacco and a third ingredient of a few shavings from a root traded from the Nez Percé added to each bowl.

3. Wildschut noted here: "During the last few moments of our talk a close friend of Two Leggings, Bull Does Not Fall Down, had silently seated himself next to me. When Two Leggings finished he spoke to me, 'I was in camp when Shows His Wing's party returned and I remember how Two Leggings, then called Big Crane, was praised. He did not tell me until many summers later that his words had not been straight. But he had only been a boy and we laughed about it.' "

4. Curtis reports the custom in reverse: If one of your father's clan brothers falls down before you it is necessary to say "Stop! Do not rise" and to present him with a gift before he stands (*The North American Indian*, Vol. IV, 1909, p. 24).

Chapter Four

1. Curtis described the Crows' first knives, which they obtained from the Gros Ventres, as having blue-dyed bone handles (*The North American Indian*, Vol. IV, 1909, p. 46).

2. Unlike the Hidatsa and Mandan, the Crows did not employ the cup-shaped bull boat for transporting men and supplies. Lowie describes

their two methods of water transportation: "In case of a small party with horses, three sticks were arranged to form a triangle, or four to make a rectangle, and a hide was spread over and fastened securely to the edges. This raft was then towed by the horses. Larger parties made their frame of parallel tipi poles with the required number of hides over them, the cargo being put on top.

"The other method was to place several buffalo hides on top of one another and run a gathering-string round the edge of the lowest one, causing the robes to assume a globular form. The articles to be kept dry were put in with a stone ballast and the skins were towed by means of a line. In shallow water the tower pulled the contrivance by hand, otherwise he swam holding the line between his teeth" (*The Material Culture of the Crow Indians*, p. 219).

3. Plenty Coups remembers a famous Chief Long Horse who was killed fighting Sioux sometime after the erection of Fort Maginniss, 1880 (Linderman, *Plenty Coups, Chief of the Crows*, pp. 278–284). Luther S. Kelly remembered riding by "the funeral lodge of Long Horse, a noted Crow chief who was killed at the head of his warriors while charging hostile Sioux concealed in thick bush and timber," in the summer of 1875 (*Yellowstone Kelly, The Memoirs of Luther S. Kelly*, ed. by M. M. Quaife. [New Haven: Yale University Press, 1926] p. 117). And a Crow chief named Long Horse signed the 1873 agreement for removal of their reservation to the Judith Basin, a treaty which, incidentally, was never ratified.

According to the Crow agency records the only chief named Crooked Arm was born in 1855, which would not only make him about five years old when he attains here the position as head chief, but would make him eight years old when, as a Sun Dance medicine man, he guides Two Leggings through his first ordeal. Plenty Coups' date would provide him with ample years to take over the office.

Untangling such discrepancies is impossible. Two Leggings' own chronology of seasons pursuing seasons suffers four complete breaks in sequence. Wildschut had little corroborative data on hand to check the discontinuous oral history. Agency records for such early years are often quite incorrect. And, sometimes more than one individual bore the same name.

4. Earlier, Two Leggings had named Grey Dog leader of the Kicked In The Bellies. Whatever the reason for the shift now, Leforge agrees that Sits In The Middle Of The Land was the leader of the Kicked In The Bellies (Marquis, *Memoirs of a White Crow Indian*, p. 142).

Known to the whites as Blackfoot, he appears to have been the most influential Crow policy maker in the third quarter of the nineteenth century. Curtis describes him as "about six foot two inches in height, proportionately heavy, and with muscles of a Hercules." He died about 1877 (*Op. cit.*, p. 51).

Chapter Five

1. There is no clear picture of the Crow pantheon. Wildschut and Curtis seem to agree that the prime creator was called Starter Of All Things (Wildschut, *Crow Indian Medicine Bundles*, p. 1), First Worker, or He First Made All Things (Curtis, *The North American Indian*, Vol. IV, 1909, p. 52). Leforge told his biographer that the English translation of the Crow word for god was First Maker (Marquis, *Memoirs of a White Crow Indian*, p. 134).

But a second term used by Leforge, Person Above (Marquis, *Op. cit.*, p. 134), appears to be the one Wildschut says is a more recent designation, The Above Person With Yellow Eyes or The Great Above Person (*Op. cit.*, p. 1). Lowie's The One Above is probably this deity (*The Crow Indians*, p. 252).

It is generally agreed that the only term Plenty Coups gave Linderman for god, "Ah-bahdt-dadt-deah," is a relatively recent attempt to approximate the white man's conception. Wildschut translates this third name as He Who Does Everything (*Op. cit.*, p. 1); Lowie as The Maker Of Everything (*Op. cit.*, p. 252); and Linderman as The One Who Made All Things (*Plenty Coups, Chief of the Crows*, p. 79).

To further confuse matters Two Leggings prays, apparently indiscriminately, to First Worker, his medicine person, the sun, Bear Above, Great Above Person, and The One In The Sky. Lowie asked: "Is he (the sun) or is he not equated with The One Above, whom the Indians sometimes addressed in prayer? Probably so, but it is impossible to tell with assurance. Is he the originator of the Indians and the shaper of the earth? That, too, remains a problem . . . . There is a real dilemma here. To treat the sun and Old Man Coyote as synonymous does indeed reserve for the single most eminent figure of ritual the role of the creator. But it also saddles the sun with all the grossness, the low cunning and lechery of the trickster [Old Man Coyote]" (*Op. cit.*, p. 252).

Linderman voices like confusion: "Their stories . . . are often without form to me, and I can understand why the sun and Old-Man, or Old Man Coyote, have so often been confounded" (*Old Man Coyote*, p. 13).

Curtis' definition of the sun as "his [He First Made All Things] counterpart" (Vol. IV, 1909, p. 52) provides a possible explanation. Lowie deduced that the Crows were "not philosophers but opportunists" (*Op. cit.*, p. 253). Old Man Coyote, the sun, and First

Worker were perhaps manifestations of the same being, each called forth upon an occasion appropriate to its characteristics. Thus this chapter's two creation stories are not mutually exclusive. When First Worker effects the first creation of man it coincides with his creation of the world and assumes an all-encompassing, epic tone. The second origin-of-mankind tale, realized through the marital advice of Old Man Coyote, has a more colloquial feeling and uses established Crow cultural features, the rock spirit and the sacred tobacco plant, as if the Crow ideological framework had existed in the absence of its adherents. Wildschut heard the rock and tobacco version more than a year before he was told the first, more common story; the same individual could find a second version suitable, and not contradictory, upon a different occasion. In the second story the emphasis is possibly on, as Wildschut parenthetically noted: "The symbolic representation of the everlasting and reoccuring fertilization of the inorganic with the organic life on earth."

2. The Crow sweat lodge is an oblong dome about six feet long, five feet wide, and four feet high, built on an east-west axis. Its framework of intertwined willow branches is covered with canvas or blankets. In the middle of the lodge a small pit is dug. A large fire is built a few yards from the eastern entrance of the lodge and in it stones are laid to heat. When the bathers are inside a helper passes four red-hot stones into the pit, one at a time, carrying them on forked sticks. Then the remaining stones are put into the pit and a bucket of water with a cup is passed inside. After the door flap is dropped one of the bathers says a prayer and pours four cups of water on the stones. Hot steam fills the darkened interior. After a while the flap is raised to let in fresh air. When it is closed a second time the "water chief" empties seven cups on the stones; following another cooling-off period he pours ten cups. After a final breather an indefinite number of cupfuls are poured, called "million wishes." When the bathers have had enough the door flap is raised a final time and they run for the river. Sometimes switches of sage or buffalo tails are used within to bring the heat upon the body. On more ceremonial occasions live coals are taken inside before any water has been sprinkled. Pine needles or bear root shavings are laid on them and prayers are spoken.

3. Wildschut noted that cannibalism was repugnant to the Crows. The eating of the heart or liver of an enemy was never practiced, and Crows believed that anyone who did this would have his mouth twisted. "Eaten" stands for the absorption of the dead soul by the winning clan.

4. Wildschut said this personage was called "Isteremurexposhe."

5. Wildschut gave this man's name as "Batseesh."

6. Two Leggings told Wildschut that the use of rock medicines depended on the instruction the dreamer received. Some rocks were war medicines, some helped to steal horses, others were used for doctoring or simply to gain wealth and live a long life. Wildschut says that the Crow name for rock medicine was *bacoritse*. He explains: "The same name applied to all peculiarly-shaped rocks, and particularly to all fossils [ammonites and baculites] found on the surface of the earth. All rocks to which this term applies are sacred, but they are not all considered medicine. This distinction is important, because all 'rocks' that are considered medicine were first seen in dreams and visions" (*Op. cit.*, p. 90).

Chapter Six

1. In 1877 Fort Custer was built on a high mesa above the junction of the Bighorn and the Little Bighorn rivers to stop the Sioux invasion of the Yellowstone Valley.

2. Edward S. Curtis photographed a Blackfeet medicine-pipe carrier from whose forehead protruded "the distinctive coiled hairdo of his station" (*The American Heritage Book of Indians* [New York: American Heritage Publishing Company, Inc., 1961] p. 332).

Chapter Seven

1. On the site of a temporary stockade erected in 1847, the trader Alexander Culbertson built this adobe fort and christened it on Christmas Day, 1850, in honor of the Missouri senator Thomas Hart Benton.

2. Built in 1866 of adobe and logs as one of the posts to protect the Bozeman trail, Fort C. F. Smith was burned to the ground in 1868 by Red Cloud's Sioux after the Government agreed that all country east of the Bighorn Mountains was to be regarded as western extension of the Sioux's Dakota reservation.

3. Curtis says of the Crow camps: "Their customary camps were along the mountain streams, where the lodges were commonly placed in a circle, but at times, where the valley was narrow, they were close together, paralleling the wooded watercourse" (*The North American Indian*, Vol. IV, 1909, p. 5). "The members of each clan camped together" (*Ibid.*, p. 25). But according to Lowie's data: "The camp circle was not regularly employed by the Crow and there was no definite arrangement of clans within it when it was used" (*The Material Culture of the Crow Indians*, p. 222). Plenty Coups recalled such a circle as a protective device: "The War-clubs [Lumpwoods]

selected a site in the Bighorn valley and ordered the village set up in seven small circles, themselves making a great circle with the chief's lodges pitched in the center. This arrangement was a warning to us all that trouble was near, that our Wolves had seen something to be afraid of" (Linderman, *Plenty Coups, Chief of the Crows*, p. 123).

Chapter Eight

1. Wildschut noted that he was unable to translate this name.

Chapter Nine

1. At this point Two Leggings interjected: "On a fast much later I dreamt about the Sun Dance doll and therefore had the right to own one of these bundles. Instead of making one I bought the bundle used during this ceremony from Goes Around All The Time [Sees The Living Bull]. Its first owner was a man I will call Has No Name and soon after I acquired it Crooked Arm told me its history." Wildschut notes that this bundle was known to have been used in at least four Sun Dance ceremonies: those of Holds The Young Buffalo Tail, Puts Earth On Top Of His Head, Shows His Face, and Sees The Living Bull (*Crow Indian Medicine Bundles*, pp. 26–29).

Chapter Ten

1. This means the tobacco plant, the core of a most important Crow ceremony. Two Leggings told Wildschut that he later used the Tobacco society's adoption ceremony to gain Sees The Living Bull's goodwill because he had heard this song.

   Lowie identifies the plant as *Nicotiana multivalvis* and explains that it was never smoked and was mystically associated with the stars (*The Crow Indians*, p. 274). Around its sowing, cultivation, and harvesting were organized an indefinite number of societal chapters which perpetuated themselves through elaborate adoption ceremonies.

2. This also happens to be the Crow word for east. Curtis says that the Crows believed the sun descended into water, passed around to another zenith, and then came out of the water (*The North American Indian*, Vol. IV, 1909, p. 191).

Chapter Twelve

1. At this point Two Leggings commented: "I did not understand what he meant. Later I realized that he was trying to tell me that I would become a well-known chief. I also think he was telling me that one day a white man would be sent to write my life in a book so that peo-

ple all over the earth would read my story. You are the one to tell about my life and it will soon travel all over the earth."

Chapter Thirteen

1. Wildschut noted that among the Crows two or more men who had been close friends and wished to strengthen this relationship could make a complete exchange of weapons and clothing. From then on they were "partners" and closer than brothers, sharing even their wives and duty bound to come to each other's aid. Lowie says that this bond, each becoming the other's *i'rapa'tse*, could even affect the next generation. He adds that men who called each other by this term and shared sweethearts would then call each other *biru'pxekyāta*, "my little father," the diminutive form of *biru'pxe*, which means father but was never used in direct address (*The Crow Indians*, p. 42).

2. Lowie identifies this as the root of a plant belonging to the carrot family (*Leptotaenia multifida* Nutt.). It is called *ise*, spelled *esah* by Wildschut, and was used as ceremonial incense and as a cure-all. Lowie was told that its name referred to the fact that bears supposedly fatten on it in winter (*Ibid.*, p. 63).

3. The impression here is that the Belt Mountains lie north of the Missouri, which is not so. Present-day River Crows, having lived almost all their lives in the Mountain Crow region where their reservation was established, have forgotten the Crow terms for locations in their old northern homeland. Only guesses can be made for many of these sites along the Missouri and northward which are named by Two Leggings.

Chapter Fourteen

1. Speaking of Crow hair styles, Curtis observed: "The Absaroke, moreover, greatly increased its natural length by working in other hair, so that sometimes the strands were so long as to almost touch the ground. Some of the men continued this fashion to within the last thirty years. On ceremonial occasions many of the young men imitated this manner of hairdressing by having many long locks fastened to a band worn at the back of the head. Both the real hair and the introduced strands were decorated from end to end with spots of red pigment" (*The North American Indian*, Vol. IV, 1909, p. 23).

These red spots were actually balls of pitch which Lowie says were matted into the inch-wide hair belts to keep the interwoven strands— which had been cut during mourning and saved—from blowing about (*The Material Culture of the Crow Indians*, p. 228).

2. See Note 2, Chapter Four.

3. When Plenty Coups saw a Plum Creek he was somewhere in the Judith Basin, less than a morning's ride from a place he called Two Buttes (Linderman, *Plenty Coups, Chief of the Crows*, p. 207). About ten miles due east of the center of the Judith River's length is a present-day settlement named Plum Creek. Two Leggings mentions Plum Creek frequently, speaks of a trader at its head and mouth, and describes its running into the Missouri. Leforge remembers trading with a man the Crows called "Blackbeard," Tom Bowyer, at his store at Fort Browning "where the Judith flows into the Missouri" (Marquis, *Memoirs of a White Crow Indian*, p. 60). The evidence indicates that Plum Creek is the Judith River, generally in the center of old River Crow territory.

Chapter Fifteen

1. Two Leggings paused to tell Wildschut: "She is still alive now, living in Lodge Grass, the grandmother of No Horse."

2. It is doubtful whether Wildschut's term for what is more commonly known among North American Indian tribes as "berdache," in Crow *baté*, is biologically correct. Lowie says: "Anatomically a berdache is said to be indistinguishable from male infants at birth, but as he grows up his weak voice sets him off from other boys" (*The Crow Indians*, p. 48). Most early accounts of the Crow note the existence of these deviates. They practised women's crafts, wore women's clothing, and pretended to have men lovers. Lowie says that this duty of cutting the first Sun Dance pole customarily fell to a berdache.

3. As Lowie explains this reluctance to ride the poles and the giving of gifts: "The police were closely watching the crowd, for the young braves now to be chosen for sitting on the logs tried to run away, since the first four—or, according to others, all twenty—thereby assumed the duty of never retreating from an enemy. So the young men would take to their heels, but were pursued by the police or the Whistler's kin, who rode fast horses. . . . In any event, the kin of all the log-straddlers put down before the young men such property as robes or beadwork, and little sticks to symbolize horses as gifts. All went to the Doll Owner, but after appropriating what he pleased he distributed the rest among the people who helped in the performances" (*Op. cit.*, pp. 313–314).

   By naming the recipients of the gifts as the pole-riders' relatives, Two Leggings is possibly meaning the clan aid upon which those relatives will draw to fulfil the obligations described by Lowie.

Chapter Sixteen

1. Curtis identified Old Dog as a Mountain Crow who belonged to the Lumpwood military club. He lost many wives to the Foxes and once had a hawk medicine reclaimed by its original owner because he took back a stolen wife, a disgraceful exhibition of weakness (*The North American Indian*, Vol. IV, 1909, p. 203).

Chapter Nineteen

1. Wildschut obtained from Cold Wind the original medicine bundle of which this was a copy. Its contents tallied exactly with Two Leggings' description, including the yellow-painted flute carved with representations of elk heads. Any Crow bundle depicting this animal and colored yellow suggests love medicine, but Cold Wind told Wildschut that although the bundle possessed that power it was never used as such.

Chapter Twenty-One

1. In Wagner and Allen's description of the post: "Hoskin and McGirl's trading post, located just below Baker's battlefield, where the town of Huntley now stands, was doing a thriving business. It was a horse market, a chamber of commerce, a social center, the Mecca toward which trails of all plainsmen eventually led" (Glendolin Damon Wagner and Dr. William A. Allen, *Blankets and Moccasins, Plenty Coups and His People, the Crows*. [Caldwell, Idaho: The Caxton Printers, Ltd., 1936] p. 167).

Chapter Twenty-Two

1. Wildschut noted that his medicine was probably obtained from a visiting Nez Percé or Gros Ventre [Hidatsa].

2. Red Bear, whom Two Leggings earlier mentioned as the chief of the Mountain Crows, is described by Curtis as a young leader of such renown that he "covered up" the older men. Besides giving him the power of prophecy, his medicine, the morning star, enabled him to "hold back the coming day when it appeared inopportunely" (*The North American Indian*, Vol. IV, 1909, p. 50).

   Curtis says that he met his death in 1862, stubbornly confronting an opposing force of Sioux and Cheyenne with only one other companion because he had been insulted by a fellow tribesman. The similarity in medicine powers and his chief's status indicates this was the same individual Two Leggings recalls, but then Curtis' date for his demise would have to be a little early, since the events in this chapter occurred circa 1869–70.

3. Curtis labels Iron Bull as "the richest man in the tribe," whose reputation came from his unusual generosity rather than his outstanding battlefield behavior. A head chief, he died in 1886 (*Ibid.*, p. 81).

Chapter Twenty-Three

1. When the wrappings on a scaffold burial wore away a relative would sometimes take home the skull. On occasion the relative would also have a dream in which the deceased would explain certain medicine powers possessed by the skull and would prescribe the skull's care and give associated songs and rituals. Usually these were the skulls of great medicine men or of people who had the ghosts as their medicine.

The central object of this bundle is said to be the skull of Braided Tail, one of the most famous Crow medicine men, who had lived five or six generations before. The bundle became an oracle to its successive owners, informing them on raids of the proximity of an enemy and telling them how many men would be killed at a certain location. In time of famine it would instruct the owner where to find game. It could tell a sick person if he were going to die or if he could be cured, and it could locate lost property. After five years of negotiations Wildschut purchased the Braided Tail bundle upon the death of its last owner, Old Alligator (*Crow Indian Medicine Bundles*, p. 77).

Chapter Twenty-Four

1. This was probably the famous signer of the 1825 friendship treaty with the United States Government. In most of the early accounts of Crow life he is known as Long Hair for the extraordinary long locks which were his medicine. Of them Lowie says: "In the early thirties of the last century travellers noted the marvellous length of Chief Long Hair's hair, which was estimated at from 9 ft. 11 inches to 10 ft. 7 inches in length, which the wearer either carried under his arm or within the folds of his robe, only loosening it on festive occasions" (*The Material Culture of the Crow Indians*, p. 228).

On September 22, 1930, Major General Hugh L. Scott and Montana House Representative Scott Leavitt were guests at a ceremony performed by Plenty Coups and Max Big Man. After ceremonial smudging Plenty Coups unwrapped a medicine bundle and unrolled a lock of Long Hair's hair measuring seventy-six hands and one inch in length—about 25 ft. 5 inches. Representative Leavitt wrote: "There was no evidence of any joining together of various locks" (Linderman, *Red Mother*, pp. 254–256).

2. Wildschut says that the central object in this medicine bundle was a stone of carved slate which One Child Woman, Sees The Living Bull's wife, found about three miles south of the old agency, on Fishtail Creek approximately twenty miles south of Columbus, Montana. The carvings of faces as shown in Wildschut's field photograph are unquestionably the work of some northwest coastal tribe; Wildschut suggests the Haida (*Crow Indian Medicine Bundles*, pp. 105–110).

Grey Bull told Lowie of this medicine's reputation, and another of Lowie's informants said that its owner had been instructed not to eat tongue, an act which forbade its unveiling at the customary occasion for the opening of rock medicines, The Singing Of The Cooked Meat. After Medicine Crow was given the medicine from his stepfather he followed this taboo (*Religion of the Crow Indians*, p. 389).

3. Among his list of ownership traits common to most plains tribes Ewers gives: "Horses individually owned, private property," and "Owner recognized his horses by their appearance and actions (no identifying marks placed on the animal)." Wildschut must have meant a herd composed of most of the horses owned by individuals in this village (John C. Ewers, *The Horse in Blackfoot Indian Culture, with Comparative Material from Other Western Tribes*. Bureau of American Ethnology, Bulletin 159. [Washington: Government Printing Office, 1955] p. 323).

Chapter Twenty-Five

1. Roe disagrees with such late use of dogs: "The Crow, while surrounded on all sides by tribes that used the dog travois, within the nineteenth century period covered by Lowie's informants and their immediate ancestors, confined their dog transport exclusively to packing, although they had formerly utilized the travois" (Frank Gilbert Roe, *The Indian and the Horse*. [Norman: University of Oklahoma Press, 1955], p. 19).

Chapter Twenty-Six

1. Pease Bottom was the site of Fort Pease, about eight miles northwest of the mouth of the Bighorn River on the north bank of the Yellowstone River. Erected in June 1875 by a trading party under the leadership of F. D. Pease, a former agent of the Crows, it was abandoned in March 1876 as a result of Sioux onslaughts.

Chapter Twenty-Eight

1. Plenty Coups told Wildschut a more detailed version of this disastrous war party: "A Crow war party discovered a Sioux camp near the

present location of Forsyth, Montana. From this camp the Crows captured about 100 horses, but they were discovered by the enemy and pursued. In the battle that followed two Crows were killed. They were Chicken Feet and White-Spot-on-the-Neck, the brother and brother-in-law of Big Shoulder.

"The Crows were camped on the Yellowstone near the site of Huntley when the returning war party reported the death of these young men, Big Shoulder then went out on the prairie, and choosing a place called Bear Home, a sharp rimrock about five miles north of present Billings, began to fast. Here he stayed for about five days before he received a vision."

In this dream Big Shoulder saw buffalo creatures playing shinny, an Indian style of hockey, and his next war medicine consisted of the balls and stick of this game (*Crow Indian Medicine Bundles*, pp. 54–55).

2. All the pipeholders' pipes collected by Wildschut have straight tubular stone bowls instead of the T-shaped calumet-style bowl used among the Sioux and other plains tribes (*Ibid.*, pp. 162–163).

Chapter Twenty-Nine

1. A communiqué of the apparent unimportance of the one being delivered here would probably have gone unrecorded. But the camp which so awed Two Leggings might have been that composed of the combined forces of Generals Terry and Crook after their 4,000 troops met on August 11, 1876. In the words of General Nelson A. Miles: "We continued our journey up the Rosebud and I reported my command to Brigadier-General Terry. We formed part of our forces during the two months following, and moved up the Rosebud, where General Terry's troops joined those under Brigadier-General Crook. This brought the two department commanders together with one of the largest bodies of troops ever marshalled in that country" (*Personal Recollections and Observations of General Nelson A. Miles.* [New York: The Werner Company, 1897] pp. 215–216).

Chapter Thirty

1. Following the Custer massacre on June 25, 1876, Sitting Bull's forces stayed at Grand River until they moved to Cedar Creek to confer with General Nelson A. Miles, and afterwards to fight with him. Vestal writes of his subsequent meanderings: "After the skirmish with Bear Coat (Miles), Sitting Bull's mounted warriors easily ran away from the walking soldiers, and the story went that Sitting Bull was engaged in a 'mad flight' to the British Possessions. Canada lay two

hundred miles due north—a matter of five or six sleeps for a man in a hurry. Yet Sitting Bull did not arrive there until months later, May, '77. In fact his flight was so 'mad,' that apparently he mistook his direction, for he 'fled' southwest and was rambling up and down the Yellowstone from the Big Horns to the Powder and eastward, most of the winter" (Stanley Vestal, *Sitting Bull, Champion of the Sioux*. [Norman: University of Oklahoma Press, 1957], p. 206).

Sitting Bull did not return to the States until July 1881, when he surrendered. If these were indeed his horses, Two Leggings and his party must have made their haul early in the winter of 1876–77 and not in the fall of 1879, as "three years after the battle of the Little Bighorn" would indicate.

Chapter Thirty-One

1. Wrote Agent E. P. Briscoe of these transportation facilities on May 10, 1888: "The military having possession of the desirable point of crossing, have established a ferry, and there is much complaint from them because they have to cross the Indians without pay" (*Annual Report of the Commissioner of Indian Affairs*, 1888, p. 155).

2. After its survey crew had been dogged by Sioux during their plotting of the route in 1871–73, the Northern Pacific Railroad, its entire Montana segment running along the Yellowstone River, was finally completed in 1886.

3. If one could be sure of Two Leggings' 1888 date for these events, Fort Custer's "Lump Nose" could possibly be identified as Colonel Nathan A. M. Dudley, Commanding Officer of the First Cavalry.

Appendix

Throughout my work on the manuscript I found myself forced to separate Two Leggings' facts from Wildschut's, or Jasper Long's, sometimes subjective interpretation of Crow life. Where something specific was recorded and explained there was little problem in tightening the passage: the unwrapping of a medicine bundle, the behavior at a certain Sun Dance, a series of camp moves. But when Wildschut attempted to evoke a mood, or to recreate Two Leggings' state of mind, the distinction grew elusive. Usually I coped with this by minimizing, through grammatical constriction and word selection, the inauthentic tone.

One question had to be settled immediately. If the manuscript had been constructed to incorporate Crow literary principles, it would be of primary importance to reconstruct these precisely. However, Robert Lowie, the anthropologist whose studies constitute the major body of research on the tribe, tells how Crow narrative techniques can escape the most assiduous linguist. Wildschut, not speaking Crow and having no formal anthropological or linguistic training, could not have been aware of the close attention the Crows paid to antithesis, parallelism, repetition, hyperbole, soliloquy, rhetorical queries, and symbolic expression. While I have carefully salvaged what traces of these features remain, the absence of word-to-word translation rendered futile the hope of preserving Crow storytelling style.

Some major changes were performed. Although I tried to parallel Wildchut's sentence order, I transformed his first-person dialogues into second-person exchanges.

Wildschut placed Four Dance's and Sees The Living Bull's stories in an appendix. Since Two Leggings mentions how greatly such tales influenced his actions, it was thought more effective to include them where he heard them.

Into the manuscript's earlier chapters Wildschut interjected his questions and Two Leggings' answers. Also, he included supplementary material in a handful of footnotes, within parentheses, and in chapter prefaces—which mostly contained unvarying descriptions of the interview situation. All this information has been either woven into the narrative, placed in the notes at the end of the text, or included in the present general introduction and chapter prefaces.

Mrs. Taylor remembers that when Two Leggings sang the songs in his narration, Wildschut requested literal translations. They have not been altered.

The following extractions illustrate the rewriting procedure.

Description

Original pp. 395–96

Around its neck I had fastened a necklace of rock swallow feathers with small bells attached to it and a stuffed hawk was also tied to this necklace. When one watches the rock swallows, it will be noticed how very swiftly they fly, even when they are thickly crowded together, yet they never collide. They have a marvellous ability to swerve. That same power of dodging, even when closely pursued by enemies, was represented by the feather necklace attached to my horse. The bells on the necklace represented the coming of a storm. When closely pursued by enemies, I would pray for a sudden storm to arise which, striking between my pursuers and myself, would retard their progress, thus giving me a chance to escape. The hawk which hung from the necklace was of a swift-flying species; they also have long endurance, both qualities I wanted to impart to my horse by attaching the hawk to the necklace.

Present Version, p. 170

Around its neck I fastened a necklace of rock swallow feathers, small bells, and a stuffed hawk. When you watch rock swallows flying in a tight bunch you never see them touch. This necklace gave my horse that same power to dodge if I was chased. The bells meant a coming storm. If I was followed by enemies I would pray for a sudden storm to come between us, slowing them down. The hawk was a fast high-flying kind that had long endurance; I wanted those qualities for my horse.

Dialogue

Original p. 404

We would probably have continued our antics a little longer had not

Present Version, pp. 173–174

We would have kept it up if Crooked Arm, the camp chief, had not ap-

Crooked Arm, Chief of our camp, approached. He apparently feared that we would go too far and now carried with him his uncovered medicine pipe. He approached me and as he offered it to me to smoke, he said:

"You who are all my children and especially you, Two-Leggings, have pity on us and smoke this pipe."

"Give him the pipe," I answered, indicating Boils-His-Leggings, "and if he accepts it, then will I smoke. It was not my fault this happened; he did the same to me first."

Boils-His-Leggings now spoke and said:

"Why should I smoke that pipe? Two-Leggings is a foolish man; he is not a medicine man and from this day on he will never again sing songs of victory or kill any more enemies."

"What!" I answered, "you think that you are a medicine man, that you have enough power to prevent me from killing any more enemies, you who never had a dream yourself and who had to obtain your medicine from White-Fox. I will soon show you that your power is nothing to me."

peared, carrying his medicine pipe uncovered. He invited us to smoke, saying we were all his children, especially me, and asked us to have pity.

I would only take the pipe if Boils His Leggings took it, since he had started this. Then Boils His Leggings said that I was foolish and not even a medicine man. From now on, he said, I would never sing victory songs or kill any enemies.

I told him that he had never received a dream and had had to buy his medicine from White Fox. I promised to show him that his power was nothing to me.

Mood

Original p. 218

This prayer completed, we all entered the sweat lodge where our Chiefs again prayed for us. After this ceremony, we all plunged in the river, smoked for a while and talked over the various events of the previous day. Interesting details were added here and before entering my lodge, I with our enemies, while many an act of bravery and cunning was heartily applauded by all of us. It was early morning before I finally sought my lodge again. I was tired but happy and there by the men who had battled

Present Version, p. 94

When we all entered a sweatbath the chiefs prayed for us again. Afterward we bathed in the river and then smoked and talked over the day before, adding details and remembering the brave things that were done. It was early morning when I returned to my tipi. All was still and the air was warm. Before going in I looked up at the sky, raised my arms, and prayed for all the powerful beings above to look at me. I told them I wanted to be a chief. I asked them to give me a long life and courage when I was in dan-

looked up in the sky. The air was warm and no breath of wind stirred the leaves of the trees. The stillness of the night was only broken by the faint noise of an occasional tired but happy singer, singing his songs of victory or love. My hands raised towards the heavens above and looking at all that was above me, I prayed:

"Oh, all you powerful beings above, look at me. I want to be a brave; I want to become a chief; give me long life and health. Help me and protect me and give me always courage in whatever danger I may be, or which may cross my path. Oh moon and stars, I humbly ask your aid."

ger. I asked the moon and stars for their help.

Action

Original pp. 325-26

One of the Piegans had a splendid horse, however, and soon rode well ahead of the rest. I knew I could outrun him, but on seeing him so far ahead of his comrades, I decided to play a trick on him and possibly kill him. As the sun was travelling toward its home in the west, we raced through coulees and over hills, maintaining about an even distance between my foremost pursuer, but all the time increasing the distance between him and the rest of his band. At last I felt safe in trying to ambush him and yet allow myself sufficient time to escape from his companions. All I needed was a suitable place to carry out my plans. With this purpose in mind I searched the country ahead of me. I had descended into the dry bed of a little creek and was urging my horse down its crooked course. I passed bend after bend but not one sharp enough for my purpose. At last my time came and I felt reasonably sure that if successful in my plans, I could mount and be on my way again long

Present Version, p. 139

One Piegan, riding a good horse, was far ahead of his friends. I could outrun him but decided to trick him. We were galloping through coulees and over hills, keeping an even distance between us. But he kept pulling away from his men. Then I entered the course of a dry creek. After passing many half bends I noticed a rocky point that made the bed turn sharply. Reining in on the other side, I tied my horse to a tree and crouched behind some bushes. As I strung my bow and pulled an arrow back I could hear his horse running on the dry stones.

216

before the rest of the Piegans were within bowshot.

Some distance ahead of me I noticed a sharp rocky abutment deflecting the course of the creek so abruptly that an almost right angle bend was formed. To this spot I urged my horse at topmost speed. Rounding it, I suddenly reined in and dismounted. Fortunately I found some gnarled trees to which I tied my horse; they also gave welcome protection to myself. My pursuer was not far behind and I could plainly hear the sound of his approaching horse.

With bow ready strung, I awaited his approach, bent low behind the shrubbery on the bank of the little stream and a few feet above the riverbed. Somehow I never even considered that I might be fighting a losing battle.

The sound of the horse racing over the pebbled bed of the stream warned me of the immediate approach of my enemy.

Index

Absaroke, xvi
American Heritage Book of Indians, 204
American Fur Company, xviii
American Museum of Natural History, 80
Amos Two Leggings, xiv, xv, xxi
annuity goods from United States Government, 177–178
Apache, 162
Arapahoes, xvii, xx, 109, 162
Arikaras, xx, 133
Arrow Creek (*see also* Pryor Creek), 20, 35, 61–62, 88, 101–104, 115–:16, 121–122, 126, 163, 188–189
Arrowhead Mountains (*see also* Pryor Mountains), 19, 60, 101, 107–108, 115, 121, 126, 129, 189
Assiniboines, xvii, xx, 177
Atkinson, Henry, General, xix
Atsina, xvii, 29, 177

Bad Mountain, 56, 58, 64
Badger Creek, 175
Ballantine, 195
Bank, 12
Bannock, 184
Bear, 55
Bear Camp, 8
Bear Creek, 3, 12, 15, 99, 166
Bear Dance Song, 95–98
Bear Grease, 134
Bear In The Water, 109, 200
Bear Looks, 91–93
Bear Song Dance, 95
Bear Up Above, 8–9
Bear White Child legend, 6–10, 108, 199–200

Beartooth Range, xvii, 172
Bearpaw Mountains, xvii
Beaver, 79
Beckwourth, James, xviii
Bell Rock, 97
Belly Robe, 52
Belt Mountains, 71, 206
Big Belly clan, 66
Big Bird Above, 182
Big Boat, 17–18
Big Crane, 1–2, 6, 115, 118, 200
Big Lake, 125–126, 156, 159
Big Man, Max, 209
Big River (*see also* Missouri River), 1, 12, 18–19, 31, 42–43, 74, 80, 89, 92–93, 95, 118, 153, 163, 169, 176, 189–190
Big Shoulder, 178–180, 211
Big Shoulder Creek, 85
Bighorn Mountains, xvii, 40, 62, 74, 88, 105, 111, 156, 159, 167, 172, 189, 204
Bighorn River, xiii, xviii, 1, 4, 19, 21, 30, 39, 44, 49, 62, 64–65, 85–87, 98, 104, 108, 121, 142, 167, 176, 186, 188, 193–194, 204, 210, 212
Bighorn Valley, 30, 35, 189, 205
Billings, Montana, 35, 58–59, 103–104
Billings *Gazette*, xv
Bird Above All The Mountains, 63
Bird Fire, 195
Bird Going Up, 146–147
Bird Has A Shirt, 145
Bird Home Mountains, 58–59, 211
Bird On The Prairie, 169
Black Buttes, 159
Black Canyon, 62, 88
Black Earth, 15

218

Black Hair, 168
Black Head, 3–4, 122–124
Black Hills, xvii
Black Lodges (*see also* River Crows),
    74–75, 78, 89
Black Lodges, xvii
Black Robes, 27
Blackfeet, xxi, 18, 29, 71, 162, 174–
    175, 200–201
*Blackfeet Raiders of the Northwest-
    ern Plains, The*, cited, 198, 200
Blood (Blackfeet band), 200
Blue Creek, 103
Blue Handle, 56
Bob Tail Wolf, 12, 124, 126, 168–169
Boiling Waters, 29
Boils His Leggings, 124, 173–174, 215
Bozeman Trail, xvi, xviii, 204
Braided Tail, 134–135, 209, 212
Briscoe, E. P., Agent, 212
Bucket Leg, 150
Buffalo Calf, 195–196
Buffalo Heart Mountain, 68, 88, 126,
    128, 156
buffalo hunts, 155
Buffalo Lump, 96–97
buffaloes:
    herds of, 90, 156
    hunting of, 19–20, 29–31, 33, 103,
        155, 193
    medicine songs for, 82, 87, 108, 157,
        159
Bull Does Not Fall Down, xiii, 37, 56,
    88, 98, 200
Bull Eye, 134–135
Bull Goes Hunting, xv, 73
Bull Mountains, 116, 121–123
Bull Shield, 81–83
Bull Water, 81
Bull Weasel, 119
Bull Well Known, 88
burials, 209
Burns Himself, 131, 145–146
Bushy Head, 40, 116–118
Bushy Pine Hill, 150

Camp, E. M., Agent, 177
Canada, 162, 192
cannibalism, 203
captives, 29
Cass, Lewis, Secretary of War, xix
Cedar Creek, 211
Chases The Enemy Wearing A

Coyote Hide On His Back, xiv–
    xv
Cherry Hill, 150
Cheyennes, xvii, xx, 40–45, 106, 109,
    111–112, 121, 185, 208
Chicago Field Museum, 73
Chicken Feet, 211
Chicken Hawk Cap, 150
chiefs, 87
childbirth, 1
Children Of The Large-Beaked Bird,
    xvi
chokecherries, 74, 96, 98, 149, 163, 177
Chouteau, Pierre, xviii
clans, 17, 66, 199–200
Clear On The Forehead, 160, 163
Cody, 20–21, 39, 68, 74, 88
Cold Wind, 109–110, 208
Columbia Fur Company, xviii
Comanches, xx
Comes Out Of The Water, 51, 176
council of chiefs, 87
coups, 34
coupstick, 178
Covers Himself With The Grass, 62
Coyote, 101, 165, 178
Coyote's Penis, 101
Crane Goes To The Wind, 45
Crazy Dog, 49
Crazy Mountains, 58–59
Crazy Sister-In-Law, 52
Crazy Wolf, 146
Crook, George, General, 184, 211
Crooked Arm, 19, 43–47, 88, 98–103,
    119, 121–122, 126, 128–129, 136,
    142, 146, 173–174, 178, 201, 205,
    214–215
Crooked River, 76
Crow Indians, The, cited, 198–202,
    205–207
Crow Indian Beadwork, xiii
Crow Indian Medicine Bundles, cited,
    xiii, 108, 198–199, 202, 205, 209,
    211
Crows (*see also* Mountain Crows;
    River Crows):
    burials of, 209
    camp life of, xxi, 71, 136, 165, 204
    ceremonials of, 22–23, 44, 47, 55, 95,
        200
    chiefs, 87
    cultural traits of, 29, 39, 55, 66, 73
    geographical names, 101

219

Crows (*cont.*)
    as hunters and warriors, 29, 90, 105, 127, 162, 193, 203
    Indian agency for, xiv, 85, 150
    religion of, 23–24, 26–27, 202
    trading post, xviii
    as U.S. cavalry scouts, 184
Culbertson, Alexander, 204
Curley, 159, 176
Curtis, Edward S., xiv, xv, xvi, xxi, 198–202, 204
Custer, George A., General, 101, 133, 184, 211
Cuts The Turnip, 68, 145

Deaf Bull, xv
Deer River, 70, 74
de Smet, Pierre, xx
Denig, Edwin T., xvi, xxi, 198
Devil's Lake, xvi
Devil's Pocket, 98
Dipper Creek, 85
Dirt Creek, 132
Discovered Plant, 51
Dockstader, Frederick J., Dr., xiv, xxi
Does Not Care For Women, 58
Does Not Turn Back, 14
dolls, Sun Dance, 44–45, 47, 49, 205, 207
dreams, 61, 116, 152, 166
Dry Creek, 163, 177
Dry Head Creek, 61
Dudley, Nathan A. M., Colonel, 212
Dwarf Buttes, 102

eagles, 34, 71, 74, 82–83, 125, 135, 151–152, 159, 179, 194
Earth Lodges, xvii
Eats The Ear, 4–5
Elk River (*see also* Yellowstone River), 1–3, 35, 49, 56, 58, 68, 78, 81, 94–95, 103–104, 106, 114, 121–122, 144, 160, 165, 177, 179–180, 185, 188, 195
Elk River Valley, 20, 103, 172, 195
Ewers, John C., xiii, xvi, xxi, 198, 200, 210

Face Turned Round, 145–146, 152
farming, 188, 193
fasting, 23–27, 38, 88, 146
Female Face, 160
Fence, 195

Few, 124
Fire Wing, 109
First Worker, 23–24, 27, 39, 202–203
Fitzpatrick, Tom, xx
Five Indian Tribes of the Upper Missouri, cited, xix
Flatt Butte, 180
Flathead, 29, 90–93, 95, 148
Flesh, 97
Fly Creek, 188, 195
Forsyth, 68, 184, 211
Fort Laramie Peace Commission, xx, 177
Forts:
    Benton, 35, 174, 177, 204
    Browning, 207
    Cass, xviii
    C. F. Smith, xv, xviii, 37, 104–105, 204
    Custer, xiii, 30, 65, 193, 196, 204, 212
    Ellis, 177
    Laramie, xx, 177
    Maginniss, 201
    Pease, 210
    Peck, xv
    Sarpy, xviii
    Union, xix, 1
    Van Buren, xviii
Four, xiv, 1
Four Dance, 58, 213
Fox warrior society, 152, 167–169, 171–174, 208

gambling, 26
Gets A Shield, 176
Getting A Sword, 81–82
ghosts, 27
Gibbon, John, General, 73, 184
Goes Around All The Time, 73, 189, 205
Goes First, 124–126
Grass Lodges, xvii
Great Above Person, 30, 36, 46–47, 50, 53–54, 58, 62–64, 68, 74–75, 88, 90, 94, 100, 102, 106, 109, 113, 118, 121, 123–124, 128, 130, 135, 140, 144–145, 150, 158, 161, 169, 176, 179–182, 190
Great Falls, 136
Great Unmarried Man, 111, 113–114
Grey Bull, 210
Grey Dog, 2, 19, 201

Gros Ventres, xvii, xx, 18, 35, 200, 208
Guadagno, Carmelo, xxi
Gun River, 18

Hairy Noses, xvii
Hairy Wolf, 83
Half Yellow Face, 20–21, 109–112, 133
Hardin, xvi, 19, 44, 49, 81, 188
Hard To Camp With, 31–32
Has A Red Feather On The Side Of His Head (*see also* Long Hair), 148
Hawk High Up, 123, 208
Hawk Medicine, 208
He First Made All Things, 202
He That Mixes, 127
Head Of A Man, 97
Heart Mountain, 192
hermaphrodites, 83, 207
Hesitates, 146
Heye Foundation, xiii, xxi
Hidatsa, xvi, xix, 29, 95, 127, 200, 208
Hide Flesher Mountain, 177
High Hawk, 163–164, 170–171, 182
High Peak In The Middle, 119
Hillside, 169
His Eyes Are Dreamy, 115
Hits Herself, 115
Hits With The Arrows (*see also* Pryor Gap), 88, 101, 121, 126
Holds By The Gun, 44, 58
Horse Creek, xx
Horse in Blackfoot Indian Culture, The, 210
horses, 33–34, 38, 40, 49, 85–86, 89, 95, 100, 105, 108, 120, 125, 176, 191, 210
Howard, Oliver, General, 29, 184
Hunkpapa (Sioux tribe), xv
Huntley, 208, 211
Hunts The Enemy, 90–93, 108, 133–142

Indian and the Horse, The, cited, 210
Indian Affairs, Bureau of, xix, 193
Indian Agency, 177, 188, 193
Interior, Department of the, 80
Iron Bull, 129, 209

Joseph, 29
Judith Basin, 201, 207

Kainah (Blackfeet band), 200
Kelly, Luther S., 201
Kicked In The Bellies, xvii, 2, 201
Kind Hearted Old Man, 169
kinship, 17
Kiowas, 29
Knife River, xvi
Knows His Ground, 174

La Verendrye, Pierre G. V., xvii
land, cession of, 188
Laramie Peace Commission, xx
Larocque, François, xviii
Leforge, Thomas H., xv, 201–202, 207
legends, xxi, 6, 24, 73, 199, 200
Lets The Women Stand, 15
Lewistown, 101
Lie In A Line, 32
Linderman, Frank Bird, xxi, 198, 201–202, 205, 207, 209
Little Belt, 145
Little Bighorn River, xxi, 29, 37, 65, 85, 98, 105, 121, 167, 188, 204
Little Face, 145
Little Fire, 56
Little Heart, 137, 141, 168
Little Horse, 135
Little Rockies, 89, 163
Little Soldier Chief, 133
Little Tipi Creek, 156
Livingston, 56, 58, 177–178, 188
Lodges At The Extreme End, xvii
Long, Jasper, xxi, 213
Long Beard, 122
Long Hair (*see also* Has A Red Feather On The Side Of His Head), xviii, xix, 209
Long Horse, 2, 19, 201
Long Mountain, 9
Long Otter, 179–180, 183
Looking Glass, 29
Looks All Over The Earth, 63
Looks At A Bull's Penis, xv, 73
Lots Of Bear, 97
Loud Hawk, 125
Loud Sounding River, 76
love medicine, 165, 208
Lowie, Robert, xii, xv, xxi, 80, 198–200, 202, 204, 206–207, 209, 213
Lump Nose, 196, 212
Lumpwood warrior society, 49, 69, 143, 167–168, 173–174, 204, 208

Man Who Can Talk English, 128
Mandans, xvi, xvii, xix, 29, 200
Many Lodges, 2, 19, 78, 175
Many Tattoos, xvii
Marquis, Thomas B., Dr., xv, 198,
   201-202, 207
marriage, 49, 74
Material Culture of the Crow Indian,
   The, cited, 198, 200, 204, 206, 209
Maximilian, Prince, xviii
McGirl, Thomas, 122
McKenzie, Alexander, xviii
medicine, 39, 43, 99, 110, 146, 172, 190,
   194, 203-204
Medicine Arrow, 5
Medicine Bear, 81, 90
medicine bird, 122
medicine bundles, 29, 43, 87, 97, 108,
   116, 149, 180, 204, 208, 210
Medicine Crow, 56-57, 62-65, 73, 75,
   103-104, 174-175, 189-192, 210
Medicine Crow, Joseph, 199
Medicine Dream Buttes, 102
medicine dreams (*see also* visions), 26,
   51
medicine father, 52, 66, 144, 146, 150-
   153, 165, 169, 179, 189
medicine men, 6, 23, 26, 71, 96, 119,
   127, 150, 159, 209
Medicine Pipe, 95, 180
Medicine Porcupine, 107
medicine songs, 46, 51, 70-71, 77, 106,
   124, 140, 163, 170-171, 182-183,
   195
Medicine Thunder, 4
Meldrum, Robert, xix
Memoirs of a White Crow Indian,
   cited, xvi, 201-202, 207
Menard, xvii
Miles, Nelson A., General, 184, 211
Miles City, 2
Missouri, xviii, xix, 206-207
Missouri Fur Company, xviii
Missouri River (*see* Big River)
Mitchell, D.D., Superintendent, xx
moon, 17, 25, 74, 94, 152
Morgan, Lewis Henry, xix
Mountain Crows, xvii, xx, 128-129,
   143-144, 155, 165, 177, 208
Mountain Lion's lodge, 114, 116-117,
   121-122, 172, 188
Mouse Walks, 62
Muddy Creek, 78, 167

murder, 27, 44
Museum of the American Indian, xi,
   xiii, xxi
Museum of Natural History, xll
Musselshell River, 12, 18, 31, 35, 49,
   52, 56, 58, 64, 72, 74, 78, 97, 99,
   101, 116-117, 121, 123, 136, 153,
   163, 165, 176-178, 189
Musselshell Valley, 163
myths, 24, 73, 200

name giving, 1, 101, 115
Neck Bone, 131-132, 145-146
Never Dies, 135-136
Nez Percés, xvii, 29, 162, 184, 200, 208
No Fears, 128
No Horse, 207
No Vitals, xvi, xvii, 127
No Wife, xiv
North American Indian, The, cited,
   xiv, xxl, 198-200, 204-206, 208
North Dakota, xvi, 120
Northern Pacific Railroad, 188, 212
Northwest Company, xviii
Not Dangerous, 149
Not Mixed clan, 66, 133

Of the Crow Nation, xviii
Old Alligator, 209
Old Baldy, 40
Old Dog, 93, 99, 115, 118, 128
Old Man Coyote, 25, 27, 202
Old Man Wolf, 7
Old Tobacco, 126
Old White Man, 169
Old Woman, 105
One Blue Bead, 122, 124-125, 181-182
One Child Woman, 210
One Eye, 6-10
One Fingered Bear, 85
One Leg, 194-196
One Up There In The Sky, 67, 194
One Who Owns The Camp, 87
One Who Owns The War Party, 11
Onion, 81
Other Side Camp, 24-27, 58, 74, 116,
   161

Painted Blanket Creek, 180-181
Paints His Body Red, 124, 170

Pale Face, 170
Park City, 59, 179–180
Passes All The Women, 58
Pease, Fellows D., 210
Pease Bottom, 165
pemmican, 96, 140
Pend d'Orielle, 133
Piegan (personal name), 41–42, 66–68, 77–78, 132–134, 136, 138–141
Piegans (Blackfeet band), xv, 6, 12–19, 29, 31–39, 70, 76, 80, 88, 97, 99, 136, 138, 140, 174, 194–197, 200, 216
Pierced Noses, xvii
Pine Ridge Hills, 20, 35, 121, 194–195
pipeholder, 11, 40, 52, 67–69, 71, 83–84, 95, 99, 102, 104, 109, 116, 128, 133, 144, 150, 153–154, 156, 165, 168, 174, 179–181, 194, 204, 211
Plain Face, 168
Plain Weasel, 15
Plenty Bear, 135, 136
Plenty Coups, 80, 199, 201, 204, 207, 209–210
Plenty Coups, Chief of the Crows, cited, 201–202, 205, 207
Plenty Screeching Owl, 62
Plum Creek, 76, 78, 91, 116–118, 175, 192, 207
Poor Face, 109
Poor Lodges, xvii
Poor Wolf, 32
Porcupine Creek, 68, 165
Porcupine Hill, 134, 136
Powder River, 101, 149, 212
Pozash, 41–43
Prairie Gros Ventres, xvii
prayer, 24, 27, 46–47, 121, 132, 146, 151, 158, 179–180, 189
Pretty Face, 30
Pretty Hawk, 3–4
Pretty Old Man, 194–196
Pretty Tail, 182
Pryor Creek (*see also* Arrow Creek), 101
Pryor Gap (*see also* Hits With The Arrows), 101
Pryor Mountains (*see also* Arrowhead Mountains), 101
Puts Earth On Top Of His Head, 44–45

Quaife, Milo M., 201

raids, 162
railroad, 188, 195, 212
Rattle Mountain, 69–71
Rawhide, 178
Red Bear, 2, 128, 151, 208
Red Cherry Creek, 34
Red Clay Woman, xiv
Red Cloud, 204
Red Coats, 18
Red Hail, 156
Red Lodge, 34, 43, 89
Red Mother, 209
Red Top Hill, 150
Religion of the Crow Indians, xv, 198–199, 210
Reno, Captain, 37, 133
reservations, 80, 155, 177, 188, 193, 196, 201, 204, 207
Rides The White Horse, 97
Rise Up, 32
River Crows (*see also* Black Lodges), xvii, xix, 44, 128–129, 132–133, 144, 155, 162, 177, 188, 206–207
rock medicine, 28, 35, 95, 108, 132, 153, 204, 210
Rock Pile, 68
Rocky Mountain Fur Company, xviii
Roe, Frank Gilbert, 210
Rolls Himself, 15
Rosebud Creek Agency, 80
Rosebud River, xviii, 185, 188
Rotten Belly, xvii, xix
Rotten Grass Creek, 65, 85, 105, 167
Roundup, 117

sacrifices, 64
St. Xavier, Mission of, 36, 50, 128
scalping raids, 36, 38, 90, 93, 164–165, 168, 171–173, 196
Scar On The Mouth, 146
Scott, Hugh L., General, 209
scouting forays, 73, 149, 157, 184, 186
See Under, 128, 146
Sees The Living Bull, 61–63, 73–78, 88, 93–94, 104, 108, 114, 127–136, 142–146, 150, 162, 205, 213
Sends Him Home, 16
Sews His Guts, 35–36
Sharp Lance, 15–16
Shell On The Neck, 93, 107
Sheridan, 111
Short Bull, 196
Short Horn, 21

Shoshonis, xvii, 20, 29, 148
Shot In The Arm, 122
Shot In The Face, 51
Shot In The Hand, 150
Shows His Face, 44–45, 47, 81
Shows His Tail, 62, 65
Shows His Wing, 12–14, 200
sign language, xiii, 77, 184
Simms, S. C., 73
Simonin, M., xx
Singing Of The Crooked Meat, 95
Sings To The Sweat Lodge, xiv
Sioux, xx, 29, 39, 67, 74, 81, 85–88,
    100, 102, 104–106, 116, 118, 122–
    126, 145, 149, 164, 168, 170–172,
    176–178, 182–188, 190–193, 196–
    197, 201, 208
Sioux Dakota Reservation, 204
Sits Down, 57
Sits In The Middle Of The Land, xx,
    19, 35, 73, 97, 201
Sits Toward The Mountain, 169
Sitting Bull, 192, 211
Sitting Bull, Champion of the Sioux,
    cited, 212
Skin On The Forehead, 102
Slayton, 78
Small Face, 131
Small Heart, 91
Small Sun, 97–98
smoke signals, 35
Snake Hill, 169–170
Snow Mountain, 59
Snowy Mountain, 19
Snowy Mountains, 35
Social Life of the Crow Indians, cited,
    198–199
soldiers, United States, 185–186, 193
songs, 55
Son Of The Morning Star, 133
Sore Tail, 2
Spotted Horse, 20, 52–53, 185–186
Stands Among Them, 160
stars, 24–25, 141, 152
Starter Of All Things, 202
Stays Among The Birds, 15
Stays Among The Buffalo, 102
Stinking Water, 39
Stone Pile, 163
Stops, Roger, 199
storytelling, 22
Straight Calf, 171

Strap, 32–33
Striped Feather Arrows, xvii
Strikes At Different Camps, xiv, 1
suicides, 27
Sully, A., Superintendent, 177
Sun, 25, 94, 104, 130, 152, 202
Sun Dance, 27, 29, 44–45, 47, 49–50,
    52, 81, 84–85, 108–109, 201, 207,
    213
Sun Dance bundle, 45, 108
Sun Dance doll, 45, 58, 81, 84, 205
Sun Dance lodge, 46, 81, 84
supplies, 156
sweat lodge, 27, 61, 64, 67–68, 70, 94,
    99–100, 104, 118–119, 130–131, 144–
    149, 162, 179, 203
Swordbearer incident, 184, 193

Taylor, Mrs. L. A., xiii, xxi
Ten Bear, 135, 138
Teton Sioux, xvii
Terry, Alfred H., General, 211
They That Cut Off Our Heads, xvii
They Who Refused The Paunch, xvi
Three Mountain, 89
Three Wolves, 40, 150
Thunderbird, 62–63, 124
Ties Up Her Bundle, xiv
Tobacco, 105, 143–145, 203, 205
    adoption dance, 143
    Dance of, 128–129, 144, 175
    society of, 66, 95, 127, 143
Toluca, 195
Tongue River, xviii, 88
trade, 76
transportation, 201, 210
Treacherous clan, 6
tribal alliances, 29
Trout Creek, 136
Trudeau, Jean Baptiste, xvii
Tullock Creek, 186
Twins, 76
Twists His Tail, 162
Two Belly, 12–14, 99–100, 103, 115,
    118–122, 126, 128, 142, 146, 155–
    162, 178, 184–186, 189
Two Leggings:
    ambitions of, 55, 102
    boyhood of, 1–2, 5–6, 61, 127
    discrepancies of stories, 201, 206
    early names of, 115, 118, 120, 127,
        133, 143

first coup of, 36
love life of, 49, 176
on pantheism, 22–23, 200
and United States Cavalry, 185, 212
Two Leggings Creek, 85–86
Two Stars, 174–175

Union Pacific Railroad, 188
Utes, xvii, 40

Vestal, Stanley, 212
visions, 49–50, 61, 64, 88, 99, 150, 153, 166

Walking Mouse, 56
Walks Toward The Two Mountains, 66
war bonnets, 185
war insignia, 34
war medicine bundles, 110, 181
war parties, 39, 64, 69, 75, 78, 86, 89, 101, 116, 145, 153, 165, 168, 172, 189, 204, 210
Warm Water, 79
warrior societies, 6, 29, 49, 87, 133, 167
Washkie, 29
weapons, 35, 190, 194
Wears A Mustache, 42
Weasel Sits Down, 117, 178
West Hill, 150
Where The Bear Sits Down Mountain, 99, 189
Where The Dog Bites, 169
Where The Gros Ventre Sun Dance Tipi Stands, 169
Where The Lightning Strikes, 153, 162–163, 169
Where The Moccasin Hangs, 101
Where The Thunderbird Sits Down Mountain, 62, 75, 88
Where The White Clay Is, 169
Where They Ran Away From Camp Creek, 180–181
Where They See The Rope, 101
whiskey peddlers, 188
White Man Above In The Sky, 75, 146
Whistling Waters clan, 1, 6–10, 73, 199
White Around The Edges, 76
White Buffalo, 14

White Child, 199
White Clay On The Forehead, 194
White Eye, 196
White Fox, 174
White From The Waist Up, 91–92
White Man Above In The Sky, 75, 146
White Man Runs Him, 101
White Mouth, 148
White On The Neck, 80–86, 211
White On The Side Of His Head, 19, 74
White Swan, 133
Wildschut, William, xi, xiii, xxi, 22, 39, 61, 73, 80, 193, 198–204, 206–207, 210, 213
Williamson, H., Agent, 184, 193
Willow Creek, 99
Willow Top, 135
Wind River Shoshonis, 80
Wise Ones, 3, 6, 22, 32, 67–68, 121
Without Fires, 8, 24–26, 43, 46, 48, 55, 70
Wolf Bear, 104, 108–109, 168–171
Wolf Cap, 12
Wolf Chaser, xv, 2–3, 17, 19–20, 33, 43, 45
Wolf Creek, 69
Wolf Goes To Drink, 21
Wolf Head, 40–41, 43
Wolf Mountains, 44, 88, 121, 168–169, 191
Wolf Runner, 64
Wolf Tail, 134
Woman Does Not Know Anything, 52–53
Woman Face, 163
Women Leggings, 58
Woody Creek, 35, 85, 98
Wraps Up His Tail, 184
Wrinkled Face, 89
Wyoming, xvii, xx, 39

Yanktonai (Sioux tribe), xv
Yellow Bull, 200
Yellow Crane, 150
Yellow Legs, xvii
Yellow Weasel, 62
Yellow Willow Creek, 136, 142
Yellowstone Kelly, The Memoirs of Luther S. Kelly, 201

Yellowstone River (*see also* Elk River), xvii, xx, 177, 188, 210–212
Yellowstone Valley, 162, 204, 212
Young Beaver, 90, 92
Young Buffalo Tail, 44

Young Curlew, 170
Young Mountain, 56, 62–71, 76–78, 90–91, 98–99, 104–106, 121–127, 168
Young Rabbit, 62